TEXTS IN GERMAN PHILOSOPHY

General Editor: CHARLES TAYLOR

Advisory Board: RÜDIGER BUBNER, RAYMOND GEUSS,
GARBIS KORTIAN, WILHELM VOSSENKUHL, MARX WARTOFSKY

SCIENCE OF KNOWLEDGE

J. G. Fichte

SCIENCE OF KNOWLEDGE

with the **First** *and* **Second Introductions**

edited and translated by
PETER HEATH
University of Virginia

JOHN LACHS
Vanderbilt University

The right of the
University of Cambridge
to print and sell
all manner of books
was granted by
Henry VIII in 1534
The University has printed
and published continuously
since 1584.

CAMBRIDGE UNIVERSITY PRESS

Cambridge
New York   Port Chester
Melbourne   Sydney

Published by the Press Syndicate of the University of Cambridge
The Pitt Building, Trumpington Street, Cambridge CB2 1RP
40 West 20th Street, New York, NY 10011, USA
10 Stamford Road, Oakleigh, Melbourne 3166, Australia

First published by Meredith Corporation 1970
Reissued by Cambridge University Press 1982
Reprinted 1984, 1988, 1991

Library of Congress catalog card number: 82-4536

British Library Cataloguing in Publication Data

Fichte, Johann Gottlieb
  Science of knowledge.–(Texts in German philosophy)
  1. Knowledge, Theory of
  I. Title II. Heath, Peter
  III. Lachs, John IV. Wissenschaftslehre.
  English V. Series
  121 BD161

ISBN 0-521-25018-8 hardback
ISBN 0-521-27050-2 paperback

Transferred to digital printing 2003

Contents

Preface   vii

On the Translation   xix

Glossary   xxi

INTRODUCTIONS TO THE SCIENCE OF KNOWLEDGE

First Introduction to the Science of Knowledge   3

Second Introduction to the Science of Knowledge, for readers who already have a philosophical system   29

FOUNDATIONS OF THE ENTIRE SCIENCE OF KNOWLEDGE

Preface   89

PART 1

FUNDAMENTAL PRINCIPLES OF THE ENTIRE SCIENCE OF KNOWLEDGE

§1. First, Absolutely Unconditioned Principle   93

§2. Second Principle, Conditioned as to Content 102

§3. Third Principle, Conditioned as to Form   105

PART II

FOUNDATION OF THEORETICAL KNOWLEDGE

§4.   First Discourse   120

    A.   Determination of the synthetic proposition to
be analyzed   122

    B.   Synthesis of the opposites contained in our
proposed principle, and in general   123

    C.   Synthesis by interdetermination of the opposites
contained in the first of the opposing principles   127

    D.   Synthesis by interdetermination of the opposites
contained in the second of the opposing principles   131

    E.   Synthetic union of the opposition between the two
types of interdetermination   138

Deduction of Presentation   203

PART III

FOUNDATION OF KNOWLEDGE OF THE PRACTICAL

§5.   Second Discourse   218

§6.   Third Discourse

    In the striving of the self there is simultaneously
posited a counterstriving of the not-self, which
holds the former in equilibrium   251

§7.   Fourth Discourse

    The self's striving, the not-self's counterstriving, and
the equilibrium between them, must be posited   253

§8.   Fifth Discourse

    Feeling itself must be posited and determined   256

§9.   Sixth Discourse

    Feeling must be further determined and limited   261

§10. Seventh Discourse

    The drive itself must be posited and determined   264

§11. Eighth Discourse

    The feelings themselves must be capable of being
opposed   281

Index   288

Preface

Philosophers who are neither narrow nor impatient will find Fichte's *The Science of Knowledge* an interesting, perhaps even exciting work. This is all the more remarkable because Fichte labors under a number of severe handicaps, not the least of which is his cumbersome, unnecessarily complex style. His thought, which may be difficult enough to follow on the clearest exposition, is obscured by the vagueness and the ambiguities of his writing. Bad punctuation, idiosyncratic sentence structure, and a dismaying overabundance of nonfunctional expletives interfere with the task of understanding, and it is ironic that a thinker in whose philosophy the requirement of unity plays such an exalted role, could have endowed this work with no more readily discernible structure than it displays. On a charitable interpretation we could say that Fichte was so intent upon his ideas that he could pay little attention to the way he communicated them. It may be more nearly correct to say that he was one of that ever increasing host of philosophers who never quite learn to write well.

Infelicities of expression are by no means the only obstacles to appreciating Fichte's work. His literary *persona*, alternating between arrogance and mock humility, and always ready for vitriolic personal attacks, is thoroughly unbearable. In addition, he can be infuriatingly careless and inconsistent in his views. Consciousness and self-consciousness, for example, are central concepts in his system, but not once throughout the *Science of Knowledge* and its two Introductions (written subsequently to the main work) does he attempt to give a serious account of them: some of his cursory remarks about them are plainly contradictory. Finally, he also suffers from the fault that has discredited much of speculative philosophy: his arguments frequently seem shallow and verbal. Not only are the meaning and referent of some of his words unclear, many of his syntheses in the theoretical part of the main work turn on what appear to be forms of obscure linguistic sleight of hand. We may well come away with the feeling that such dialectical involutions can have little to do with reality.

In the light of such an impressive list of faults, the reader may ask what Fichte might have to offer to him, and even what conceivable reason we might have had to spend our time translating his work. It is not easy to answer such a blunt challenge without simply asking the reader to complete the book and see for himself. What one finds interesting or profitable is surely a personal matter; but it should be possible to give some reasons for going to the trouble of reading such a difficult volume, or at least to mention some of the features that seem to us to recommend it.

From the first page of the First Introduction it is evident that we are dealing with a major and independent voice, a philosophical principal. Although Kant set the stage, developed the terms, and even largely determined the rules with which Fichte operates, it would be wrong to view our author simply as a follower of Kant or an expositor of Kant's system. Part of the interest of Fichte's work derives precisely from the fact that, accepting so much of both the matter and form of the critical philosophy, he is in a position to explode it from the inside. The person interested in the remarkable logic shown in the history of philosophical systems will find Fichte's work a fascinating case study.

Whatever we may think of its ultimate success, the scope and conception of the Fichtean enterprise are truly impressive. The aim is to present an account of the nature of man that would at once be an account of the nature of reality. Fichte wishes to show the essential unity of human faculties and to establish that as acting, willing agents we are independent of the sensible world and enjoy a radical, untrammelled freedom. It is the self through its cognitive faculties that creates and determines the objects which constitute the external world: reality exists only in and for the conscious mind.

Fichte attempts, in short, to establish a tenable idealism as a natural outgrowth of the Kantian critical philosophy. A careful study of his work shows that he draws freely on Spinoza and Leibniz; but he wishes to retain their positive insights incorporated in a more sophisticated, critical system than they could develop. Use of the Kantian transcendental method of proof and an elaborate dialectic indeed made it possible for Fichte to work out the details of his system with a subtlety and sophistication that are difficult to match. Even his apparently sophistical arguments bear second scrutiny: such intensive reading is frequently rewarded with surprising insights into their meaning or significance. It is clear that Fichte's philosophy represents one of the few major attempts to develop and defend a complete idealism: this by itself would make it well worth serious study.

The author of the *Science of Knowledge* is not alone among philosophers in paying too little attention to his fundamental presuppositions and in making virtually no attempt to communicate them. For this reason, it may be appropriate for us to spend a little time discussing them here. We might begin by asking what Fichte thought he was doing when he engaged in the task of developing a philosophy.

Fichte was convinced that there is a single, fundamental question of philosophy, which functions as a watershed: our answer to it determines the total complexion of our philosophical commitments. The task of philosophical science according to Fichte is to explain how our experience of a world of spatio-temporal, law-governed objects is possible. The question that must be answered first and foremost concerns the ground or foundation of experience. There are only two possible answers: one identifies the self-conscious self as the sole source of experience, the other maintains that cognition of an objective world could never arise without the influence on the self of independently existing objects. Accordingly, there are only two fundamental types of philosophy: idealism, with its insistence on the all-sufficiency of the self, and what Fichte variously calls "realism" or "dogmatism," with its claim that objects exist independently of the mind.

It is clear to Fichte from the first that dogmatism is not a tenable philosophy. His main argument against it is that it cannot account for the existence of conscious selves. But, interestingly enough, he is of two minds about the force of this argument against the dogmatist. In some places he asserts that, given their premises, both philosophies are consistent and, that since argument about fundamental principles is impossible, each is secure in its sphere and irrefutable. On this view, the choice between the theories is a matter of "inclination and interest," and what can be said for idealism is not so much that it is true as that it is something we *ought* to believe, for only according to the idealist are we free and responsible agents. Fichte cannot resist taking this opportunity to intimate that his opponents, since they believe in a "mechanically" determined world of which the self is a part, themselves lack the free agency which is the mark of the human and the indispensable condition of morality. In other places, however, he argues that idealism is demonstrably superior to a realistic view, but such a demonstration is, in fact, nowhere provided. It is fairly obvious that Fichte thought the view that the conscious self is "an accident of unconscious physical nature" nearly absurd, and was convinced that if his idealist deductions could be successfully accomplished, realism, even in the minimal form in which it involves the existence of a mind-independent but unknowable thing-in-itself, would lose all its plausibility.

In ordinary experience and in our action we are convinced that there is a world existing independently of us. Fichte wishes to make allowance for this and he readily admits that a simple and uncritical idealism cannot adequately account for it. There must be a not-self to serve as the counterpart of the knowing subject, and this not-self must be empirically real, viz. independent of the finite consciousness that apprehends it. The task of a critical idealism is to show that even though this not-self is opposed to the self on the level of conscious experience, it nonetheless has its source in the self on a deeper level. From the point of view of the ultimate conditions of knowing, which never come to explicit consciousness except in the reflections of the philosopher, the not-self is the creation of and exists only for the primordial activity that Fichte designates as the absolute self. In the Kantian terms Fichte adopts, we could say that for critical idealism the world of objects is empirically real but transcendentally ideal.

What is to be the method of such a critical idealism? Much has been made of Fichte's geometrical method which, it is sometimes said, parallels Spinoza's. In the works printed here, at least, there is little sign of any such procedure. One can indeed detect geometrical models behind some of Fichte's thought, but it would be grossly misleading to say that his aim in the *Science of Knowledge* is to provide logically rigorous deductions of his theses. When he uses the word "deduction," he is thinking not of the forms of inference we know from logic and geometry, but rather of the transcendental method of Kant. This latter method of proof enables us to argue from some actual structure of experience to the conditions indispensable for it: for Kant, to "deduce" a certain concept in this sense is simply to show that the activity it designates is a necessary prerequisite for having the sort of experience we in fact have.

Now Fichte is in fundamental agreement with Kant about the correct method of philosophizing. But whereas Kant takes as his conditioned, whose conditions he is to discover, our experience of spatio-temporal objects in causal connection with each other, Fichte maintains that the deduction must have as its point of departure our immediate but nonsensible acquaintance (what he calls "intellectual intuition") with an absolute and infinite self. The task of the philosopher is to inquire into what is contained in or required by the concept of an absolute self. When the deduction is completed and the concept has yielded up all that was tacitly present in it or implied by it, we should arrive at nothing short of the totality of all the structures of experience. If any of the fundamental structures of experience could not be deduced from the concept of the absolute self, critical idealism would be shown to be an inadequate philosophy.

This interpretation of Fichte's method is borne out by various hints throughout the works in this volume, as well as by his actual procedure in the *Science of Knowledge*. It also helps to explain the obscure passage at the end of the First Introduction, which compares the philosopher to the chemist. The philosopher does indeed "see" the a priori: without any reference to experience he develops the system of conditions of the pure activity Fichte calls the absolute self. The test of the correctness and adequacy of critical idealism is that this system of conditions derived from the absolute self is identical with the structures or generic features of experience (the "a posteriori" in the passage at issue) as actually lived.

One could argue that this procedure of seeking out the conditions of the self goes counter to Fichte's original postulation of the self as absolute. The absolute self must be unconditioned: the current procedure exhibits it as the most highly conditioned of all activities. The objection is well founded but is not, for that reason, damaging to Fichte's method. In characteristic fashion, he embraces both the thesis that the self is simple and unconditioned and the view that it is the most dispersed and highly conditioned of realities. The point strikes at the heart of Fichte's metaphysics, and we shall have more to say about it presently. For now it is enough to remark that in his view nothing can be an absolute self without at once limiting itself; this determination or limitation is what gives rise to the finite, conditioned self and its counterpart, the objective world of the non-ego. It is this necessary and immediate, we could almost say automatic, self-limitation of the self that Fichte has in mind when he describes the philosopher's task as that of simply observing the self-development of his fundamental concept. Once the concept of the absolute self is clearly in focus, it appears to generate, as if without our help and by means of its dialectical force alone, an entire galaxy of subsidiary judgments and ideas.

There are two further comments that should be made in connection with Fichte's ideas on philosophical method. It is interesting to note that it never occurred to him to question the adequacy of the transcendental method to yield philosophical truth. Had he reflected on his use of that method as distinct from the use made of it by Kant, Fichte might have considered that in seeking out the necessary conditions of experience, the sets of conditions deduced will vary according to the experiential structure selected as our point of departure. Kant's deductions may be no less impeccable than Fichte's, and other philosophers could no doubt develop scores of faultless, imaginative, and characteristically different accounts of the conditions of experience. How could we conceivably choose between them? Surely not by the consistency and skill with which they are carried through. Instead, we would have to argue that a certain structure of experience is more fundamental, and hence better adapted to serve as a starting point than all the others. With this argument, however, the transcendental method of proof offers us no help. Fichte himself is silent on the issue, and in choosing self-connectedness as the fundamental structure of all experience (as distinct, say, from temporality), he has laid himself open to the charge of assuming what he set out to prove, or at least of loading the dice in his own favor.

Secondly, it is appropriate to call attention tó a subsidiary method Fichte uses in his elaborate deduction of the conditions of experience. This dialectical procedure is the means by which the transcendental deduction actually progresses. The first moment of the dialectic is the analysis of a given concept until apparently contradictory results are reached. Since such contradictions could not be allowed to stand without detriment to the unity of consciousness and hence tò the unity of the self, they have to be reconciled or "synthesized." The synthesis of the apparently contradictory judgments always occurs by the introduction of a new concept which, in turn, is itself soon found to contain an apparent contradiction. Perhaps the clearest example of this procedure is the original synthesis of the *Science of Knowledge*, which proceeds to derive from the concept of the absolute self the opposition of self and not-self, only to unite the two apparently incompatible concepts through the new idea of divisibility. By the movement of this dialectic, Fichte is driven beyond the theoretical part of his study: theoretical reason leaves us with contradictions that can be reconciled only when we enter the sphere of will, which is reason in its relation to human action. When the last contradiction will have been shown to be merely apparent, we should have in our possession the complete and adequate system of universal reason.

Before we take a closer look at some of the main concepts of Fichte's philosophy, we ought to examine a mysterious operation that appears to be fundamental to much of what he says. We have in mind the operation designated by the German word *setzen*, which we have variously translated as "assert," and more frequently as "posit." At certain points in the *Science of Knowledge* Fichte writes almost as if *setzen* and its compounds were the only verbs in the German language. Unfortunately, this is one of those words that reminds translators of the ultimate hopelessness of their task: it would have to be rendered by a paragraph in every case. "Assert" captures part of its meaning, but suffers from being too closely

associated with language or propositions. "Posit" falls short because it is a colorless word that has little value in philosophy and
none in ordinary language, and completely lacks the rich suggestive-
ess of the German original.

By *setzen* Fichte refers to a nontemporal, causal activity that
can be performed only by minds. We can be conscious of performing the activity of positing, but Fichte seems to be of two minds as
to whether or not this activity itself is endowed with consciousness.
Perhaps the most fundamental meaning of the word in ordinary
German is to put, place, set up, or establish: as such, it implies
creative causal endeavor. In a linguistic or intellectual context it
can be used to convey the assertion of some proposition or the
establishment of some truth. When we say that the self *setzt* itself,
the English phrase "self-assertion" perhaps comes closest to an
adequate rendering of what is meant. The particular feature of the
word— lost in translation but central for Fichte—is that when
used in connection with the assertion of propositions, it makes
contact with the intellect, while when signifying affirmation, it
properly belongs in the sphere of will. Reason, Fichte points out, is
the capacity for positing: through the creative power of reason whatever is posited is made real. Positing, then, is a primordial act, in
which the theoretical and the practical coincide, and in which an
undivided self is totally engaged in a single creative, all-encompass-
ing enterprise.

The fundamental premise of Fichte's philosophy is just such
a self positing or asserting itself, and positing itself as engaging in this
enterprise of self-assertion. This thought invites comparison with
the concept of Aristotle's Prime Mover, eternally engaged in con-
templation of himself, and would perhaps be identical with it, were
it not for the practical, volitional element involved in self-assertion.
A more compelling similarity is with Spinoza's idea of the eternal
potency-in-act—the inner core of his one Substance. The striking
similarity to Spinoza is sustained throughout the *Science of Knowledge*, and Fichte frequently pays tribute to him as the greatest
and most consistent of dogmatists. Fichte appears to be saying that
only the fundamental premise of Spinoza was wrong; he gave the
wrong answer to the watershed question of philosophy, conceiving
of this potency-in-act in impersonal terms.

Unfortunately, Fichte does not think it necessary to explain what it means for a primordial, undifferentiated activity to be personal. He quickly answers the charge of egotism by reminding us that his absolute self is no member of a world of finite persons, and altogether lacks the individuated subjectivity essential to it if such an accusation is to have meaning. But if the primordial activity is devoid of all the features of individual personality (and that is the only idea of personality we have), what sense could it make to call it a self? In a number of passages Fichte suggests that the absolute self is conscious of itself, or at least that it consists of an activity that is conscious: perhaps for Fichte these are the features that render the primordial activity a self. In one place indeed he goes so far as to exclaim categorically: *Was für sich nicht ist, ist kein Ich*—what is not conscious of itself is not a self. But both of these suggestions appear to go against other central views he espouses, for he frequently assures us that no consciousness is possible without self-consciousness, and no self-consciousness without a consciousness of objects. But the absolute self, as such, is logically prior to all objects, and hence must be at best a necessary condition of consciousness, without itself being conscious. Another possible reason Fichte might offer for calling the infinite potency-in-act a self is that it is within the experience of a knowing subject that we have immediate nonsensible contact with it. But this suggestion comes to immediate grief: it is simply a fallacy to suppose that whatever a self cognizes is, for that very reason, itself a self.

That the primordial activity cannot bear the features of personality is further supported by the fact that its reality must be affirmed in what Fichte calls a "thetic judgment." Such a judgment, of which "I am" is "the first and foremost" example, is devoid of what we would conventionally call a predicate. The concept of its subject, therefore, remains unrelated to any other concept: only the reality of the subject is asserted without any reference to what class it might belong to or what property it may possess. But if the original potency-in-act must be infinitely indeterminate, it certainly cannot possess the property of being a conscious self.

In this primordial activity—conceived perhaps on the model of Aristotle's *energeia*—agent, activity, and product are indistinguishably united. Even though some passages appear to contradict this, it is evident that Fichte thinks of his absolute self as unitary and singular. There is but one such activity, not a different one for each empirical self. This single activity is the source of all there is, not through arbitrary choice but in a necessary, yet perfectly free fashion. Its operation is both free and necessary for the same reason: it acts by the necessity of its own nature independently of any external influence. It gives rise to the totality of all experience, including our experience of an external world, by an inevitable, non-temporal activity of self-determination.

Since to be is to have some limitations, the absolute self could not even be real if it were perfectly indeterminate. But the unavoidability of its self-determination, which is at once a self-fragmenting and self-limitation, is best understood by reflecting that as soon as we add a single predicate to the thetic judgment which affirms the reality of the self, we have related it to a class or property and thereby made it to some extent determinate. If we attach the predicate of infinity—certainly an appropriate one—to the absolute self, we instantly destroy its infinite indeterminateness. The moment, therefore, that the primordial activity is conceived as infinite, it sheds its infinity and displays itself as finite. We could also say that its infinity requires its finitude and, if we wished to identify such a dialectical relation with causation, that the infinite necessarily gives rise to the finite.

It is here that Fichte feels he can improve upon the system of Kant. Two great weaknesses of the critical philosophy, Fichte notes, are that it provides no compelling deduction of the pure forms of intuition and the categories from the fundamental laws of the intellect, and that it is unable to account for the manifold of sense without postulating an independently existing but totally unknowable thing-in-itself. Fichte proceeds at once to give a deduction of the categories on the basis of the self-determining activity of the self alone. In the deduction within the theoretical part of the *Science of Knowledge* he also shows how the absolute self posits the not-self and through that restricts itself to the status of finite knowing subject. But the question of why the absolute self should give rise to an objective world of spatio-temporal multiplicity is not ultimately resolved until we reach some of the chronically obscure sections of the practical part. It is particularly difficult to get a just measure of Fichte's system because the relation of the structures deduced in the theoretical and the practical parts of his work is almost completely indeterminate. We must combine plain talk with some conjecture in order to arrive at a reasonably clear and accurate statement of what he might have had in mind.

If the question of why the absolute self creates the objective world is taken as a request for reasons, in Fichte's view it simply does not admit of an answer. A reason or ground must always be a consideration that goes beyond what we wish to account for. But there is nothing extraneous to, different from, or "beyond" the absolute self in its infinity, and in any case if there were reasons for what it creates, its activity would be determined and not free. The absolute self creates freely and in that sense unaccountably. In another sense, however, we can find an excellent reason for why the absolute self should create; and this is a reason that accounts, at once, also for what its creations will necessarily be. The reason is, of course, the nature and structure of the primordial activity: everything real and everything ideal alike must flow from this by necessity.

The self is an active, striving being. In particular, it has two fundamental drives, which impose upon it two different but closely interrelated tasks. The practical drive of the self is "to fill out infinity"; this drive urges it on to engage in the activity of self-assertion without end, to transform everything into its own image, and to subject a whole world to its autonomous laws. The theoretical drive, by contrast, is one that moves the self to reflect upon itself and to know itself in splendid unity. If the practical drive is conceived as a line of activity stretching outward from the self to infinity, the drive to reflection must be thought of as checking that activity at a certain point and making it revert back toward the self.

Now Fichte maintains that these two drives presuppose each other. Without the drive to infinite activity the drive to reflection would have nothing to restrict. And, since any direction presupposes its opposite, without the self-directed line of activity initiated by the drive to reflection, the outward-moving activity of the practical drive would be impossible. But we must also note that the two drives cannot be satisfied together. Reflection necessarily imposes limits on infinite activity, while activity, when it is infinite, makes reflection impossible. Since both drives are primordial, neither can permanently overcome the other: they vie with each other and are satisfied by turn, though never completely. The result is a continued alternation in the direction of activity at a certain point beyond the self: the ensuing *Schweben*, a wavering or oscillation, is what Fichte calls the imagination — the source of all presentations and hence the locus of the physical world. This interplay of the self with itself, a sort of self-conflict, results in frustration, incapacity, and restraint. These, in turn, are manifested in the self in the form of feeling, which is the source of the sense of necessity that accompanies presentations thought to come to us unbidden from the external world. Thus the task of giving the ground of experience, in Fichte's narrow sense of this word, in which it designates the totality of presentations accompanied by the feeling of necessity, and the one of giving an account of the creation of the not-self, supposed by him to be equivalent, are both completed. It only remains for us to remark that, in his view, the positing of physical nature also has the salutary effect of providing for the self a stage for its moral action, an opponent to overcome in its striving, and a recalcitrant force that sets it the repeated task of extending the sway of its law without limit. The ultimate value of creation is that it makes it possible for the self to do its duty.

Whatever view we may take of the success of Fichte's deduction of experience and the physical world, there can be little doubt that it is remarkable in its design and impressive in its execution. We may indeed have severe reservations about the claim that he deals with concepts of pure reason when his work abounds in empirical analogies, and many of his central conceptions hide only thinly the physical models from which, perhaps unconsciously, they were derived. But even if we allow for this and Fichte's other, all too obvious faults, the worst a stringent critic could say of the *Science of Knowledge* and its two Introductions is that they are, like so many works that stud the history of philosophy, the brilliant labor of abortive genius.

On the translation

The *Wissenschaftslehre* is not a particularly long book, but its difficulty has evidently been a deterrent to translators. Our sole predecessor in English, that we know of, is a mutilated version first published in the United States by A. E. Kroeger (*Fichte's Science of Knowledge*, 1868). Though the industrious Mr. Kroeger subsequently went on to translate a number of Fichte's other writings, his incompetence for the task was in due course exposed, with characteristic and memorable violence, by the early G. E. Moore.[1] It is fortunate that all these travesties are now out of print. Despite some disconcerting blunders, the French version by F. Grimblot (*Doctrine de la Science*, 1843) is generally much superior in style and accuracy, but even of this work we have made very little use. Our aim in the present translation has been to offer a complete and reliable text, reproducing the author's often involved meaning as exactly as is possible without departure from the canons of good, or at least tolerable, English. To that end we have not hesitated to vary the rendering of particular terms where sense and context seemed to demand it, to refashion a few obscure or unnatural phrases, or to modify gross eccentricities of punctuation. This, we feel, is the more excusable, since Fichte's own work, intended primarily as a handbook to his lectures, is by no means a polished specimen of the prose-writer's art. To translate him literally is thus to do no service, either to himself or to his present-day reader; free adaptation and

[1] *International Journal of Ethics*, Vol. 9 (1898), pp. 92–97.

paraphrase, though tempting, are, on the other hand, equally un-acceptable, involving as they do a degree of interpretation which it is not our function to provide. The best that can be done, we think, is to keep close to the sense of the original, while avoiding such awkward turns of expression as would bother the reader, or remind him too insistently of the language of origin. For the same reason, we have abstained from the device of interpolating German equivalents for the technical terms employed. These will be found, consolidated, in the Glossary. We have similarly been content to present a plain text, without noting separately the minor variations which distinguish the three versions of the work that Fichte pub-lished (Leipzig 1794–5; Tübingen 1802; Jena and Leipzig 1802). Wherever appropriate, these variants have been silently incorpor-ated in the text, which otherwise follows that of F. Medicus (1922), itself based on the third edition and now handily reprinted in one volume by the Meiner Verlag. The fine new variorum edition of the Bayerische Akademie has also been consulted, and occasionally found helpful. The numerous italicized words and phrases, and the curiosities of punctuation that remain, are almost invariably those of Fichte himself. The marginal page-numberings refer, as is customary, to the *Gesamtausgabe* of I. H. Fichte (1834–46). The two Introductions of 1797, though prefixed to the main text, are other-wise similarly treated, and again follow the Meiner reprint of Medicus. The first of them is the work of Dr. Lachs, who also contributes the prefatory material; the remainder of the translation, the Glossary, and the Index are due to Mr. Heath. Each, however, has checked the work of the other, and striven to preserve him from error; each, on occasion, has followed his own preference, though without serious dispute; each, at all events, has retained sufficient confidence in the other's judgement to be willing to blame him for any resulting mistakes; and both will be grateful to readers and reviewers who may be able to point them out.

P. L. H.

J. L.

A few corrections and improvements have been made in the text of this reissue. We are grateful to Prof. Fritz Marti for suggesting them.

Glossary

Anschauen, —d, —ung Intuit, intuitant, intuition
Anstoss Check
Auffassen, —ung Apprehend, apprehension
Aufheben Annul, annihilate, abolish, destroy, eliminate
Aufstellen Establish, postulate, suppose
Bedingen, —ung Condition
Befriedigen, —ung Satisfy, satisfaction
Beifall Inclination
Beschaffenheit Constitution
Bestimmen, —d, —ung Determine, define, determinant, determination
Bestimmt Determinate, definite, specific
Bestimmtheit, bestimmbarkeit Determinacy, determinability
Bewirkte (Causal) product
Beziehung Conjunction, connection, relation
Eingreifen Intrusion, incursion
Empfindung Sensation
Entäussern, —ung Alienate, alienation
Entgegen(Gegen-)setzen Oppose, set in opposition to, counter-posit
Fixieren Stabilize, fixate
Forderung Demand, requirement
Gefühl Feeling
Gegenseitig Mutual
Gegenstand Object
Gegenteil Opposite, contrary, counterpart
Gehalt Content
Gleich Alike, equal, equivalent, identical, same, similar
Gleichsetzen Compare, liken, equate

Grenze   Boundary, limit
Handeln, —ung   Act, action, activity
Hemmen   Curb, impede
Ich   Self
Inbegriff   Essence
Leiden   Passivity
Missfall   Disinclination
Mittelbarkeit   Mediacy
Schranke, Einschränken, beschränken   Limit, bound, restrict, confine
Schweben   Waver, oscillate
Sehnen   Longing
Sein   Existence, being
Setzen   Posit, assert
Stoff   Matter
Streben, gegenstreben, widerstreben   Striving, counter-striving, resistance
Tathandlung   Act
Tätigkeit   Activity
Trieb   Drive
Übergehen   Transition
Übertragen   Transfer, transference
Urteilskraft   Judgement
Verhältnis   Relation, relationship
Verwechslung   Interchange
Vorstellung   Presentation, representation
Wechsel, —n   Change, exchange, reciprocity, interplay
Wechselbestimmung   Interdetermination
Wechseltun   Interaction
Wesen   Essence, nature
Wirksamkeit   Efficacy
Wirkung   Causal process
Zurückgehend (in sich selbst)   Self-reverting
Zusammenfassen   Bring together, conjoin
Zusammenhang   Connection
Zusammentreffen   Encounter, clash
Zutun   Cooperation
Zwang   Compulsion

INTRODUCTIONS TO THE SCIENCE
OF KNOWLEDGE

FIRST INTRODUCTION TO THE SCIENCE OF KNOWLEDGE

PREFATORY NOTE

De re, quae agitur, petimus, ut homines, eam non opinionem sed opus esse, cogitent, ac pro certo habeant, non sectae nos alicujus, aut placiti, sed utilitatis et amplitudinis humanae fundamenta moliri. Deinde, ut suis commodis aequi, in commune consulant, et ipsi in partem veniant.

—Baco de Verulamio

On a modest acquaintance with the philosophical literature since the appearance of the Kantian Critiques I soon came to the conclusion that the enterprise of this great man, the radical revision of our current conceptions of philosophy, and hence of all science, has been a complete failure; since not a single one of his numerous followers perceives what is really being said. Believing that I did, I decided to dedicate my life to a presentation, quite independent of Kant, of that great discovery, and will not relent in this determination. Whether I shall have greater success in making myself intelligible to my own generation, only time will tell. In any case, I know that nothing true or useful is lost again once it has entered the world of men; even if only a remote posterity may know how to use it.

In pursuit of my academic duties, I at first wrote for my students in the classroom, where I had it in my power to continue with verbal explanations until I was understood.

. . . in behalf of the matter which is in hand I entreat men to believe that it is not an opinion to be held, but a work to be done; and to be well assured that I am laboring to lay the foundation, not of any sect or doctrine, but of human utility and power. Next I ask that they fairly consult their common advantage, . . . and themselves participate in the remaining labors . . .

—Francis Bacon, *The Great Instauration*, Preface. [Editors' translation]

3

I, 420   I need not here attest how many reasons I have for being satisfied with my students and for entertaining of very many of them the highest hopes for science. The manuscript in question also became known outside the university, and there are numerous ideas about it among the learned. Except from my students, I have neither read nor heard a judgment in which there was even a pretense of argument, but plenty of derision, abuse, and general evidence that people are passionately opposed to this theory, and also that they do not understand it. As to the latter, I take full responsibility for it, until people have become familiar with the content of my system in a different form and may find perchance that the exposition there is not, after all, so wholly unclear; or I shall assume the responsibility unconditionally and forever if this may incline the reader to study the present account, in which I shall endeavor to achieve the utmost clarity. I shall continue this exposition until I am convinced that I am writing wholly in vain. But I do write in vain, if no one examines my arguments.

I still owe the reader the following reminders. I have long asserted, and repeat once more, that my system is nothing other than the *Kantian;* this means that it contains the same view of things, but is in method quite independent of the *Kantian* presentation. I have said this not to hide behind a great authority, nor to seek an external support for my teaching, but to speak the truth and to be just.

After some twenty years it should be possible to prove this. Except for a recent suggestion, of which more anon, Kant is to this day a closed book, and what people have read into him is precisely what will not fit there, and what he wished to refute.

My writings seek neither to explain *Kant* nor to be explained
I, 421   by him; they must stand on their own, and *Kant* does not come into it at all. My aim—to express it directly—is not the correction and completion of the philosophical concepts now in circulation, whether anti-Kantian or Kantian; it is rather the total eradication and complete reversal of current modes of thought on these topics, so that in all seriousness, and not only in a manner of speaking, the object shall be posited and determined by the cognitive faculty, and not the cognitive faculty by the object. My

system can therefore be examined on its own basis alone, not on the presuppositions of some other philosophy; it is to agree only with itself, it can be explained, proved, or refuted in its own terms alone; one must accept or reject it as a whole.

"If this system were true, certain propositions cannot hold" gets no reply from me: for I certainly do not consider that anything should hold, if this system contradicts it.

"I do not understand this work" means nothing more to me than just that; and I consider such an admission most uninteresting and uninstructive. My writings cannot be understood, and ought not to be understood by those who have not studied them; for they do not contain the repetition of a lesson already learned beforehand, but, since *Kant* has not been understood, something that is quite new in our day.

Unreasoned disparagement tells me no more than that this theory is not liked, and such an avowal is also extremely unimportant; the question is not whether it pleases you or not, but whether it has been demonstrated. In order to assist the testing of its foundations, I shall add indications throughout this exposition as to where the system needs to be attacked. I write only for those who still retain an inner feeling for the certainty or dubiousness, the clarity or confusion of their knowledge, to whom science and conviction matter, and who are driven by a burning zeal to seek them. I have nothing to do with those who, through protracted spiritual slavery, have lost themselves and with themselves their sense of private conviction, and their belief in the conviction of others; to whom it is folly for anyone to seek independently for truth; who see nothing more in the sciences than a comfortable way of earning a living, and who shrink back from any extension of knowledge, as from a new burden of work; to whom no means are shameful to suppress the destroyer of their trade.

I would be sorry if they understood me. Until now it has gone according to my wishes with these people; and I hope even now that this exordium will so bewilder them that from now on they see nothing but letters on the page, while what passes for mind in them is torn hither and thither by the caged anger within.

I, 422

INTRODUCTION

1

Attend to yourself: turn your attention away from everything that surrounds you and towards your inner life; this is the first demand that philosophy makes of its disciple. Our concern is not with anything that lies outside you, but only with yourself.

Even the most cursory introspection will reveal to anyone a remarkable difference between the various immediate modifications of his consciousness, or what we may also call his presentations. Some of them appear to us as completely dependent on our freedom, but it is impossible for us to believe that there is anything answering to them outside us, independently of our activity. Our imagination and will appear to us to be free. Others of our presentations we refer to a reality which we take to be established independently of us, as to their model; and we find ourselves limited in determining these presentations by the condition that they must correspond to this reality. In regard to the content of cognition, we do not consider ourselves free. In brief, we may say that some of our presentations are accompanied by the feeling of freedom, others by the feeling of necessity.

The question, "Why are the presentations which depend on freedom determined precisely as they are, and not otherwise?" cannot reasonably arise, because in postulating that they depend on freedom all application of the concept of "wherefore" is rejected; they are so because I have so determined them, and if I had determined them otherwise, they would be otherwise.

But the question, "What is the source of the system of presentations which are accompanied by the feeling of necessity, and of this feeling of necessity itself?" is one that is surely worthy of reflection. It is the task of philosophy to provide an answer to this question, and in my opinion nothing is philosophy save the science which performs this task. The system of presentations accompanied by the feeling of necessity is also called *experience*, both internal and external. Philosophy, in other words, must therefore furnish the ground of all experience.

I, 423

Only three objections may be brought against the above. A person might deny that presentations occur in consciousness which are accompanied by the feeling of necessity and referred to a reality which is taken to be determined without our assistance. Such a person would either deny against his better knowledge or be differently constituted from other people; if so, there would actually be nothing there for him to deny, and no denial, and we could disregard his objection without further ado. Secondly, someone might say that the question thus raised is completely unanswerable, for we are, and must remain, in insurmountable ignorance on this issue. It is quite unnecessary to discuss arguments and counterarguments with such a person. He is best refuted by providing the actual answer to the question, and then nothing remains for him to do but to examine our attempt and to indicate where and why it does not appear to him sufficient. Finally, someone might lay claim to the name and maintain that philosophy is entirely different from what has been indicated, or that it is something over and above this. It would be easy to show him that precisely what I have set forth has from the earliest been considered to be philosophy by all competent exponents, that everything he might wish to pass off as such has a different name already, and that if this word is to designate anything specific, it must designate precisely this science.

I, 424

However, since we are not inclined to engage in this essentially fruitless controversy about a word, we have ourselves long ago surrendered this name and called the science which is expressly committed to solving the problem indicated, *the Science of Knowledge.*

2

One can ask for a reason only in the case of something judged to be contingent, viz., where it is assumed that it could also have been otherwise, and yet is not a matter of determination through freedom; and it is precisely the fact that he inquires as to its ground that makes it, for the inquirer, contingent. The task of seeking the ground of something contingent means: to exhibit some other thing whose properties reveal why, of all the manifold deter-

minations that the explicandum might have had, it actually has just
those that it does. By virtue of its mere notion, the ground falls
outside what it grounds; both ground and grounded are, as such,
opposed and yet linked to each other, so that the former explains
the latter.

Now philosophy must discover the ground of all experience;
thus its object necessarily lies outside all experience. This proposition holds good of all philosophy, and really did hold universally
until the time of the Kantians and their facts of consciousness,
and thus of inner experience.

There can be no objection at all to the proposition here
established: for the premise of our argument is the mere analysis
of our proposed concept of philosophy, and it is from this that our
conclusion follows. Should someone say perhaps that the concept
of ground ought to be explained in some other way, we certainly
cannot prevent him from thinking what he likes in using this
expression: however, it is our right to declare that under the
above description of philosophy *we* wish nothing to be understood
beyond what has been said. If this meaning be not accepted, the
possibility of philosophy in our sense would accordingly have to
be denied; and we have already attended to that alternative above.

3

A finite rational being has nothing beyond experience; it is
this that comprises the entire staple of his thought. The philosopher is necessarily in the same position; it seems, therefore,
incomprehensible how he could raise himself above experience.

But he is able to abstract; that is, he can separate what is
conjoined in experience through the freedom of thought. *The
thing*, which must be determined independently of our freedom
and to which our knowledge must conform, and *the intelligence,*
which must know, are in experience inseparably connected. The
philosopher can leave one of the two out of consideration, and he
has then abstracted from experience and raised himself above it.
If he leaves out the former, he retains an intelligence in itself,
that is, abstracted from its relation to experience, as a basis for
explaining experience; if he leaves out the latter, he retains a

thing-in-itself, that is, abstracted from the fact that it occurs in experience, as a similar basis of explanation. The first method of procedure is called *idealism,* the second *dogmatism.*

The present discussion should have convinced anyone that these two are the only philosophical systems possible. According to the former system, the presentations accompanied by the feeling of necessity are products of the intelligence which must be presupposed in their explanation; according to the latter, they are products of a thing-in-itself which must be assumed to precede them.

Should someone wish to deny this proposition, he would have to prove either that there is a way, other than that of abstraction, by which to rise above experience, or that the consciousness of experience consists of more constituents than the two mentioned.

Now in regard to the first system, it will indeed become clear later on that what is to rank as intelligence is not something produced merely by abstraction, but under a different predicate really has its place in consciousness; it will nonetheless emerge, however, that the consciousness thereof is conditioned by an abstraction, of a kind that is, of course, natural to man.

It is not at all denied that a person might fuse together a whole from fragments of these heterogeneous systems, or that idle work of this nature has in fact very often been done: but it is denied that, given a consistent procedure, there are any other systems possible besides these two.

4

Between the objects—we shall call the explanatory ground of experience that a philosophy establishes *the object of that* I, 427   *philosophy,* since only through and for the latter does it appear to exist—between the object of *idealism* and that of *dogmatism,* there is, in respect of their relation to consciousness in general, a remarkable difference. Everything of which I am conscious is an object of consciousness. Such an object may stand in three relations to the subject. The object appears either as having first been created by the presentation of the intellect, or as existing without the aid of the intellect; and, in the latter case, either as determined in its nature, as well, or as present merely in its existence, while its essence is determinable by the free intellect.

The first relation amounts to a mere inventing, with or without an aim, the second to an object of experience, the third to a single object only, as we shall demonstrate forthwith.

I can freely determine myself to think this or that; for example, the thing-in-itself of the dogmatic philosophers. If I now abstract from what is thought and observe only myself, I become to myself in this object the content of a specific presentation. That I appear to myself to be determined precisely so and not otherwise, as thinking, and as thinking, of all possible thoughts, the thing-in-itself, should in my opinion depend on my self-determination: I have freely made myself into such an object. But I have not made myself as it is in itself; on the contrary, I am compelled to presuppose myself as that which is to be determined by self-determination. I myself, however, am an object for myself whose nature depends, under certain conditions, on the intellect alone, but whose existence must always be presupposed.

Now the object of idealism is precisely this self-in-itself.[1] The object of this system, therefore, actually occurs as something real in consciousness, not as a *thing-in-itself*, whereby idealism would cease to be what it is and would transform itself into dogmatism, but as a *self-in-itself;* not as an object of experience, for it is not determined but will only be determined by me, and without this determination is nothing, and does not even exist; but as something that is raised above all experience.

By contrast, the object of dogmatism belongs to those of the first group, which are produced solely by free thought; the thing-in-itself is a pure invention and has no reality whatever. It does not occur in experience: for the system of experience is nothing other than thinking accompanied by the feeling of necessity, and not even the dogmatist, who like any other philosopher must exhibit its ground, can pass it off as anything else. The dogmatist

[1] I have avoided this expression until now, in order not to engender the idea of a self as a *thing*-in-itself. My caution was in vain: for this reason I now abandon it, for I do not see whom I should need to protect.

wants, indeed, to assure to that thing reality, that is, the necessity of being thought as the ground of all experience, and will do it if he proves that experience can really be explained by means of it, and cannot be explained without it; but that is the very question at issue, and what has to be proved should not be presupposed.

Thus the object of idealism has this advantage over the object of dogmatism, that it may be demonstrated, not as the ground of the explanation of experience, which would be contradictory and would turn this system itself into a part of experience, but still in general in consciousness; whereas the latter object cannot be looked upon as anything other than a pure invention, which expects its conversion into reality only from the success of the system.

This is adduced only to promote clear insight into the differences between the two systems, and not in order to infer from it something against dogmatism. That the object of every philosophy, as the ground of the explanation of experience, must lie outside experience, is demanded simply by the nature of philosophy, and is far from proving a disadvantage to a system. We have not as yet found the reasons why this object should furthermore occur in a special manner in consciousness.

I, 429

Should somebody be unable to convince himself of what has just been asserted, then, since this is only a passing remark, his conviction as to the whole is not yet made impossible thereby. Nevertheless, in accordance with my plan, I shall consider possible objections even here. One could deny the claim that there is immediate self-consciousness involved in a free action of the spirit. We would only have to remind such a person once more of the conditions of self-consciousness we have detailed. This self-consciousness does not force itself into being and is not its own source; one must really act freely and then abstract from objects and concentrate only upon oneself. No one can be compelled to do this, and even if he pretends to, one can never know if he proceeds correctly and in the requisite way. In a word, this consciousness cannot be demonstrated to anyone; each person must freely create it in himself. One could only object to the second assertion, viz., that the thing-in-itself is a sheer invention, by reason of having misunderstood it. We would refer such a person to the above description of the origin of this concept.

5

Neither of these two systems can directly refute its opposite, for their quarrel is about the first principle, which admits of no derivation from anything beyond it; each of the two, if only its first principle is granted, refutes that of the other; each denies everything in its opposite, and they have no point at all in common from which they could arrive at mutual understanding and unity. Even if they appear to agree about the words in a sentence, each takes them in a different sense.[2]

I, 430   First of all, idealism cannot refute dogmatism. As we have seen, the former, indeed, has this advantage over the latter, that it is able to exhibit the presence in consciousness of the freely acting intellect, which is the basis of its explanation of experience. This fact, as such, even the dogmatist must concede, for otherwise he disqualifies himself from any further discussion with the idealist; but through a valid inference from his principle he converts it into appearance and illusion, and thereby renders it unfit to serve as an explanation of anything else, since in his philosophy it cannot even validate itself. According to him, everything that appears in our consciousness, along with our presumed determinations through freedom and the very belief that we are free, is the

---

[2]This is why *Kant* has not been understood and the Science of Knowledge has not found favor and is not soon likely to do so. The Kantian system and the Science of Knowledge are, not in the usual vague sense of the word, but in the precise sense just specified, idealistic; the modern philosophers, however, are one and all *dogmatists*, and firmly determined to remain so. *Kant* has been tolerated only because it was possible to make him into a dogmatist; the Science of Knowledge, which does not admit of such a transformation, is necessarily intolerable to these sages. The rapid diffusion of *Kantian* philosophy, once understood—as best it has been—is a proof not of the profundity, but of the shallowness of the age. In part, in its current form, it is the most fantastic abortion that has ever been produced by the human imagination, and it reflects little credit on the perspicacity of its defenders that they do not recognize this: in part, it is easy to prove that it has recommended itself only because people have thereby thought to rid themselves of all serious speculation and to provide themselves with a royal charter to go on cultivating their beloved, superficial empiricism.

product of a thing-in-itself. This latter belief is evoked in us by the operation of the thing, and the determinations which we deduce from our freedom are brought about by the same cause: but this we do not know, and hence we attribute them to no cause, and thus to freedom. Every consistent dogmatist is necessarily a fatalist: he does not deny the fact of consciousness that we consider ourselves free, for that would be contrary to reason; but he demonstrates, on the basis of his principle, the falsity of this belief. —He completely denies the independence of the self upon which the idealist relies, and construes the self merely as a product of things, an accident of the world; the consistent dogmatist is necessarily also a materialist. He could be refuted only on the basis of the postulate of the freedom and independence of the self; but it is precisely this that he denies.

I, 431

The dogmatist is no less incapable of refuting the idealist.

The thing-in-itself, which is the fundamental principle of the dogmatist, is nothing and has no reality, as even its exponents must concede, apart from what it is alleged to acquire through the circumstance that experience can be explained only on its basis. The idealist destroys this proof by explaining experience in another way: thus he denies precisely what the dogmatist relies on. The thing-in-itself becomes completely chimerical; there no longer appears to be any reason at all to assume one; and with this the entire edifice of dogmatism collapses.

From what has been said the absolute incompatibility of the two systems appears at once, in that what follows from one of them annihilates the conclusions of the other; hence their fusion necessarily leads to inconsistency. Wherever it is attempted, the parts do not mesh, and at some juncture an immense hiatus ensues. Whoever would wish to take issue with what has just been asserted would have to demonstrate the possibility of such a combination, which presupposes a continued passage from matter to spirit or its reverse, or what is the same, a continued passage from necessity to freedom.

So far as we can yet see, from the speculative point of view the two systems appear to be of equal value: they cannot coexist, but neither one can make any headway against the other. In this light, it is interesting to ask what might motivate the person who sees this—and it is easy enough to see—to prefer one of the systems over the other, and how it is that skepticism, as the total surrender of the attempt to solve the problem presented, does not become universal.

The dispute between the idealist and the dogmatist is, in reality, about whether the independence of the thing should be sacrificed to the independence of the self or, conversely, the independence of the self to that of the thing. What is it, then, that motivates a reasonable man to declare his preference for one over the other?

From the given vantage point, which a person must necessarily adopt if he is to be counted a philosopher, and to which one comes sooner or later, even without meaning to, in the course of reflection, the philosopher finds nothing but *that he must present himself as free* and that there are determinate things outside him. It is impossible for a person to rest content with this thought; the thought of a mere presentation is only a half-thought, the fragment of a thought; something must be superadded which corresponds to the presentation independently of the presenting. In other words, the presentation cannot exist for itself alone: it is something only when conjoined with something else, and for itself it is nothing. It is precisely this necessity of thought which drives us on from that standpoint to the question, "What is the ground of presentations?" or, what comes to the very same, "What is it that corresponds thereto?"

Now the presentation of the independence of the self, and that of the thing, can assuredly coexist, but not the independence of both. Only one of them can be the first, the initiatory, the independent one: the second, by virtue of being second, necessarily becomes dependent on the first, with which it is to be conjoined.

Now which of the two should be taken as primary? Reason provides no principle of choice; for we deal here not with the addition of a link in the chain of reasoning, which is all that rational grounds extend to, but with the beginning of the whole chain, which, as an absolutely primary act, depends solely upon the freedom of thought. Hence the choice is governed by caprice, and since even a capricious decision must have some source, it is governed by *inclination* and *interest*. The ultimate basis of the difference between idealists and dogmatists is thus the difference of their interests.

The highest interest and the ground of all others is self-interest. This is also true of the philosopher. The desire not to lose, but to maintain and assert himself in the rational process, is the interest which invisibly governs all his thought. Now there are two levels of humanity, and before the second level is reached by everyone in the progress of our species, two major types of man. Some, who have not yet raised themselves to full consciousness of their freedom and absolute independence, find themselves only in the presentation of things; they have only that dispersed self-consciousness which attaches to objects, and has to be gleaned from their multiplicity. Their image is reflected back at them only by things, as by a mirror; if these were taken from them, their self would be lost as well; for the sake of their self they cannot give up the belief in the independence of things, for they themselves exist only if things do. Everything they are, they have really become through the external world. Whoever is in fact a product of things, will never see himself as anything else; and he will be right so long as he speaks only of himself and of others like him. The principle of the dogmatists is belief in things for the sake of the self: indirect belief, therefore, in their own scattered self sustained only by objects.

The man who becomes conscious of his self-sufficiency and independence of everything that is outside himself, however— and this can be achieved only by making oneself into something independently of everything else—does not need things for the support of himself, and cannot use them, because they destroy that self-sufficiency, and convert it into mere appearance. The self which he possesses, and which is the subject of his interest, annuls this belief in things; he believes in his independence out of inclination, he embraces it with feeling. His belief in himself is direct.

This interest also explains the emotions which usually enter into the defense of philosophical systems. The attack on his

I, 434

system in fact exposes the dogmatist to the danger of losing his self; yet he is not armed against this attack, because there is something within him that sides with the attacker; hence he defends himself with passion and animosity. By contrast, the idealist cannot readily refrain from regarding the dogmatist with a certain contempt, for the latter can tell him nothing save what he has long since known and already discarded as erroneous; for one reaches idealism, if not through dogmatism itself, at least through the inclination thereto. The dogmatist flies into a passion, distorts, and would persecute if he had the power: the idealist is cool and in danger of deriding the dogmatist.

What sort of philosophy one chooses depends, therefore, on what sort of man one is; for a philosophical system is not a dead piece of furniture that we can reject or accept as we wish; it is rather a thing animated by the soul of the person who holds it. A person indolent by nature or dulled and distorted by mental servitude, learned luxury, and vanity will never raise himself to the level of idealism.

We can show the dogmatist the inadequacy and incoherence of his system, of which we shall speak in a moment: we can bewilder and harass him from all sides; but we cannot convince him, because he is incapable of calmly receiving and coolly assessing a theory which he absolutely cannot endure. If idealism should prove to be the only true philosophy, it is necessary to be born, raised, and self-educated as a philosopher: but one cannot be made so by human contrivance. Our science expects few converts, therefore, among those *already formed;* if it may have any hopes at all, they are set, rather, upon the young whose innate power has not yet foundered in the indolence of our age.

I, 435

6

But dogmatism is completely unable to explain what it must, and this demonstrates its untenability.

It must explain the fact of presentation, and undertakes to render it intelligible on the basis of the influence of the thing-in-itself. Now it must not deny what our immediate consciousness tells us about presentation. —What, then, does it say about presentation? It is not my intention here to conceptualize what can only be intuited internally, nor to treat exhaustively of that to whose discussion a large part of the Science of Knowledge is dedicated. I merely wish to recall what everybody who has taken just one good look into himself must have discovered long ago.

The intellect as such *observes itself;* and this self-observation is directed immediately upon its every feature. The nature of intelligence consists in this *immediate* unity of being and seeing. What is in it, and what it is in general, it is *for itself;* and it is that, *qua* intellect, only in so far as it is that for itself. I think of this or that object: what, then, does this involve, and how, then, do I appear to myself in this thinking? In no other way than this: when the object is a merely imaginary one, I create certain determinations in myself; when the object is to be something real, these determinations are present without my aid: *and I observe that creation and this being.* They are in me only in so far as I observe them: seeing and being are inseparably united. —A thing, to be sure, is supposed to have a diversity of features, but as soon as the question arises: *"For whom,* then, is it to have them?"* no one who understands the words will answer: "For itself"; for we must still subjoin in thought an intellect *for* which it exists. The intellect is, by contrast, necessarily what it is for itself, and requires nothing subjoined to it in thought. By being posited as intellect, that for which it exists is already posited with it. In the intellect, therefore—to speak figuratively—there is a double series, of being and of seeing, of the real and of the ideal; and its essence consists in the inseparability of these two (it is synthetic); while the thing has only a single series, that of the real (a mere being posited). Intellect and thing are thus exact opposites: they inhabit two worlds between which there is no bridge.

It is by the principle of causality that dogmatism wishes to explain this constitution of intellect in general, as well as its particular determinations: it is to be an effect and the second member in the series.

But the principle of causality holds of a single *real* series, not of a double one. The power of the cause is transferred to something else that lies outside it, opposed to it, and creates a being

I, 436

therein and nothing more; a being for a possible intellect outside it and not for the being itself. If you endow the object acted upon with mechanical power only, it will transfer the received impulse to its neighbor, and thus the motion originating in the first member may proceed through a whole series, however long you wish to make it; but nowhere in it will you find a member which reacts upon itself. Or if you endow the object acted upon with the highest quality you can give to a thing, that of sensitivity, so that

I, 437

it governs itself on its own account and in accordance with the laws of its own nature, not according to the law given it by its cause, as in the series of mere mechanism, then it certainly reacts back upon the stimulus, and the determining ground of its being in this action lies not in the cause, but only in the requirement to be something at all; yet it is and remains a bare, simple being: a being for a possible intellect outside of itself. You cannot lay hold of the intellect if you do not subjoin it in thought as a primary absolute, whose connection with that being independent of it may be difficult for you to explain. —The series is simple, and after your explanation it remains so, and what was to be explained is not explained at all. The dogmatists were supposed to demonstrate the passage from being to presentation; this they do not, and cannot, do; for their principle contains only the ground of a being, but not that of presentation, which is the exact opposite of being. They take an enormous leap into a world quite alien to their principle.

They seek to conceal this leap in a variety of ways. Strictly— and that is the procedure of consistent dogmatism, which becomes materialism at once—the soul should not be a thing at all, and should be nothing whatever but a product, simply the result of the interaction of things among themselves.

But by this means there arises something in the things only, and never anything apart from them, unless an intellect, which observes things, is supplied in thought. The analogies the dogmatists present to make their system intelligible—that of harmony, for example, which arises out of the concord of several instruments—actually make its irrationality apparent. The concord and the harmony are not in the instruments; they are only in the mind of the listener who unifies the manifold in himself; and unless such a listener is supplied, they are nothing at all.

And yet, who is to prevent the dogmatist from assuming a soul as one of the things-in-themselves? This would then belong among the postulates he assumes for the solution of the problem, and only so is the principle of the action of things on the soul applicable, for in materialism there is only an interaction among things whereby thought is supposed to be produced. In order to make the inconceivable thinkable, he has sought to postulate the active thing, or the soul, or both, to be such that through their action presentations could result. The *acting thing* was to be such that its actions could become presentations, much like *God* in *Berkeley's* system (which is a dogmatic, and not at all an idealistic one). This leaves us no better off; we understand only mechanical action, and it is absolutely impossible for us to think of any other; the above proposal, therefore, consists of mere words without any sense. Or again, the soul is to be such that every action upon it becomes a presentation. But with this we fare exactly as with the previous principle: we simply cannot understand it.

This is the course dogmatism takes everywhere and in every form in which it appears. In the immense hiatus left to it between things and presentations, it inserts some empty words instead of an explanation. To be sure, these words can be memorized and repeated, but nobody at all has ever had, nor ever will have, a thought connected to them. For if one tries to conceive distinctly *how* the above occurs, the whole notion vanishes in an empty froth.

Thus dogmatism can only repeat its principle, and then reiterate it under various guises; it can state it, and then state it again; but it cannot get from this to the explanandum, and deduce the latter. Yet philosophy consists precisely of this deduction. Hence dogmatism, even from the speculative viewpoint, is no philosophy at all, but merely an impotent claim and assurance.

Idealism is left as the only possible philosophy.

What is here established has nothing to do with the objections of the reader, for there is absolutely nothing to be said against the latter; its concern is, rather, with the absolute incapacity of many to understand it. Nobody who even understands the words can deny that all causation is mechanical and that no presentation comes about through mechanism. But this is precisely where the difficulty lies. A grasp of the nature of intelligence as depicted, upon which our entire refutation of dogmatism is founded, presupposes a degree of independence and freedom of mind. Now many people have progressed no further in their thinking than to grasp the simple sequence of the mechanism of nature; so it is very natural that presentations, if they wish to think of them, should also fall for them in this series, the only one that has entered their minds. The presentation becomes for them a kind of thing: a singular confusion, of which we find traces in the most famous of philosophical authors. Dogmatism is enough for such men; there is no hiatus for them, because for them the opposing world does not even exist. —Hence the dogmatist cannot be refuted by the argument we have given, however clear it may be; for it cannot be brought home to him, since he lacks the power to grasp its premise.

The manner in which we deal here with dogmatism also offends against the indulgent logic of our age, which, though uncommonly widespread in every period, has only in our own been raised to the level of a maxim expressed in words: one need not be so strict in reasoning, proofs are not to be taken so rigorously in philosophy as they are, say, in mathematics. Whenever thinkers of this type observe even a couple of links in the chain of reasoning, and catch sight of the rule of inference, they at once supply the remainder pell-mell by imagination, without

I, 440 further investigation of what it consists of. If an Alexander perforce tells them: Everything is determined by natural necessity: our presentations are dependent upon the disposition of things and our will upon the nature of our presentations; hence all our volitions are determined by natural necessity and our belief in free will is an illusion; they find this wonderfully intelligible and clear, and go off convinced and amazed at the brilliance of this demonstration, in spite of the fact that there is no sense to it. I beg to observe that the Science of Knowledge neither proceeds from nor counts upon this indulgent logic. If even a single member of the long chain that it must establish be not rigorously joined to the next, it will have proved nothing whatever.

7

As already stated above, idealism explains the determinations of consciousness on the basis of the activity of the intellect. The intellect, for it, is only active and absolute, never passive; it is not passive because it is postulated to be first and highest, preceded by nothing which could account for a passivity therein. For the same reason, it also has no *being* proper, no subsistence, for this is the result of an interaction and there is nothing either present or assumed with which the intellect could be set to interact. The intellect, for idealism, is an *act*, and absolutely nothing more; we should not even call it an *active* something, for this expression refers to something subsistent in which activity inheres. But idealism has no reason to assume such a thing, since it is not included in its principle and everything else must first be deduced. Now out of the activity of this intellect we must deduce *specific* presentations: of a world, of a material, spatially located world existing without our aid, etc., which notoriously occur in consciousness. But a determinate cannot be deduced from an indeterminate: the grounding principle, which is the rule of all deduction, is inapplicable here. Hence this primordial action of the intellect must needs be a determinate one, and, since the intellect is itself the highest ground of explanation, an action determined by the intellect and its nature, and not by something outside it. The presupposition of idealism will, therefore, be as follows: the intellect acts, but owing to its nature, it can act only in a certain fashion. If we think of this necessary way of acting in abstraction from the action itself, we shall call it, most appropriately, the law of action: hence there are necessary laws of the intellect.—This, then, also renders immediately intelligible the feeling of necessity that accompanies specific presentations: for here the intellect does not register some external impression, but feels in this action the limits of its own being. So far as idealism makes this one and only rationally determined and genuinely explanatory assumption, that the intellect has necessary laws, it is called critical, or also transcendental idealism. A transcendent idealism would be a system that deduced determinate presentations from the free and

I, 441

totally lawless action of the intellect; a completely contradictory
hypothesis, for surely, as has just been remarked, the principle of
grounding is inapplicable to such an action.

As surely as they are to be grounded in the unitary being of
the intellect, the intellect's assumed laws of operation themselves
constitute a system. This means that the fact that the intellect
operates in just such a way under this specific condition can be
further explained by the fact that it has a definite mode of
operation under a condition in general; and the latter in turn may
be explained on the basis of a single fundamental law: the
intellect gives its laws to itself in the course of its operation; and
this legislation itself occurs through a higher necessary action, or
presentation. The law of causality, for example, is not a primordial law, but is merely one of several ways of connecting the
manifold, and can be deduced from the fundamental law of this
connection: and the law of this connection of the manifold, along
with the manifold itself, can again be deduced from higher laws.

I, 442

In accordance with this remark, critical idealism itself can
now proceed in two different ways. On the one hand, it may
really deduce the system of the necessary modes of operation, and
with it concurrently the objective presentations created thereby,
from the fundamental laws of the intellect, and so allow the whole
compass of our presentations to come gradually into being before
the eyes of its readers or listeners. On the other hand, it may
conceive these laws as already and immediately applied to objects,
that is, as applied somewhere, upon their lowest level (at which
stage they are called categories), and then maintain that it is by
means of them that objects are ordered and determined.

Now how can the critical philosopher of the latter sort, who
does not deduce the accepted laws of the intellect from the nature
thereof, obtain even a mere material knowledge of them—the
knowledge that they are precisely these, viz., the laws of substantiality and causality? For I will not yet burden him with the
question of how he knows that they are mere immanent laws of
the intellect. They are the laws that are applied directly to objects: and he can have formed them only by abstraction from
these objects, and hence only from experience. It avails nothing if

he borrows them in some roundabout way from logic; for logic itself has arisen for him no otherwise than by abstraction from objects, and he merely does indirectly what, if done directly, would too obviously catch our eyes. Hence he can in no way confirm that his postulated laws of thought are really laws of thought, really nothing but immanent laws of the intellect. The dogmatist maintains against him that they are universal properties of things grounded in the nature of the latter, and it is past seeing why we should give more credence to the unproved assertion of the one than to the unproved assertion of the other.—This method yields no knowledge that the intellect must act precisely thus, nor why it must do so. In order to promote such understanding, something would have to be set forth in the premises that is the unique possession of the intellect, and those laws of thought would have to be deduced from these premises before our very eyes.

I, 443

It is especially difficult to see, how, according to this method, the object itself arises; for, even if we grant the critical philosopher his unproved postulate, it explains nothing beyond the *dispositions* and *relations* of the thing; that, for example, it is in space, that it manifests itself in time, that its accidents must be related to something substantial, and so on. But whence comes that which has these relations and dispositions; whence the stuff that is organized in these forms? It is in this stuff that dogmatism takes refuge, and you have merely made a bad situation worse.

We know well enough that the thing comes into being surely through an action in accord with these laws, that it is nothing else but the *totality of these relations unified by the imagination,* and that all these relations together constitute the thing; the object is surely the original synthesis of all these concepts. Form and matter are not separate items; the totality of form is the matter, and it is through analysis that we first obtain individual forms. But the critical philosopher who follows the present method can only assure us of this; and it is in fact a mystery how he knows it himself, if indeed he does. So long as the thing is not made to arise as a whole in front of the thinker's eyes, dogmatism is not hounded to its last refuge. But this is possible only by dealing with the intellect in its total, and not in its partial conformity to law.

Such an idealism is, therefore, unproved and unprovable. It has no other weapon against dogmatism save the assurance that it is right; and against the higher, perfected critical philosophy, nothing save impotent rage and the assertion that one can go no further, the assurance that beyond it there is no more ground, that from there one becomes unintelligible to *it*, and the like; all of which means nothing whatever.

Finally, in such a system only those laws are established whereby the purely subsumptive faculty of judgment determines the objects of external experience alone. But this is by far the smallest part of the system of reason. Since it lacks insight into the whole procedure of reason, this halfhearted critical philosophy gropes around in the sphere of practical reason and reflective judgment just as blindly as the mere imitator and copies out, just as artlessly, expressions totally unintelligible to it.[3]

In another place[4] I have already set forth in full clarity the methods of the perfected transcendental idealism established by the Science of Knowledge. I cannot explain how people could

I, 444

I, 445

[3]Such a critical idealism has been propounded by *Professor Beck* in his *Einzig möglichen Standpunkte.* . . . Although I find in this view the weaknesses objected to above, that should not deter me from the public expression of due respect to the man who, on his own account, has raised himself out of the confusion of our age to the insight that the philosophy of Kant is not a dogmatism but a transcendental idealism, and that, according to it, the object is given neither in whole nor in half, but is rather made; and from expecting that in time he will raise himself even higher. I consider the above work as the most suitable present that could have been made to our age, and recommend it as the best preparation for those who wish to study the Science of Knowledge from my writings. It does not lead to this latter system; but destroys the most powerful obstacle which closes it off for many people. —Some have fancied themselves insulted by the tone of that work, and just recently a well-meaning reviewer in a famous journal demands in clear terms: *crustula, elementa velit ut discere prima.* For my part, I find its tone, if anything, too mild: for I truly do not think that we should, of all things, thank certain writers for having confused and debased the richest and noblest teaching for a decade or more, nor see why we should first ask their permission to be right. —As regards the hastiness with which the same author, in another group, which is far below him, pounces upon books that his own conscience ought to tell him he does not understand, and cannot even rightly know how deep their matter may go, I can feel sorry only on his own account.

[4]In the work, *Über den Begriff der Wissenschaftslehre.* Weimar, 1794.

have failed to understand that exposition; at any rate, it is asserted that some have not understood it.

I am forced, therefore, to repeat what has been said before,
and warn that in this science everything turns on the understanding thereof.

This idealism proceeds from a single fundamental principle
of reason, which it demonstrates directly in consciousness. In so
doing it proceeds as follows. It calls upon the listener or reader to
think a certain concept freely; were he to do so, he would find
himself obliged to proceed in a certain way. [We must distinguish
two things here: the required mode of thinking—this is accomplished through freedom, and whoever does not achieve it with us
will see nothing of what the Science of Knowledge reveals—and
the necessary manner in which it is to be accomplished, which
latter is not dependent on the will, being grounded in the nature
of the intellect; it is something *necessary,* which emerges, however, only in and upon the occurrence of a free action; something
found, though its discovery is conditioned by freedom.]

So far idealism demonstrates its claims in our immediate
consciousness. But that the above necessity is the fundamental
law of all reason, that from it one can deduce the whole system of
our necessary presentations—not only of a world whose objects
are determined by the subsuming and reflective judgment, but
also of ourselves as free practical beings under laws—this is a
I, 446   mere hypothesis. Idealism must prove this hypothesis by an actual deduction, and this precisely is its proper task.

In so doing it proceeds in the following fashion. *It shows that
what is first set up as fundamental principle and directly demonstrated in consciousness, is impossible unless something else occurs along with it, and that this something else is impossible unless
a third something also takes place, and so on until the conditions
of what was first exhibited are completely exhausted, and this
latter is, with respect to its possibility, fully intelligible.* Its course
is an unbroken progression from conditioned to condition; each
condition becomes, in turn, a conditioned whose condition must
be sought out.

If the hypothesis of idealism is correct and the reasoning in

goal of idealism

the deduction is valid, the system of all necessary presentations or the entirety of experience (this identity is established not in philosophy but only beyond it) must emerge as the final result, as the totality of the conditions of the original premise.

Now idealism does not keep this experience, as the antecedently known goal at which it must arrive, constantly in mind; in its method it knows nothing of experience and takes no account of it at all; it proceeds from its starting point in accordance with its rule, unconcerned about what will emerge in the end. It has been given the right angle from which to draw its straight line; does it then still need a point to draw it to? In my opinion, all the points on its line are given along with it. Suppose that you are given a certain number. You surmise it to be the product of certain factors. Your task then is simply to seek out, by the rule well known to you, the product of these factors. Whether or not it agrees with the given number will turn out later, once you have the product. The given number is the entirety of experience; the factors are the principle demonstrated in consciousness and the laws of thought; the multiplication is the activity of philosophiz-

I, 447   ing. Those who advise you always to keep an eye on experience when you philosophize are recommending that you change the factors a bit and multiply falsely on occasion, so that the numbers you get may, after all, match: a procedure as dishonest as it is superficial.

To the extent that these final results of idealism are viewed as such, as consequences of reasoning, they constitute the a priori in the human mind; and to the extent that they are regarded, where reasoning and experience really agree, as given in experience, they are called a posteriori. For a completed idealism the a priori and the a posteriori are by no means twofold, but perfectly unitary; they are merely two points of view, to be distinguished solely by the mode of our approach. Philosophy anticipates the entirety of experience and *thinks* it only as necessary, and to that extent it is, by comparison with real experience, a priori. To the extent that it is regarded as given, the number is a posteriori; the same number is a priori insofar as it is derived as a product of the factors. Anyone who thinks otherwise, simply does not know what he is talking about.

A philosophy whose results do not agree with experience is surely false, for it has not fulfilled its promise to deduce the entirety of experience and to explain it on the basis of the necessary action of the intellect. Either the hypothesis of transcendental idealism is, therefore, completely false, or it has merely been wrongly handled in the particular version which fails to perform its task. Since the demand for an explanation of experience is surely founded in human reason; since no reasonable man will accept that reason can impose a demand whose satisfaction is absolutely impossible; since there are only two roads to its satisfaction, that of dogmatism and that of transcendental idealism, and it can be proved without further ado that the former cannot fulfill its promise; for these reasons, the resolute thinker will always prefer the latter, holding that the hypothesis as such is completely right and that error has occurred only in the reasoning; nor will any vain attempt deter him from trying again, until finally success is achieved.

I, 448

The course of this idealism runs, as can be seen, from something that occurs in consciousness, albeit only as the result of a free act of thought, to the entirety of experience. What lies between these two is its proper field. This latter is not a fact of consciousness and does not lie within the compass of experience; how could anything that did so ever be called philosophy, when philosophy has to exhibit the ground of experience, and the ground lies necessarily outside of what it grounds. It is something brought forth by means of free but law-governed thought. —This will become entirely clear as soon as we take a closer look at the fundamental assertion of idealism.

The absolutely postulated is impossible, so idealism shows, without the condition of a second something, this second without a third, and so on; that is, of all that it establishes nothing is possible alone, and it is only in conjunction with them all that each individual item is possible. Hence, by its own admission, only the whole occurs in consciousness, and this totality is in fact experience. Idealism seeks a closer acquaintance with this whole, and so must analyze it, and this not by a blind groping, but according to the definite rule of composition, so that it may see the whole take form under its eyes. It can do this because it can abstract; because in free thought it is surely able to grasp the individual alone. For not only the necessity of presentations, but also their freedom is present in consciousness: and this freedom, again, can proceed either lawfully or capriciously. The whole is given to it from the standpoint of necessary consciousness; it discovers it, just as it discovers itself. The series created by the unification of this whole emerges only through freedom. Whoever performs this act of freedom will come to be aware of it, and lay out, as it were, a new field in his consciousness: for one who does not perform it, that which the act conditions does not exist at all. —The chemist synthesizes a body, say a certain metal, from its elements. The ordinary man sees the metal familiar to him; the chemist, the union of these specific elements. Do they then see different things? I should think not! They see the same thing, though in different ways. What the chemist sees is the a priori, for he sees the individual elements: what the common man sees is the a posteriori, for he sees the whole. —But there is this difference here: the chemist must first analyze the whole before he can compound it, since he is dealing with an object whose rule of composition he cannot know prior to the analysis; but the philosopher can synthesize without prior analysis, because he already knows the rule that governs his object, reason.

No reality other than that of necessary thought falls, therefore, within the compass of philosophy, given that one wishes to think about the ground of experience at all. Philosophy maintains that the intellect can be thought only as active, and active only in this particular way. This reality is completely adequate for it; since it follows from philosophy that there is in fact no other.

It is the complete critical idealism here described that the Science of Knowledge intends to establish. What has just been said contains the concept of this former, and I shall entertain no objections to it, for no one can know better than I what I propose to do. Proofs of the impossibility of a project that will be accomplished, and in part already is so, are simply ridiculous. One has only to attend to the course of the argument, and examine whether or not it fulfills its promise.

I, 449

funny

SECOND INTRODUCTION TO THE SCIENCE
OF KNOWLEDGE

For readers who already have a philosophical system

Philosophisches Journal, V, pp. 319–78; VI, pp. 1–40 (1797).

1

I, 453 I believe the introduction given in the first part of this journal to be perfectly adequate for the unprejudiced reader, that is, for those who betake themselves to the author without preconceived opinions, and neither assist him, nor yet withstand him. It is otherwise with those who already have a philosophical system. From the construction of the latter they have abstracted certain maxims, which have become a matter of principle with them; anything not brought about in accordance with these rules they dismiss without further inquiry, or even the need to read it, as false; it is bound to be false, indeed, for it has been done in defiance of their uniquely valid method. If these people are not to be given up altogether—and why should they be?—we require at the outset to get rid of this obstacle, which deprives us of their attention; we must imbue them with a mistrust of their own rules.

This preliminary inquiry into method is most particularly necessary in regard to the Science of Knowledge, whose entire structure and significance are utterly different from those of the philosophical systems that have been customary hitherto. The system-makers I have in mind proceed from some concept or other; without caring in the least where they got it from, or

I, 454 whence they have concocted it, they analyze it, combine it with others to whose origin they are equally indifferent, and in reason-

29

ings such as these their philosophy itself is comprised. It consists, in consequence, of their own thoughts. The Science of Knowledge is a very different matter. Its chosen topic of consideration is not a lifeless concept, passively exposed to its inquiry merely, of which it makes something only by its own thought, but a living and active thing which engenders insights from and through itself, and which the philosopher merely contemplates. His role in the affair goes no further than to translate this living force into purposeful activity, to observe the activity in question, to apprehend it and grasp it as a unity. He undertakes an experiment. His affair it is, to put the object of inquiry in a position where precisely those observations that were intended can be made; his affair also, to take note of the phenomena, to follow them correctly, and to connect them together; but how the object manifests is not his affair, but that of the object itself, and he would be operating directly counter to his own aim if he did not leave it to itself, and sought to intervene in the development of the phenomenon. The philosopher of the first type, by contrast, is fashioning an artefact. In the object of his labours he reckons only upon the matter, not upon an inner, self-active force thereof. Before he goes to work, this inner force must already have been killed, or it would offer resistance to his efforts. From this dead mass he fashions something, purely through his own powers, and in accordance only with his own concept, already devised beforehand. In the Science of Knowledge there are two very different sequences of mental acts: that of the self, which the philosopher observes, and that of the philosopher's observations. In the opposite philosophies just referred to, there is only *one* sequence of thought: that of the philosopher's meditations; for the content thereof is not itself introduced as thinking. A major source of misunderstanding, and

I, 455 many irrelevant objections to the Science of Knowledge arise from either not distinguishing these two series at all, or confounding what belongs to the one with what belongs to the other; and this has come about because the critics encounter only one sequence in their philosophy. The act of one who fashions an artefact is assuredly the phenomenon itself, for his material is inert; but the report of one who undertakes an experiment is not the specific phenomenon under scrutiny, but the concept thereof.[1]

2

After these preliminary remarks, whose further application will be found in the discussion now in hand—how is the Science of Knowledge to go about the solution of its problem?

⌈The question it has to answer is, as we know, the following: Whence arises the system of presentations accompanied by the feeling of necessity? or: How do we come to attribute objective validity to what in fact is only subjective? or, since objective validity is described as existence: How do we come to believe in an existent? Since this question arises from a reversion into oneself, from observing that the immediate object of consciousness is in fact only consciousness itself, it can refer to no other existence than an existence for us; and it would be perfectly absurd to assimilate it to the question as to an existence unrelated to consciousness.⌋Yet it is precisely the greatest absurdities that

I, 456

---

[1]It would be owing to a similar confusion of the two sequences of thought in transcendental idealism, were anyone to think it possible to have an equally basic and consistent *realist* system, *alongside* and *extraneous to* idealism. The realism that overtakes us all, and even the most hardened idealist, when it comes to acting—that is, the assumption that things exist outside and quite independently of us—is itself rooted in idealism and is explained and deduced thereby; and the deduction of an objective truth, alike in the world of appearances and in the intelligible world, is assuredly the one aim of all philosophy. —The philosopher says only in *his own* name: Everything that exists for the self, exists through the self. The self, however, itself says in its own philosophy: As surely as I am and live, something exists outside me, which is not there by my doing. How it arrives at such a claim, the philosopher explains by the principles of his philosophy. The first standpoint is that of pure speculation; the second, that of life and scientific knowledge (in a sense contrasted with that of the Science of Knowledge). The second is only intelligible on the basis of the first; realism has grounds, indeed, apart from that, for we are constrained to it by our own nature, but it has no *known* and *comprehensible* grounds: yet the first standpoint, again, exists only for the purpose of making the second intelligible. Idealism can never be a *mode of thought*, it is merely a *speculative* point of view.

seem most commonly to be put forth by the philosophers of our day.

The question proposed, namely: How is an existent possible for us? itself abstracts from all existence: which is to say, not that it supposes a nonexistence, whereby this concept would be neither negated, nor yet abstracted from, but that it does not entertain the concept of existence in general at all, either positively or negatively. It inquires as to the ground of the predicate of existence in general, imputed or withheld, as the case may be; but the ground is always external to the grounded, that is, it is opposed to the atter. The answer, if it is to be an answer to *this* question, and genuinely seeks to be addressed thereto, must similarly abstract from all existence. To maintain a priori, in advance of the attempt, that such abstraction is not possible in the answer, because it is not possible in general, is to maintain that it is also impossible in the question, and hence that the question, as put, is itself impossible; and therefore that the demand for a metaphysic, in the sense indicated, whereby we inquire as to the ground of existence for us, is not a demand of reason. The irrationality of this question cannot be proved on objective grounds against those who defend it; for the latter hold its possibility and necessity to be based on the highest law of reason, that of autonomy (practical legislation), to which all other rational laws are subject, and which grounds them all, while at the same time determining and I, 457 confining them to their sphere of validity. Those who defend the question will grant the opponent his arguments, while denying their pertinence to the issue in hand; how justifiably, the opponent can judge only if he joins them in mounting to their highest law; whereby, however, he comes at the same time to require an answer to the question in dispute, and so ceases to be their opponent. The antagonism can have arisen only from a subjective incapacity: from awareness of never having raised this question in one's own case, or felt the need to secure an answer. As against this, the defenders, too, can put forward nothing on objective rational grounds; for the state in which this doubt automatically ensues is based on preceding acts of freedom, which no demonstration can serve to compel.

3

Who is it now, who performs the required abstraction from all existence: in which of the two series does it lie? Obviously, in that of philosophical ratiocination; no other series has so far made its appearance.

The only thing the philosopher adheres to, and from which he proposes to account for what is to be explained, is the conscious being, or subject, which he will therefore have to conceive as stripped of any presentation of existence, in order first to point therein to the ground of all existence—existence for itself, naturally. But when all existence of or for the subject is taken away, it has nothing left but an act; more especially in relation to existence, it is that which acts. So he will therefore have to view it in its acting, and from this point on the double series will first commence.

The basic contention of the philosopher, as such, is as follows: Though the self may exist only for itself, there necessarily arises for it at once an existence external to it; the ground of the latter lies in the former, and is conditioned thereby: self-consciousness and consciousness of something that is to be—not ourselves,—are necessarily connected; but the first is to be regarded as the conditioning factor, and the second as the conditioned. To establish this claim, not by argument, indeed—as valid for a system of existence-in-itself—but, by observation of the original procedure of reason, as valid for reason, he will have to show, firstly, how the self is and may be for itself; then, that this existence of itself for itself would be impossible, unless there also at once arose for it an existence outside itself.

I, 458

Thus the first question would be: How does the self exist for itself? The first postulate: Think of yourself, frame the concept of yourself; and notice how you do it.

Everyone who does no more than this, so the philosopher claims, will find that in the thinking of this concept his activity as an intelligence reverts into itself and makes itself its own object.

Now if this be correct, and once it is admitted, we know the mode of construction of the self, the manner in which it exists for itself (and no other existence is in question here); the philosopher can thereupon proceed to his demonstration that this act would be impossible without another, whereby there arises for the self an existence outside itself.

Thus, as we have now described it, does the Science of Knowledge knit its investigations together. We next have to consider its right to proceed in this fashion.

4

First of all, what elements in the act described are to be assigned to the philosopher as such, —and what to the self that is to be observed by him? The self has nothing beyond the reversion into itself; everything else pertains to the relation thereto of the philosopher, for whom the entire system of experience is already given as a mere fact, which is to be brought into being before his eyes by the self, so that he may come to know the manner of its genesis.

I, 459   The self, we say, reverts *into itself*. So is it not therefore already present for itself before the occurrence of this reversion, and independently thereof? Must it not already be there for itself, in order that it may make itself the object of an act? And if so, doesn't your philosophy in that case already presuppose what it was meant to explain?

I answer: Not at all. It is only through this act, and first by means of it, by an act upon an act itself, which specific act is preceded by no other whatever, that the self *originally* comes to exist for itself. Only *for the philosopher* is it there beforehand, as a fact, since he himself has already run through the whole course of experience. He is obliged to express himself as he does, if only to be understood; and is able so to express himself, because he has already long since acquired all the concepts that are needed for the purpose.

Now what—to look first at the self under observation—is this reversion it makes into itself; to what class of modifications of consciousness is it to be assigned? It is not a *conceiving;* this it only becomes by contrast with a not-self, and through determination of the self within this opposition. Hence it is a mere intuition. —It is also, accordingly, no consciousness, not even a consciousness of self; and simply because no consciousness comes about through this mere act, we may indeed infer further to another act, whereby a not-self arises for us; only so can we make progress in our philosophical argument, and derive as required the system of experience. By the act described, the self is merely endowed with the possibility of self-consciousness, and therewith of all other consciousness; but no true consciousness comes into being as yet. The act in question is merely a part, and a part not originally separated, but only to be distinguished by the philosopher, of that entire enterprise of the intellect, whereby it brings its consciousness into being.

How does it fare, on the other hand, with the philosopher as such?

I, 460 This self-constructing self is none other than his own. He can intuit the aforementioned act of the self in himself only, and in order that he may intuit it, he has to carry it out. Freely, and by his own choice, he brings it about in himself.

But—it may be asked, and asked it has been—if this whole philosophy is erected on something brought about by an act of mere arbitrary choice, does it not thereby become a fancy of the brain, a mere fabrication? How then is the philosopher to ensure the objectivity of this purely subjective act? How is he to accord this primordial character to what is obviously empirical merely, and occurs at a time—the time when he sets about philosophizing. How is he to prove that this current free thought of his, in the middle of his series of presentations, corresponds to the necessary thought whereby he came to exist for himself at all, and which ties the whole sequence of these presentations together? I answer: This act is by its nature objective. That I exist for myself, is a fact. Now I can only have come about for myself through acting, for I am free; and through this particular act only; for by this I come about for myself at every instant, and by every other, something wholly different comes about for me. The act in question is simply the concept of the self, and the concept of the self is the concept of this act; both are exactly the same; and by means of this concept nothing else is thought, nor can be thought, save what we

have referred to. It *is* so, because I *make* it so. The philosopher
merely makes clear to himself what he actually thinks, and always has thought, when he thinks of *himself;* that he thinks of
himself is, however, an immediate fact of consciousness for him
—The query about objectivity is based on the strange assumption
that the self is something over and above its own thought of itself,
and that this thought is underlaid by something else—Heaven
knows what!—apart from the thought itself, and whose true
nature is a matter of concern. If people wish to make inquiry
concerning such an objective validity of thought, or the bond
between this object and the subject, I confess that the Science of
Knowledge can give no information on the point. Let them set out
on their own to discover such a bond, in this or any other case;
until they bethink themselves, perhaps, that this unknown they
are in search of is still their own thought, and that what they may
again wish to lay beneath it is also merely a thought of theirs, and
so on forever; and that they are wholly unable to inquire or to
speak about anything, without in fact thinking of it.

I, 461

    In this act, then, which for the philosopher as such is arbi-
trary and temporal, but for the self is that which he necessarily
and primarily constructs for himself, as by right now established,
for the observations and inferences that are to follow—in this act,
I say, the philosopher contemplates himself, scans his act directly, knows what he does, because *he*—*does* it.

    Does, then, a consciousness arise for him therein? Undoubt-
edly: for he not only intuits, but also *conceives.* He conceives his
act as an *acting in general,* of which he already has a concept in
consequence of his previous experience; and as this *specific, self-
reverting act,* as he intuits it in himself; by this characteristic
difference he singles it out from the sphere of action in general.
—What acting is, can only be intuited, not evolved from concepts
or communicated thereby; but the import of this intuition is
grasped by contrast with mere *being.* Acting is not being, and
being is not acting; the mere concept furnishes no other determination; for the true nature of things, one must have recourse to
intuition.

    Now *to me,* at least, this whole procedure of the philosopher appears very possible, very easy, very natural, and I can scarcely conceive how it should appear otherwise to my readers, or how they should find anything strange and mysterious therein. Everybody, one hopes, will be able to think *of himself.* He will become aware, one hopes, that, in that he is summoned to think thus, he is summoned to something dependent on his self-activity, to an *inward action,* and that if he does what is asked, and really affects himself through self-activity, he is, in consequence, acting. Let us hope, too, that he will be able to distinguish *this* act from the *opposite* one, whereby he thinks of objects outside him, and to find that in the latter the thinker and the thought are opposed, so that his activity has to be addressed to something distinct from himself, whereas in the act required of him, thinker and thought are the same, so that his activity has therefore to revert into itself. He will perceive, let us hope, that, since this is the *only* way for the thought of himself to arise in him—since, as he has found, an opposite mode of thinking produces in him a wholly different thought—that, as I say, the thought of himself is nothing other than the thought of this act, and the word 'I' nothing other than the designation thereof; that *self* and *self-reverting act* are perfectly identical concepts. Let him but assume provisionally, with transcendental idealism, that all consciousness rests on, and is conditioned by, self-consciousness. This assumption he makes anyway, if he does but turn an attentive eye upon himself and has risen to the point of requiring a philosophy; but its correctness is to be categorically shown him in philosophy itself by complete deduction of all experience from the possibility of self-consciousness. He will thereupon grasp, let us hope, that he is then obliged to *think* of this self-reversion as preceding and conditioning all other acts of consciousness, or—what comes to the same—must think of it as the most primordial act of the subject. And since nothing exists for him that is not in consciousness, while everything else therein is conditioned by this very act, and so cannot again condition it in the same respect, he will grasp it, moreover, as *for him* a wholly unconditioned and thus absolute act. He will then, we trust, realize accordingly that the *presupposition in question,* and the *thought of the self as originally posited*

I, 462

I, 463

by itself, are again perfectly identical; and that transcendental idealism, if it is to go to work systematically, cannot possibly proceed in any other way than it does in the Science of Knowledge.

Should anyone henceforth have occasion to object to this procedure, it will lessen the chances of beating the air if I simply refer him to the description just given, and beg him to tell me the precise step in the sequence to which he takes exception.

5

This intuiting of himself that is required of the philosopher, in performing the act whereby the self arises for him, I refer to as *intellectual intuition*. It is the immediate consciousness that I act, and what I enact: it is that whereby I know something because I do it. We cannot prove from concepts that this power of intellectual intuition exists, nor evolve from them what it may be. Everyone must discover it immediately in himself, or he will never make its acquaintance. The demand to have it proved for one by reasoning is vastly more extraordinary than would be the demand of a person born blind to have it explained to him what colors are, without his needing to see.

Everyone, to be sure, can be shown, in his own admitted experience, that this intellectual intuition occurs at every moment of his consciousness. I cannot take a step, move hand or foot, without an intellectual intuition of my self-consciousness in these acts; only so do I know that *I* do it, only so do I distinguish my action, and myself therein, from the object of action before me. Whosoever ascribes an activity to himself, appeals to this intuition. The source of life is contained therein, and without it there is death.

This intuition, however, never occurs in isolation, as a complete act of consciousness; any more than sensory intuition occurs
I, 464   singly or renders consciousness complete; for both must be *brought under concepts*. Nor is this all, indeed, for intellectual intuition is also constantly conjoined with an intuition of *sense*. I cannot find myself in action without discovering an object on which I act, in the form of a conceptualized sensory intuition;

without projecting a picture, no less conceptual, of what I wish to bring about. For how do I know what I seek to accomplish, and how could I know this, without having an immediate regard to myself, in projecting the target-concept as an act? —Only this whole set of circumstances, in uniting the given manifold, completes the sphere of consciousness. It is only the concepts of object and goal that I come to be aware of, however, not the two intuitions that underlie them.

It may be simply this that the enemies of intellectual intuition are anxious to urge against it, namely that it is possible only in conjunction with a sensory intuition; an observation which is certainly of importance, and which the Science of Knowledge assuredly does not contest. But if anyone should think himself justified thereby in rejecting intellectual intuition, he could with equal justice deny sensory intuition as well, for it too is possible only in conjunction with the intellectual, seeing that everything that is to be *my* presentation has got to be related to myself; the consciousness of self, however, comes solely from intellectual intuition. (It is a curious feature of the more recent history of philosophy, that it has not been realized how everything that can be said against the claim to an intellectual intuition also holds against the claim to sensory intuition, so that the blows aimed at the opposition fall also upon those who deliver them.)

But, if it has to be admitted that there is no immediate, isolated consciousness of intellectual intuition, how does the philosopher then arrive at the knowledge and isolated presentation of the same? I answer: by the same process, undoubtedly, that leads him to the knowledge and isolated presentation of sensory intuition, namely, an inference from the obvious facts of consciousness. The inference whereby the philosopher arrives at this claim to intellectual intuition is as follows: I propose to think of some determinate thing or other, and the required thought ensues; I propose to do some determinate thing or other, and the presentation of its occurrence ensues. This is a fact of consciousness. Were I to view it by the laws of merely sensory consciousness, it would contain no more than has just been given, a sequence of particular presentations; this sequence in the time-series is all I would be

I, 465

conscious of, and all I could assert. I could say only: I know that the presentation of that particular thought, with the indication that it was to occur, was immediately followed in time by a presentation of the same thought, with the indication that it actually was occurring; that presentation of that particular phenomenon, as one that was to happen, was immediately followed by its presentation as really taking place; I could not, however, enunciate the utterly different proposition, that the first presentation contains the *real ground* of the second; that through thinking the first, the second *came about* for me. I remain merely passive, the inert stage on which presentations succeed one another, not the active principle which might bring them forth. Yet I make the latter assumption, and cannot abandon it without abandoning myself; how do I arrive at this? There is no basis for it in the sensory ingredients referred to; hence it is a special consciousness, viz. an immediate consciousness or intuition, albeit not a sensory intuition relating to a material, static existent, but an intuition of sheer activity, not static but dynamic; not a matter of existence, but of life.

The philosopher thereby discovers this intellectual intuition as a fact of consciousness (for him it is a fact; for the original self an Act); yet he discovers it, not immediately, as an isolated item in consciousness, but rather by distinguishing what appears in combination in the ordinary consciousness, and resolving the whole into its constituent parts.

I, 466   It is a wholly different task to explain this intellectual intuition—here presupposed as fact—in terms of its *possibility,* and, by this deduction from the system of reason as a whole, to defend it against the suspicion of fallacy and delusion which it incurs by conflicting with the dogmatic mode of thought that is no less grounded in reason; to confirm on yet higher grounds the *belief* in its reality, from which, by our own express admission, transcendental idealism assuredly sets out, and to vindicate in reason even the interest on which it is based. This comes about solely by exhibition of the moral law in us, wherein the self is presented as a thing sublime beyond all original modifications effected by that law; is credited with an absolute activity founded only in itself and in nothing else whatever; and is thus characterized as an absolute agency. The consciousness of this law, which itself is doubtless an immediate consciousness derived from no other, forms the basis for the intuition of self-activity and freedom; I am given to myself, by myself, as something that is to be active in a certain fashion, and am thereby given to myself as active in general; I have life within me, and draw it from myself. Only through this medium of the moral law do I behold *myself;* and in thus seeing myself, I necessarily see myself as self-active; and thereby arises for me the wholly alien factor of my self's real efficacy, in a consciousness that would otherwise be merely that of a succession among my presentations.⌉

Intellectual intuition is the only firm standpoint for all philosophy. From thence we can explain everything that occurs in consciousness; and moreover, only from thence. Without self-consciousness there is no consciousness whatever; but self-consciousness is possible only in the manner indicated: I am simply active.

I, 467   Beyond that I can be driven no further; here my philosophy becomes wholly independent of anything arbitrary, and a product of iron necessity, insofar as the free reason is subject to the latter: a product, that is, of *practical* necessity. I *can* go no further from this standpoint, because I *may* not go any further; and transcendental idealism thus appears at the same time as the only dutiful mode of thought in philosophy, as that mode wherein speculation and the moral law are most intimately united. I *ought* in my thinking to set out from the pure self, and to think of the latter as absolutely self-active; not as determined by things, but as determining them.

The concept of action, which becomes possible only through this intellectual intuition of the self-active self, is the only concept which unites the two worlds that exist for us, the sensible and the intelligible. That which stands opposed to my action—I must oppose something to it, for I am finite—is the sensible world; that which is to come about through my action is the intelligible world.

There are those who, on mention of an intelligible intuition, put on a familiar air of superiority;² I should like to know how

---

²As is done, for instance, by the Raphael among the critics, in his review in the *Allgemeine Literatur Zeitung* of Schelling's essay *On the Self.*

they view the consciousness of the moral law; or how they would undertake to construct the concepts of right, virtue and so forth, which they yet undoubtedly possess. According to them there are but two intuitions a priori, time and space. They undoubtedly frame these concepts in time, the form of inner sense, yet assuredly do not suppose them to be time itself, but merely a certain filling of time. Now what is it, then, that they fill time with, and on which they found their construction of these concepts? They have nothing left to them but space, and so their right would have to turn out square, say, and their virtue circular; just as all the concepts of sensory intuition they construct, such as those of a tree or an animal, etc., are nothing but specific limitations of space. They do not think of right and virtue thus. So what is the basis of their construction? If they look properly, they will find that it is action in general, or freedom. The concepts of both right and virtue, for them, are specific limitations of action in general, just as all their sensory concepts are specific limitations of space. But now how do they arrive at this basis for their construction? They have not, let us hope, derived action from the dead persistency of matter, or freedom from the mechanism of Nature; they must have got it through immediate intuition, and hence there is also a third intuition besides their other two.

I, 468

It is therefore not so trivial a matter as it seems to some, whether philosophy starts out from a fact or an Act (that is, from a pure activity which presupposes no object, but itself produces it, and in which the acting, therefore, immediately becomes the *deed*). If it proceeds from the fact, it places itself in the world of existence and finitude, and will find it difficult to discover a road from thence to the infinite and supersensible; if it sets out from the Act, it stands precisely at the point joining the two worlds, from whence they can be surveyed with a single glance.

6

It is not the way of the Science of Knowledge, or of its author, to seek the protection of any authority. If a person must first look to see whether this science conforms to the doctrine of some other writer, before he is willing to be persuaded by it, instead of seeing whether it conforms to the demands of his own reason, our theory does not count on him at all, since he lacks the absolute self-activity, the wholly independent belief in himself, which that theory presupposes. It is for reasons quite other, therefore, than those of recommending his doctrine, that the author of this work has come forward with the preliminary obser-

I, 469   vation that it is perfectly in accordance with the teaching of Kant, and is nothing other than Kantianism properly understood. In this view he has been increasingly confirmed by the continuing elaboration of his system, and the many-sided application that he has been led to give to its principles. All who rank as well-acquainted with the Kantian philosophy, and have given their opinion on the matter—both friends and foes of the Science of Knowledge—are unanimous in affirming the contrary,[3] and *at their urging* the same has been said by Kant himself, who, after all, must undoubtedly understand himself the best.[4] If the author of this

I, 470   work were capable of a certain way of thinking, this would

---

[3]The accomplished author of the review of the first four volumes of this philosophical journal in the *Allgemeine Literatur Zeitung* (F. Schlegel), who likewise invites proof of this claim, forbears to give his own opinion as to the consiliency or otherwise of the two systems; so he is in no way referred to here.

[4]Herr Forberg, who is cited by the *Allgemeine Literatur Zeitung,* the *Salzburger Literarische Zeitung* and others as the author of *Fragmente aus meinen Papieren,* (Jena 1796) can affirm (p. 77) "on the *best* authority (presumably a written statement from Kant), that Kant considers my system to differ entirely from the Kantian." I, for my part, have so far found it impossible to learn, on the best or on any authority, the Kantian opinion of the Science of Knowledge; moreover, I am very far from expecting that reverend sage, who has surely earned his position, to plunge into a train of thought quite new, quite strange to him and quite at variance with his own style, simply in order to utter a verdict which beyond all doubt the age will already pronounce without him; and that Kant is not given to judging what he has not read, is something I know only too well. For all that, I must in fairness believe Herr Forberg, until I can prove otherwise. It may thus be true that Kant should have voiced such an opinion. But the question then is whether he was speaking of the Science of Knowledge *genuinely perused and understood,* or rather, it may be, of the rash miscarriages which its expositor was pleased to bring forth, under the name of the Science of Knowledge, in the philosophical *Annals;* which *Annals,* as the Editor thereof will know, have directed attention to the weaknesses of the Science in question.

necessarily be very welcome to him. Since he holds it no shame at
all to understand Kant wrongly, and foresees that the opinion that
it really is no shame will shortly become general, he could take
upon himself the minor disgrace of having once expounded Kant
amiss; and would conversely gain the honor of ranking as the first
discoverer of a viewpoint that will certainly obtain general curren-
cy, and will effect a most beneficial revolution among mankind. It
is well-nigh inexplicable, why both friends and foes of the Science
of Knowledge should so ardently contest our claim, and should so
earnestly summon the claimant to the proof thereof, which he
never promised, which he expressly abjured, and which would
have its place in the eventual history of the Science of Knowledge, not in its exposition. The foes, at least, do not do this out of
any tender concern for the author's honor; and the friends could
spare themselves that trouble, since I myself have no mind for
such an honor, and seek the honor that I do recognize in another
quarter. Can it be, to obviate the reproach, that they may not
have understood Kant's writings? Such an allegation is at least no
reproof in the mouth of the author of this work, who confesses as
loudly as he may that he too has failed to understand them, and
that only after first discovering the Science of Knowledge by his
own route, did he find in them a sound and self-consistent meaning; and it is to be hoped that the above allegation will soon cease
to serve as a reproof in any mouth. If my opponents are particularly concerned to rebut the accusation of not recognizing their
own doctrine, which they have defended with all the forces at
their command, when it was presented to them in a strange guise,
I would also be very glad to spare them that assuredly grave
reproach, if I did not have an interest which seems to me higher
than theirs and to which theirs *ought* to be sacrificed. For I will
I, 471　　not for an instant be taken for more than I am, or allow myself to
be credited with an achievement that is not my own.

　　So for once I must embark upon the proof so often demanded; and therefore take the opportunity which offers itself here.

　　As we have just seen, the Science of Knowledge sets out
from an intellectual intuition, that of the absolute self-activity of
the self.

But now it is undeniable, and is there before the eyes of all who read Kant's writings, that there is nothing he is more decidedly—one might almost say, disdainfully—against, than the claim to possess a faculty of intellectual intuition. After all the further elaboration of his system since the appearance of the *Critique of Pure Reason,* whereby its principles have obviously achieved far greater clarity and finish in his mind, as will be apparent to anyone who attentively compares his earlier writings with the latter—after all this, I say, the attitude in question is so deeply rooted in the nature of Kantian philosophy, that even in one of his latest productions ("On Fine Airs in Philosophy," *Berliner Monatsschrift,* May 1796) he reiterates it as sharply as ever; deriving from the delusion of an intellectual intuition the fashion in philosophy for despising work of any kind, and in general the most unmitigated fanaticism.

Could further testimony be needed, that a philosophy erected on precisely what Kantianism thus forcibly condemns must be the complete antithesis of that system, and the very same unmitigated and unmeaning system that Kant is referring to in the essay in question? Before building on this argument, it would be advisable to consider whether entirely different concepts might not be expressed in the two systems by means of the same word. In the Kantian terminology, all intuition is directed to existence of some kind (a posited or permanent); intellectual intuition would thus be the immediate consciousness of a nonsensuous entity; the immediate consciousness of the thing-in-itself, and that by way of pure thought; hence a creation of the thing-in-itself by means of the concept (much as those who prove the existence of God from the mere concept are obliged to regard God's existence as a mere consequence of their thinking). In terms of its chosen route, the Kantian system may have need in this fashion to shut out the thing-in-itself; the Science of Knowledge has disposed of it by other means; we recognize it to be the uttermost perversion of reason, and a concept perfectly absurd; all existence, for us, is necessarily *sensory* in character, for we first derive the entire concept of existence from the form of sensibility; and are thus completely protected against the claim to any connection with the thing-in-

I, 472

itself. Intellectual intuition in the Kantian sense is a wraith which
fades in our grasp when we try to think it, and deserves not even
a name. The intellectual intuition alluded to in the Science of
Knowledge refers, not to existence at all, but rather to action, and
simply finds no mention in Kant (unless, perhaps, under the title
of *pure apperception*). Yet it is nonetheless possible to point out
also in the Kantian system the precise point at which it should
have been mentioned. Since Kant, we have all heard, surely, of
the categorical imperative? Now what sort of consciousness is
that? Kant forgot to ask himself this question, since he nowhere
dealt with the foundation of *all* philosophy, but treated in the
Critique of Pure Reason only of its theoretical aspect, in which
the categorical imperative could make no appearance; and in the
Critique of Practical Reason, only of its practical side, in which
the concern was solely with content, and questions about the type
of consciousness involved could not arise. —This consciousness is
undoubtedly immediate, but not sensory; hence it is precisely
what I call "intellectual intuition," and—seeing there are no
canonical authors in philosophy—call it so with no less right than
Kant had in thereby denominating something else, which does not
exist. By the same right I may demand that people should inform
themselves of the meaning I give to the term, before passing
judgment on my system.

I, 473   My worthy friend, Court Chaplain Schulz, to whom I communicated the still vague idea I had of basing the whole of
philosophy on the pure self, long ago, before I was clear about it,
and whom I found nearer and less averse to it than anyone else,
has a notable passage on this subject. In his examination of
Kant's *Critique of Pure Reason,* part 2, p. 159, he says: "Just
because it can and must teach us immediately, we ought not to
confuse the pure active self-consciousness in which every self
properly consists, with the *faculty of intuition*, or maybe conclude
therefrom that we possess a *nonsensory, intellectual power of
intuition.*" (Precisely what the Science of Knowledge has since
maintained.) "For *intuition* signifies a *presentation* that is *immediately* related to the object. Pure self-consciousness, however, is
not presentation, but rather *that* whereby every presentation—

first properly becomes such." —"When I say, I present something to myself, this is as much as to say: I am conscious that I have a presentation of this object," etc. Thus, according to Herr Schulz, a presentation is that of which consciousness is possible. Now he is speaking at this very point of pure self-consciousness. Undoubtedly he knows what he is talking about; and as a philosopher, therefore, he certainly has a presentation of pure self-consciousness. —But it is the original self-consciousness he is referring to, rather than that of the philosopher; and the meaning of his contention is therefore as follows: Originally, that is, in the ordinary consciousness untouched by philosophical reflection, pure self-consciousness does not constitute a complete consciousness, but is merely a necessary factor whereby the latter first becomes possible. But if *sensory* intuition does constitute a consciousness, is it then anything else but that also whereby a presentation first

I, 474   becomes such? Intuitions without concepts, are they not blind? In what sense is Herr Schulz entitled to call (sensory) intuition, in the absence of self-consciousness, a presentation? From the philosopher's standpoint, self-consciousness, as we have seen, is as much a presentation as intuitions are; from the standpoint of original presentation, *they* are no more presentations than self-consciousness is. Or does the concept constitute a presentation? Concepts without intuitions we know to be empty. Self-consciousness, sensory intuitions and concepts, taken in isolation, are one and all, not presentations, but merely that whereby presentations become possible. For Kant, for Schulz and for myself, a complete presentation involves three factors: that whereby the presentation is related to an object, and becomes the presentation of *something*, and which we are all agreed in calling sensory intuition; —(this is so, even if I am myself the object of the intuition; I become for myself a permanent in time)—that whereby it is related to the subject, and becomes *my* presentation, and which according to Kant and Schulz is not to be called intuition, but is so called by me, because it stands in the same relation to the complete presentation as sensory intuition; and finally, that whereby both are united, and in this union alone become presentation, which we again agree in calling the concept.

So what then, in a couple of words, is the import of the Science of Knowledge? It is this: reason is absolutely independent; it exists only for itself; but for it, too, it is all that exists. So everything that it is must be founded in itself, and explained solely from itself, and not from anything outside it, to which it could never get out without abrogating itself; in short, the Science of Knowledge is transcendental idealism. And what then, in a couple of words, is the import of the Kantian philosophy? How are we to characterize Kant's system? I confess I am unable to conceive how one could understand a single proposition in Kant, or reconcile it to other propositions, without making the same

I, 475

assumption, which I believe to be displayed at every point: I admit that one of my reasons for declining to provide the proof requested was that it seemed to me a trifle ludicrous, and a trifle tedious, to point out the wood by counting the individual trees.

I will cite here just one key passage from Kant. He says (*C.P.R.*, B136—Kemp Smith translation): "The supreme principle of the possibility of all intuition, in its relation to understanding, is that all the manifold of intuition should be subject to conditions of the original synthetic unity of apperception." Which means, in other words, that the *thinking* of an intuited item is possible only if the possibility of the original unity of apperception can be sustained therein. Now for Kant, even an intuition is itself possible only if it is thought and conceived, since intuitions without concepts are, for him, blind, that is to say, nothing at all. I conclude, therefore, since intuition itself stands under the conditions of the possibility of thinking, that for Kant it is not only thinking in its immediacy, but by means of this also the intuiting conditioned thereby, and thus *all consciousness,* which stands under conditions of the original unity of apperception.

What is the condition? —Kant speaks here indeed of conditions, but in fact proposes only one as the basic condition—what, then, is the condition of the original unity of apperception? §16 gives it as follows: that it should be *possible* for my presentations to be accompanied by the '*I* think', that is, that *I am what thinks* in this thinking.

Which 'I' is being spoken of here? That, perchance, which

the Kantians blithely piece together from a manifold of presentations, in none of which it was contained individually, though it is present in all together; so that the above-cited words of Kant would mean *this:* I, who think D, am the same I who thought C and B and A, and through the thinking of my manifold thoughts I first become I for myself, namely that which is *identical* in the manifold? In that case Kant would be just such a miserable babbler as the said Kantians; for then, according to him, the possibility of all thinking would be conditioned by another thinking, and by the thinking of this thinking, and I should like to know how we are ever to arrive at any thinking at all.[5]

However, we shall not merely argue here, but will cite the words of Kant himself. At B 132 he says: "But this representation ('I think') is an act of *spontaneity,* that is, it cannot be regarded as belonging to sensibility." (Hence not to inner sense either, I would add, which is where the above-described identity of consciousness assuredly belongs.) "I call it *pure apperception,* to distinguish it from empirical apperception (just mentioned). . . . because it is that self-consciousness which, while generating the representation '*I think*' (a representation which must be capable of accompanying all other representations, and which *in all consciousness is one and the same*),[6] cannot itself be accompanied by any further representation." Here the nature of pure self-consciousness is clearly described. In all consciousness it is the same; hence undeterminable by any contingent feature of consciousness; the self therein is determined solely by itself, and is absolutely determined. —Nor can Kant understand by this pure apperception the consciousness of our individuality, or confuse the one with the other; for the consciousness of individuality is necessarily accompanied by another consciousness, that of a *Thou,* and is possible only on this condition.

We therefore find quite definitely in Kant the concept of the

[5]Even if we were willing to pass over this, bad as it is, the conflation of these many presentations would still yield only a manifold *thinking,* as *a thinking in general,* not anything *that thinks* in this manifold thinking.

[6][The last italics are Fichte's, not Kant's, Tr.]

pure self, exactly as it is framed in the Science of Knowledge.
—And how, in the above passage, does *Kant* think this pure self
to be related to all consciousness? As *conditioning the same.*
Hence, for Kant, the possibility of all consciousness will be conditioned by the possibility of the self, or of pure self-consciousness,
exactly as in the Science of Knowledge. The conditioning factor is
presupposed in the thinking of the conditioned; for this is just
what the given relationship signifies: so for Kant, therefore, a
systematic derivation of all consciousness, or, what comes to the
same, a system of philosophy, would have to set out from the pure
self, exactly as is done in the Science of Knowledge, and the idea
of such a science will thus have been furnished by Kant himself.

But one may perhaps wish to invalidate this argument by
the following distinction: *conditioned* is one thing, and *determined* another.

According to Kant, all consciousness is merely conditioned
by self-consciousness, that is, its content can be founded upon
something outside self-consciousness; now the results of this
foundation are simply not supposed to *contradict* the conditions of
self-consciousness; simply not to eliminate the possibility thereof;
but they are not required actually to *emerge* from it.

According to the Science of Knowledge, all consciousness is
determined by self-consciousness, that is, everything that occurs in
consciousness is founded, given and introduced by the conditions
of self-consciousness; and there is simply no ground whatever for
it outside self-consciousness. —I must explain that in our case the
determinacy follows directly from the *fact of being conditioned,*
and that here, therefore, the distinction in question does not
operate at all, and says nothing. Anyone who says here: All
consciousness is conditioned by the possibility of self-
consciousness, *and so I will now regard it,* still knows nothing
about consciousness in this inquiry, and is abstracting from everything that he may fancy he knows about it. He derives what is
required from the proposed principle; and only what he has thus
derived as consciousness is consciousness for him, and everything
else is and remains nothing. Thus derivability from self-
consciousness therefore *determines* for him the scope of what he
counts as consciousness, because he starts from the presupposi-

I, 477

I, 478

tion, that all consciousness is *conditioned* by the possibility of self-consciousness.

Now I am very well aware that *Kant* by no means *established* a system of the aforementioned kind; for in that case the present author would have saved himself the trouble and chosen some other branch of human knowledge as the scene of his labors. *I* am aware that he by no means *proved* the categories he set up to be conditions of self-consciousness, but merely said that they were so: that still less did he derive space and time as conditions thereof, or that which is *inseparable* from them in the original consciousness and fills them both; in that he never once says of them, as he expressly does of the categories, that they are such conditions, but merely implies it by way of the argument given above. However, I think I also know with equal certainty that *Kant envisaged* such a system; that everything that he actually propounds consists of fragments and consequences of such a system, and that his claims have sense and coherence only on this assumption. Whether he had not thought out this system for himself to a pitch of clarity and precision where he *could* also have expounded it to others, or whether he had in fact done so, and simply did not *want* to expound it, as certain passages seem to indicate,[7] might well, as it seems to me, remain wholly unex-

[7]For example, *C.P.R.*, B 108: "In this treatise, I purposely omit the definitions of the categories, *although I may be in possession of them.*" The categories can only be defined, *each by its determinate relation to the possibility of self-consciousness,* and anyone in possession of these definitions is necessarily in possession of the Science of Knowledge. —B 109: *"In a system of pure reason,* definitions of the categories would rightly be demanded, but in *this* treatise they would merely divert attention from the main object of the enquiry." In this passage the *system of pure reason* and *this* treatise (the *Critique of Pure Reason*) are opposed, and the latter is not put forward as constituting the former. It is not easy to understand how, since *Reinhold's* time particularly, the question should have been raised as to the foundations and completeness of the Kantian inquiry, nor how, failing the publication by *Kant* of a system of pure reason, the *Critique* should have been transformed into such a system by its mere antiquity, nor again why the further questions admittedly allowed for in this passage, once actually raised, should have been somewhat rudely brushed aside. —For me, now, the *Critique of Pure Reason* is in no way devoid of foundations; they are very plainly there: only nothing has been built on them, and the building -materials—though already neatly prepared—lie about on top of one another in a very arbitrary order.

plored, or if it is to be looked into, someone else may do it; for on this point I have never expressed any view. However such an inquiry might turn out, the eminent author still retains unique credit for *this* achievement, of having first knowingly diverted philosophy away from external objects and directed it into ourselves. This is the spirit[8] and inmost heart of his whole philosophy, as it is also the spirit and heart of the Science of Knowledge.

I, 480

But I am confronted with a major difference that is alleged to lie between the Kantian system and the Science of Knowledge. This difference has again quite recently been asserted by one who has long had—what few others could say—the justified impression of having understood Kant, and by now has also shown himself to have grasped the Science of Knowledge. *Reinhold* it is, who seeks to show (on p. 341 of his *Auswahl vermischter Schriften*, part 2, Jena 1797) that in the claim I have just repeated and vindicated I am unjust *to himself*, and, what certainly follows from that, *to other adepts of Kant's writings as well.* He says: "The basis of our claim that there is something outside us corresponding to our presentations assuredly also lies, according to the *Critique of Pure Reason,* in the *self;* but only

---

[8]We are surely obliged to read by the *spirit,* if reading by the *letter* gets us no further. Kant himself, in the modest admission that he was not specially conscious of a gift for clarity, attaches no great value to the letter of his doctrine, and in the Preface to the Second Edition of the *Critique of Pure Reason,* B xliv, himself recommends that his writings be interpreted by their *interconnection* and according to the *idea* of the whole, and thus by the *spirit and intention* that individual passages may display. In his *Über eine Entdeckung,* etc., (1790) p. 119 ff., he himself provides a notable example of interpretation according to the spirit, in his exposition of Leibniz, every statement whereof proceeds from the premise: is it really credible that Leibniz should have wished to say this, and this, and this? On p. 122 he says that one should not be put out over the explanation (given in express terms by Leibniz) of *sensibility as a confused form of presentation,* but should rather *replace it* by one adapted to his intention, *since otherwise his system would be inconsistent with itself.* Similarly, the alleged innateness of certain concepts would be wholly misunderstood *if it were taken literally.* The last are Kant's own words. —The upshot would seem to be this: an original philosopher (there can be no reference here to mere expositors, since these are compared to their authors, if the latter are still extant) is to be interpreted according to the spirit *actually residing in him,* and not according to a spirit that *allegedly ought so to reside.*

insofar as *empirical knowledge* (experience) occurs therein as a fact; and insofar as this knowledge must be grounded, as to its *transcendental* content (which merely constitutes its *form*), *solely* in the *mere* self—while as to its *empirical content,* whereby it has objective reality, it must be grounded in the self *through something* that is *different* from the self. No scientific form of philosophy was possible so long as this something *different from the self,* as ground of the objective reality of the transcendental, had to be looked for solely *outside the self.*"

I shall neither have persuaded my readers, nor proved my case to the full, if I do not dispose of this objection.

The (purely historical) question is this: Did *Kant* really base experience, as to its empirical content, on *something different from the self?*

I am well aware that all Kantians, with the sole exception of Herr *Beck,* whose work in what here concerns us, the standpoint, appeared after the Science of Knowledge,[9] have understood Kant thus. So he is understood even by the commentator he has recently endorsed, Herr *Schulz,* whom I cite here for that reason. How often the latter concedes to Herr *Eberhard* that *the objective ground of appearances lies in something that is the thing-in-itself* (e.g., *Examination,* etc., part 2, p. 99); that hence they are *phenomena bene fundata,* and the like. How *Reinhold,* to this very hour, expounds Kant, we have just had occasion to see.

It may appear arrogant and disparaging to others when a solitary person appears and says: Till this moment, among a crowd of worthy scholars who have devoted their time and energies to the exposition of a certain book, there is not one who has understood this book in anything but a *completely distorted* fashion; they have discovered in it the very opposite system to that which is propounded therein; dogmatism instead of transcendental idealism: *I alone, however, understand it aright.* Yet in truth this arrogance should only seem to be such; for it is to be hoped that hereafter others, too, will understand the book, and the soli-

I, 481

---

[9]I do not reckon Herr *Schelling* among the expositors of Kant, any more than I have ever laid claim to that honor myself, save in respect of the assertion under discussion, and of what I say in the present context.

tary one no longer remain alone. Other reasons why in fact it should not be held arrogant if one ventures to contradict the whole body of Kantians, I shall not put forward here.

Yet—and this is the oddest feature of the affair—the discovery that Kant knows nothing of any somewhat distinct from the self is anything but new. For ten years every one has been able to see in print the most thorough and complete proof of it. It is to be found in Jacobi's *Idealismus und Realismus, ein Gespräch* (Breslau 1787) in the supplement *Über den transzendentalen Idealismus*, p. 207 ff. Jacobi has there cited and gathered together the most decisive and palpably evident of Kant's statements on this point, in the latter's own words. I have no need to do again what has been done already and could not well be done better, and refer the reader the more gladly to the work in question,

I, 482 since the whole book, like all of Jacobi's philosophical writings, could assuredly even now be profitable reading for the present generation.

These expositors of Kant will perhaps allow me to address just a few questions to them. How broadly, then, according to *Kant,* does the applicability of all the categories extend, and in particular that of causality? Only over the realm of appearances; and thus only over what is already for us and in us. And how, then, could one arrive at the assumption of a something distinct from the self, as a ground of the empirical content of knowledge? Only, I take it, by an inference from the grounded to the ground; hence, by application of the concept of causality. That is Kant's own view of the matter (p. 211 of Jacobi's book); and that reason alone is enough for him to reject the assumption of *things existing in themselves outside us.* But our expositors permit him for once to forget the basic contention of his system, as to the validity of the categories in general, and by a bold inference to issue forth from the world of appearances and arrive at things existing in themselves outside us. *Aenesidemus,* who, for his part, certainly also interprets Kant in this fashion, and whose skepticism locates the truth of our knowledge in its conformity to things-in-themselves, exactly as our Kantians do, has denounced this arrant inconsistency with sufficient distinctness. What answer, then, have the commentators given him on the point? —Kant speaks, after all, of a thing-in-itself? Well, what is this thing for him? A *noumenon,* as we can read in many passages of his works. In *Reinhold* and *Schulz* it is the same also, namely a mere noumenon. But what, then, is a noumenon? According to *Kant,* to *Reinhold* and to *Schulz,* it is something which we merely append *in thought* to appearances, according to laws of thought that call for demonstration, and were demonstrated by Kant, and which we are *obliged* to append, according to these laws;[10] *something, therefore, which arises only through our thinking;* but something that exists, not through our *free* thinking, but through a thinking *necessary* on the presupposition of selfhood—and exists, therefore, only *for our thinking,* for ourselves as thinking beings. And this noumenon, or thing-in-itself, what further use do these commentators wish to make of it? This thought of a thing-in-itself is grounded upon sensation, and sensation they again wish to have grounded upon the thought of a thing-in-itself. Their earth reposes on a mighty elephant, and the mighty elephant—reposes on their earth. Their thing-in-itself, which is a mere thought, is supposed to *operate* upon the self! Have they again forgotten what they first said; and is their thing-in-itself, which a moment ago was a mere thought, now something other than that? Or do they wish in all earnest to attribute to a mere thought the exclusive predicate of reality, that of efficacy? And were these the bemarvelled discoveries of the towering genius whose torch illumined the philosophy of the declining century?

That the above-described system is indeed the Kantianism of

I, 483

[10]Here lies the foundation-stone of Kantian realism. —To think of something as a thing-in-itself, that is, as existing independently of *myself, the empirical, I must* think of myself from the point of view of life, where I am merely the empirical; and for that very reason know nothing of my activity in this thinking, *because it is not free.* Only from the philosophical viewpoint can I *infer* in my thinking to this activity. This may be the reason why the clearest thinker of our age, to whose work I refer above, refused to accept the quite correctly stated view of transcendental idealism, and even thought to destroy it by the mere exposition thereof, because he was not clear about this distinction of the two points of view, and supposed that the idealist way of thinking was called for in *life;* an expectation which only requires stating in fact, to come to destruction. —Just as, in my opinion, it is owing to this very fact that others, who profess this idealism, are also desirous of accepting a realist system *in addition to* the idealist, to which they will never find an entry.

the Kantians; that it indeed consists in a reckless juxtaposition of
the crudest dogmatism, which has things-in-themselves making
impressions upon us, with the most inveterate idealism, which has
all existence arising solely out of the thinking of the intellect, and
I, 484   knows nothing of any other, is something I know only too well. I
except from what I shall say of it the two estimable gentlemen
already referred to: *Reinhold,* because, with a sagacity and love
of truth which do the highest honor to head and heart alike, he
has rejected this system (which he still, however, continues to
believe the Kantian—a historical question on which alone I differ
with him); and *Schulz,* because for a long time, and especially
since the latest inquiries, he has voiced no opinion in philosophy,
and may thus be fairly assumed to have grown doubtful about his
own earlier system. But in general, everyone who is master of his
inner sense to the mere extent of being able to distinguish thought
and existence, and not lumping them together, is bound to perceive that such a system, in which both are admittedly jumbled
together, receives all-too-much honor in being seriously alluded
to. It is surely to be expected of few men indeed that they should
conquer the natural propensity to dogmatism and aspire to the
free flight of speculation. And if a man of superior endowments,
such as Jacobi, was unable to do this, how should one expect it of
certain others, whom out of respect I do not mention here? Would
that they might have always been and remained dogmatists! But
that these inveterate dogmatists should have been able to fancy
that *Kant's Critique* had such a meaning for them; that because
Kant's critical writings—Heaven knows by what chance—were
praised in a well-known journal, they should have supposed they
could equally follow the fashion and become Kantians; that for
years past in their frenzy they should have filled many reams of
costly paper, without during this long period having ever once
come to their senses, or understood a sentence of what they
themselves had written; that to this day, after having been somewhat palpably shaken, they should have been unable to rub the
sleep from their eyes, but have preferred, rather, to struggle
tooth and nail against the unwanted disturbers of the peace; that
the culture-starved German public should have eagerly purchased

I, 485   these blackened sheets and sought to imbibe their drift, and actually copied and recopied the same a third time without so much as realizing that there was no sense in them; this will remain forever in the annals of philosophy as the scandal of our generation, and posterity will be able to account for the events of this time no otherwise than by postulating a mental epidemic that was raging therein.

But, I shall be told, if we disregard the cited work of Jacobi, which admittedly hits us hard owing to Kant's own words, your argument amounts to no more than this: the view in question is absurd, so *Kant* never asserted it. Now even admitting the former—as unfortunately we must—why should not Kant have been able to declare this absurdity as well as the rest of us, among whom there are some whose achievements even you acknowledge, and whose common sense you will not presumably deny altogether? —I reply: The inventor of a system is one thing, and his commentators and disciples are another. What proves a not absolute want of common sense in the latter, would prove it of the former. The reason is this: The followers do not yet have the idea of the whole; for if they had it, they would not require to study the new system; they are obliged first to piece together this idea out of *the parts* that the inventor provides for them; and all these parts are in fact not wholly determined, rounded and polished in their minds, so long as they do not constitute a natural whole. Now this apprehension of the parts may perhaps require some time, and during this period it may happen that they are falsely specified in detail, so that *in relation to the yet-to-be-completed whole,* which is actually not yet available, they fall into contradiction to one another. By contrast, the inventor proceeds from the idea of the whole, in which all the parts are united, and sets forth these parts individually, because only by means of them can he communicate the whole. The business of the followers is to synthe-

I, 486   size what they still by no means possess, but are only to obtain by the synthesis; the business of the inventor is to analyze what he already has in his possession. It follows not at all that the former really perceive that contradiction of the individual parts, in relation to a whole to be constituted therefrom, which another who conjoins these parts may subsequently find there; how can they, if they have not yet arrived at the point of integration? But it follows very surely that a person proceeding from the true conjunction should perceive, or think he perceives, the contradiction obtaining among the items in his account; for *he* would quite certainly have the parts set out before him. There is no absurdity in first entertaining dogmatism, and then transcendental idealism: we can all do that, and are bound to do so, if we philosophize about the two systems in question; but it is absurd to wish to entertain both systems *as one*. The expositor of the Kantian system does not necessarily do this, but the founder of the system would surely have done so, if his system proceeded from the union of the two.

To impute this absurdity to any man still in possession of his reason is, for me at least, impossible; how could I attribute it to Kant? So long, therefore, as Kant does not expressly declare in so many words, *that he derives sensation from an impression given by the thing-in-itself;* or, to employ his own terminology, *that sensation is to be explained in philosophy from a transcendental object existing in itself outside us,* for so long I shall decline to believe what his expositors have to tell of him. If he does issue such a declaration, however, I would sooner regard the *Critique of Pure Reason* as a product of the most singular accident than as the work of a human head.

But now Kant, say the critics, tells us in plain terms (B 33) that "objects are given to us"—that "this . . . is only possible . . . insofar as the mind is affected in a certain way"—that "the capacity . . . for receiving representations through the mode in which we are affected by objects, is entitled *sensibility*." He even says (B 1), "For how should our faculty of knowledge be awakened into action did not objects affecting our senses partly of themselves produce representations, partly arouse the activity of our understanding to compare these representations, and by combining or separating them, work up *the raw material* of the sensible impressions into that knowledge of objects which is entitled experience?" —These, too, will be about all the passages that they are able to cite on their behalf. In this context, passage

I, 487

against passage merely, and word against word, and disregarding that idea of the whole which in my view these interpreters still knew nothing of, I ask in the first place: If these passages are really irreconcilable with the endlessly repeated later statements, that there can be no question at all of the operation of a transcendental object existing in itself outside us, how comes it, then, that our interpreters have preferred to sacrifice, to the *few* passages which they take to be expounding dogmatism, the *innumerable* passages teaching a transcendental idealism, rather than the other way about? Undoubtedly because they have not entered without preconception upon the study of Kant's work, but have already brought with them as a standard of interpretation their own deep-rooted dogmatism, as the only correct system, which a sound thinker like Kant must surely also have held to; and have sought no instruction upon dogmatism from Kant, but only a confirmation of that view.

But are these apparently conflicting assertions really incapable of reconciliation? Kant speaks in these passages of *objects*. As to the meaning he attaches to this term, our business is assuredly not to define it, but to attend to Kant's own account of the matter. "The understanding," says Kant (p. 221 of Jacobi's treatise) "is that which adds the object to appearance, in that it *combines* the manifold thereof in *a single consciousness*. We thereupon speak of recognizing the *object* when we have effected synthetic unity in the manifold of intuition, and the concept of this unity is the representation of the object $= X$. *But this $= X$ is not the transcendental object* (that is, the thing-in-itself), *for of that we do not know even this much.*" What, then, is the object? *That which is added* to appearances by the understanding, *a mere thought.* —The object affects us; *something that is merely thought affects us.* What does this mean? If I have even a scintilla of logic in me, the meaning is simply: it affects us insofar as it exists, that is, *it is merely thought of as affecting us.* "The capacity . . . for receiving representations through the mode in which we are affected by objects" —what now is this? Since we merely think the affection itself, we undoubtedly also merely think the general capacity for this; it too is simply a mere thought. If you posit an object with

I, 488

the thought that it has affected you, you conceive yourself *in this case affected;* and if you suppose that this happens with *all* the objects of your perception, you conceive yourself as *susceptible to affection in general,* or in other words, *by this thinking of yours* you ascribe to yourself receptivity or sensibility. Thus the object as given *also* becomes *merely thought:* and hence the passage taken from Kant's Introduction is also merely taken at the empirical level from the system *of necessary thought,* which is first to be explained and derived by means of the Critique that follows.

Is there then assumed to be no *contact,* no *affection* whatever in accounting for knowledge? To put the difference in a word: certainly our knowledge all proceeds from *an affection;* but not affection *by an object.* This is *Kant's* view, and also that of the Science of Knowledge. Since Herr *Beck,* if I understand him rightly, has overlooked this important circumstance, and Herr *Reinhold*[11] also pays insufficient attention to that which conditions the positing of a not-self, and alone makes it possible, I deem it appropriate on this occasion to give a brief explanation of the matter. In this I shall make use of my own terminology, rather than that of Kant, since I naturally have a better command of the former than I have of the latter.

As surely as I posit myself, I posit myself as something restricted, in consequence of the intuition of my self-positing. In virtue of this intuition I am finite.

This restrictedness of mine, since it conditions my own positing of myself, is primordial in character. —One might wish at this point to account further, either for the restrictedness of myself *qua* object of reflection, as due to my necessary restrictedness as the reflecting subject, so that I would be finite to myself because I can only think the finite; or conversely, for the restrictedness of the reflecting subject, as due to the restrictedness of the object reflected upon, so that I should be able to think the finite only, because I myself am finite; but such an account would explain nothing; for initially I am neither the reflecting subject nor the reflected object, and neither of the two is conditioned by the

I, 489

[11]In his discussion of the leading features of the Science of Knowledge, in the *Vermischte Schriften* already referred to.

other, since I am *both in combination;* though this union I cannot indeed think, since in the act of doing so I separate the reflected from that which reflects.

In virtue of the intuition and the concept thereof, all restrictedness is *through and through determinate,* but not, indeed, a restrictedness in general.

From the possibility of the self we have evidently now derived the necessity *of its restrictedness in general.* Yet the *determinacy* thereof is not derivable, for that itself, as we can see, is what conditions all selfhood. Here, therefore, all deduction comes to an end. This determinacy appears as the absolutely contingent, and provides the *merely empirical* constituent of our knowledge. It is that, for example, whereby among possible rational beings I am a *man,* and among men am this *particular* person, and so forth.

I, 490

This restrictedness of myself, in its determinate form, is evinced in a limitation of my practical capacity (it is at this point that philosophy is pushed out of the theoretical field and over into the practical); the immediate perception of this limitation is a *feeling* (as I call it, in preference to Kant's term *sensation:* it only becomes sensation through relation to an object, by means of thought): the feeling of sweet, red, cold and the like.

Forgetfulness of this original feeling leads to an extravagant form of transcendental idealism, and an incomplete philosophy which cannot account for the merely sensible predicates of objects. *Beck* seems to me to have gone astray in this fashion, and *Reinhold* to imagine that the Science of Knowledge has done so.

The wish to explain this original feeling further, by attributing it to the efficacy of a *somewhat,* is the dogmatism of the Kantians, which I have just been pointing out, and which they would be happy to impose upon Kant. This somewhat of theirs is necessarily the ill-starred thing-in-itself. With immediate feeling, all *transcendental* explanation comes to an end, for the reason indicated above. Its feeling is certainly explained for itself, however, by the *empirical* self, as seen from the transcendental point of view; its law is, nothing limited without a limitant; by intuition it creates for itself an extended matter, to which it carries over, by thought, this purely subjective element of feeling, as to its ground, and by this synthesis alone it fashions for itself an object. The continuing analysis and explanation of its own state gives it its system of the world; and observation of the laws of this explanation provides the philosopher with his science. Herein lies Kant's *empirical realism*, which is also a *transcendental idealism*.

This whole determinacy, and hence also the sum of feelings it makes possible, is to be regarded as a priori, that is, absolute, and determined without any contribution on our part; it is Kant's *receptivity*, and an item thereof is what he calls an *affection*. Without it, consciousness is assuredly inexplicable.

I, 491   It is undoubtedly an immediate fact of consciousness that I feel *myself* to be determined in this fashion or that. If our much-applauded philosophers are now desirous of *explaining* this feeling, they do not realize that they are thereby attempting to attach something to it, which does not reside immediately in the fact; and how can they do this save by thinking, and by thinking under a category at that—in this case the principle of a real ground? Given that they have no kind of immediate intuition of the thing-in-itself and its relationships, what else do they know of this principle, save that they are obliged to think in accordance with it? They therefore assert no more than that they are obliged to append in thought an object as ground. This we concede them, indeed, from the point of view they occupy, and insist on it just as they do. Their thing is a product of their own thinking; but now straightway it is again supposed to be a thing-in-itself, that is, not a product of thought. I really fail to understand them; I can neither think this thought for myself, nor conceive an understanding able to think it, and would wish by this explanation to have done with them forever.

7

After this digression, we return to our original purpose, namely to describe the course of the Science of Knowledge, and to vindicate it against the animadversions of certain philosophers. As we said earlier (Section 5), the philosopher contemplates himself in that act whereby he constructs for himself the concept of himself; and—I now assert further—*he thinks this act.* —The philosopher undoubtedly knows of that whereof he speaks: but a mere intuition yields no consciousness; we know only of that which we grasp and apprehend in thought. As has likewise been pointed out previously, this apprehension of his act is assuredly quite possible for the philosopher, who is already in possession of experience. For he has a concept of *action in general and as such,* in contrast to the *existence* which is equally familiar to him already. And he also has a concept of this *particular action,* in that it is partly an act of the *intellect* as such, a purely ideal activity, and in no way a real efficacy of our practical powers in the narrow sense; and is partly that act, among the possible exercises of this intellect as such, which merely *reverts into itself,* and is not directed outwards to an object.

I, 492

In this connection, however, as everywhere else, there should be no losing sight of the fact that intuition is and remains the basis of the concept, the thing that is apprehended therein. We cannot think anything up for ourselves, in any absolute sense, or fabricate anything by an act of thought; the immediately intuited is all we can think; a thinking that rests upon no intuition, that does not include an intuiting, present in the same undivided moment, is an empty thinking, and indeed no thinking at all. At best it may be the thought of a mere sign of the concept, and if this sign be a word—as well it may—an unthinking enunciation of this word. I determine my intuition for myself by thinking of an opposite thereto; this and this alone is what is meant by the phrase: I apprehend the intuition.

By this thinking, the action he thinks of in himself becomes, for the philosopher, *objective,* that is, present to his mind as something which, insofar as he thinks it, restrains the freedom (or indeterminacy) of his thinking. This is the true and original significance of objectivity. As surely as I think, I think something determinate; for otherwise I would not have thought, and would have thought nothing. The freedom of my thinking, in other words, which might have addressed itself, according as I posit, to an infinite multiplicity of objects, is now on this occasion directed only to this restricted sphere of the thinking of my present object.

It is confined thereto. If I have regard to myself, I hold myself
freely in this sphere. If I have regard to the object merely, and in
thinking of it forget my own thinking, I *am held* and restricted by
this sphere; as happens throughout from the standpoint of ordinary thought.

The above remarks may serve to rectify the following objections and misunderstandings.

All thinking, say some, is necessarily addressed to an existent. Now the self which the Science of Knowledge starts from is
not to be credited with existence; hence it is unthinkable; and the
entire   science   erected   on   something   so   thoroughly   self-
contradictory is thus empty and futile.

I must first be permitted to make a general observation on
the state of mind from which this objection proceeds. In that these
sages receive the self-concept proposed by the Science of Knowledge into the school of their logic, and examine it according to the
rules thereof, they undoubtedly entertain this concept; for how
else could they compare and relate it? If they were really incapable of thinking it, they would be equally unable to say the least
thing about it; it would remain absolutely unknown to them in
every respect. But, as we see, they have successfully contrived to
think it, and so must certainly be able to. But since, according to
the rules they once learnt by heart and have misunderstood, they
ought not to be capable of this, they would sooner deny the
possibility of an act in the very moment of performing it, than
jettison their rules; and have more belief in some old book or
other, than in their own most intimate consciousness. How little
can these folk be aware of what they themselves are doing! How
mechanically, with what lack of insight and spirit, must their scraps
of philosophizing have been brought into being! Even M. Jour-
dain believed that he had been talking prose all his life without
knowing it, notwithstanding his astonishment at the fact; they, for
their part, would claim to have proved in the most elegant prose
that they could not have been talking prose, since they were not
aware of its rules, and the conditions for the possibility of a thing
ought surely to precede the reality thereof. If critical idealism
continues to give them trouble, we may expect them next to seek

I, 493

I, 494

counsel from Aristotle, as to whether they are really alive, or already dead and buried. In casting doubt on their ability to recognize their own freedom and selfhood, they are covertly uneasy on this latter point already.

Their objection could thus be fittingly dismissed out of hand, for it is self-contradictory and therefore demolishes itself. But let us see where the source of misunderstanding may actually lie. —All thinking necessarily proceeds from an existent; what can this mean? If we are to construe thereunder the principle just enunciated and developed by ourselves, namely that all thinking involves something thought, an object of thinking, to which this particular thinking confines itself, and by which it appears confined, then their premise must undoubtedly be conceded, and it is not the Science of Knowledge that seeks to deny it. This objectivity for mere thought is also undoubtedly to be attributed to the self from which the Science of Knowledge proceeds, or what amounts to the same, to the act whereby that self constructs itself for itself. Only through thinking does it obtain, and only for thinking does it possess, the objectivity in question; it is merely an ideal existent. —But if the existent of our opponents' principle is to be understood, not as a mere *ideal,* but as a *real* existent, that is, as something that restricts not merely the ideal but also the really efficacious, truly practical activity of the self, a permanent in time and subsistent (resistant) in space, and if they wish to maintain in earnest that only such things can be thought of, then this is an entirely new and unheard-of claim, which they certainly ought to have furnished with a meticulous proof. If they were right, then assuredly no metaphysics would be possible; for the concept of the self would be unthinkable; but then, however, no self-consciousness, and therefore no consciousness at all would be possible either. We should certainly have to give up philosophizing; but they would have gained nothing thereby, since they, too, would have to give up trying to refute us. But is the situation such as they represent it, even in their own particular case? Do they not think of themselves at every moment of life as free and efficacious? Do they not fancy themselves, for example, the spontaneous originators of the very shrewd and very novel objections

I, 495

which from time to time they bring against our system? And is this "themselves," then, a thing that resists their exertions, or is it not rather the very opposite of a resistant, namely that which itself makes the exertion? On this point I must refer them to what was said earlier (Section 5). If such an existence were ascribed to the self, it would cease to be a self; it would become a thing, and its concept would be abolished. Later, to be sure—not in time, but in the order of dependence of thought—even the self, though still remaining, as it must, a self in our sense of the word, will also be credited with existence of this sort; in part with extension and subsistence in space, and in this respect it becomes a determinate body; in part with identity and duration in time, and in this respect it becomes a soul. But it is the business of philosophy to demonstrate and explain genetically how the self comes to think of itself in this fashion; and so all this belongs, not to what we have to assume, but to what we have to derive. —It comes, then, to this: the self is originally a doing, merely; even if we think of it only as active, we already have an empirical concept of it, and so one that has first to be derived.[12]

I, 496

But our opponents are not willing to see their aforementioned principle brought forward so entirely without proof. They wish to demonstrate it by logic, and even, God willing, by the principle of noncontradiction.

If anything plainly shows the lamentable condition of present-day philosophy as a scientific pursuit, it is events of this nature. Were a writer on mathematics, natural philosophy or any of the sciences to vent opinions that revealed him to be in absolute ignorance as to the very rudiments of that science, he

---

[12]Let me briefly summarize the position here: *all existence* signifies *a restriction of free activity*. Now this activity *may* be regarded as an activity of *the mere intellect* (the subject of consciousness). Anything posited as merely restrictive of this activity is credited solely with *an ideal existence: mere objectivity in relation to consciousness*. This objectivity is present in every presentation, even that of the self, that of virtue, that of the moral law, etc.; or in complete fantasies, such as a round square, a sphinx, etc., is the *object of mere* presentation.

Alternatively, the free activity is regarded as *efficacious*, as *possessing causality*; in that case, whatever restricts it is credited with *real existence*. It is part of the *real world*.

would at once be sent back to the schoolroom from which he had escaped too soon. Is it only in philosophy that we are not allowed to do this? If someone thus exposes himself here, are we to do reverence to his sagacity, while giving him in public the private instruction that he needs, without a frown of impatience or a smile of derision? In two thousand years, have the philosophers not brought forth a single principle, which they might thenceforth be allowed to assume among the experts without further proof? If there be such a principle, it is certainly that of the difference between logic, as a purely formal science, and real philosophy, or metaphysics. —And what, then, is the import of this fearsome law of noncontradiction, whereby our system is to be laid low at a stroke? To my knowledge, it is no more than this, that *if* a concept be already determined by a given property, it must not be determined by another in opposition to the first; but by *what* property a concept is to be originally determined, it neither says, nor can it by nature say; for it presupposes the original determination as having already occurred, and only has application insofar as this is supposed to have taken place. Concerning the original determination, we are obliged to seek advice from some other science.

I, 497   These sages, we hear, consider it *contradictory* that some concept should not be determined by the predicate of real existence. But how could a contradiction result, save in the case where they had already determined this concept by this predicate, and later wanted to dispossess it thereof, while still insisting it to be the same concept? But then who told them to determine the concept thus? Do these logical virtuosi not perceive that they are postulating the principle, and thus obviously maneuvering in a circle? As to whether there really is a concept which originally, by the laws of synthesizing rather than merely analytical reason, *is not determined by this predicate of real existence*, that is something of which only intuition can inform them. Logic will have warned them only that if they have already denied it to be determinable thereby, then they should not subsequently attach this predicate to the concept—in the same respect, of course, that they denied it. But if they, in their own persons, have not yet risen *to consciousness* of that intuition in which no existence is presented—the intuition itself they possess, for the nature of reason has already seen to that—if, I say, they are not yet conscious of this intuition, then *all their* concepts, which can have arisen only from sensory intuition, will certainly be determined by the predicate of real existence; and they will merely have gone wrong in naming it, if they suppose themselves to know this by logic, since in fact they know it only through the intuition of their wretched empirical selves. In their own persons, therefore, they would indeed be contradicting themselves, if they subsequently conceived one of *their* concepts without this predicate. So let them keep to their rule, which in the sphere of their possible thinking is certainly everywhere valid, and let them always have scrupulous regard thereto, so that they do not fall foul of it. For ourselves, we can make no use of it; for we have a few other concepts besides theirs, whose range this rule does not extend to, and of which they

I, 498   cannot judge, since it simply does not exist for them. Let them go about their business, and leave us to pursue our own. Even insofar as we grant them the principle, that in all thinking there must be an object of thought, it is not by any means a logical principle, but one that is presupposed in logic, and alone makes the latter possible. To think and to determine objects (in the sense referred to above) are exactly the same thing; the two concepts are identical. Logic provides the *rules* for this determination; and hence, I should have thought, it presupposes determination in general as a fact of consciousness. That all thinking has an object can be shown only in intuition. Think, and attend in this thinking to the way you do it; you will undoubtedly find that you counterposit to your thinking an object thereof.

Another objection, related to that just dealt with, is as follows: If you proceed from nothing existent, how can you be able to derive an existent without falling into inconsistency? From what you take to work on, you will never extract anything but what you already have in it; so long as you otherwise proceed honestly and do not resort to legerdemain.

I reply: We are certainly deriving no existent, in the sense that you commonly give to that word: no *existent-in-itself*. What the philosopher takes to work on is an agency according to laws, and what he establishes is the series of the necessary acts of this agency. Among them there emerges one which appears to the agent himself as an existent, and must necessarily so appear to him, by demonstrable laws. For the philosopher, looking from a higher point of view, it is and remains an act. There is existence only for the self that is observed; the latter thinks realistically; for the philosopher, there is acting and nothing else but acting; for his thinking *qua* philosopher, is idealistic.

I, 499 Let me take this opportunity of stating the matter for once with full clarity: the essence of transcendental idealism in general, and of its presentation in the Science of Knowledge in particular, consists in the fact that the concept of existence is by no means regarded as a *primary* and *original* concept, but is viewed merely as *derivative,* as a concept derived, at that, through opposition to àctivity, and hence as a merely *negative* concept. To the idealist, the only positive thing is freedom; existence, for him, is a mere negation of the latter. On this condition alone does idealism have a firm foundation, and remains consistent with itself. To the dogmatist, on the other hand, who thought himself to be reposing safely on existence, as a thing requiring no further inquiry or foundation, this claim is a folly and an abomination; for this alone threatens his very being. That in which he could always take refuge, under all afflictions that might now and then assail him, some primordial existence or other, were it only that of some completely raw and formless matter, is now utterly snatched from his midst, and he stands there naked and alone. To this attack he has no answer, save the evidence of his distress, and the assurance that he has no understanding whatever, no willingness or ability to think of what is required of him. We are very happy to accept this assurance, and only ask in reply that a similar credence be given to our own assurance that for our part we are perfectly well able to comprehend our own system. Indeed, should even this prove too hard for them, we may ourselves remit this demand, and allow them to think what they please about it.

That we cannot compel them to accept our system, since its adoption depends upon freedom, has been solemnly conceded on numerous occasions already. —The assurance of his incapacity— a purely subjective matter—is, as I was saying, all that the dogmatist has left to him; for the notion of sheltering behind ordinary logic and invoking the shade of the Stagirite, though at a loss about his very body, is quite new, and will find few imitators even amid the general desperation; for in order to disdain this refuge, it needs only the smallest smattering of what logic is actually about.

I, 500

One should not be deceived when such critics ape the language of idealism, pay it lip service, and assure us of their realization that the reference here can be only to an *existent for us*. They are dogmatists. For anyone who here maintains that all thought and consciousness must proceed from an existent, is treating existence as something fundamental, and that is just what dogmatism consists in. By such confusion of language they demonstrate all the more clearly the total confusion of their ideas; for an *existent merely for us*, which is nonetheless to be a *fundamental* existent that cannot be further derived—what can be meant by that? Who can the *we* be, for whom alone this existent exists? *Intelligences*, as such? If so, the principle that something exists for the intellect would surely amount to this, that it is presented thereby; and that it exists *only* for the intellect, would mean that it is *merely* presented. Thus the concept of an existent that is supposed, from a certain viewpoint, to subsist independently of presentation, would still require to be derived from presentation, since only thereby is it held to exist: and these people would thus be in closer agreement with the Science of Knowledge than they themselves might have imagined. Alternatively, *we*, in this context, are ourselves things, primordial things, and thus things-in-themselves. But then how is anything to exist *for* such things, and how are they to exist for themselves? For in the concept of a thing it is implicit that it exists merely, not that anything exists *for it*. What does the little word '*for*' mean to our opponents? Can it be merely a harmless bit of decoration, which they have adopted to keep up with the fashion?

8

We cannot abstract from the self, says the Science of Knowledge. This claim can be looked at from two points of view. *Either* from that of ordinary consciousness, in which case it would assert:

I, 501 We never have any other presentation save that of ourselves; at every moment, throughout our whole life, we are always thinking I, I, I, and never anything else but I. *Or else* it may be viewed from the standpoint of the philosopher, and would then signify as follows: To everything thought of as occurring in consciousness, the self must necessarily be appended in thought; in the elucidation of states of mind we may never abstract from the self, or, as Kant puts it: it must be possible for all my presentations to be accompanied, to be thought of as accompanied, by the 'I think'. What nonsense would be involved in advancing the principle in its first meaning, and how paltry to refute it in this sense! If taken in the second meaning, surely no one so much as capable of understanding it will have anything to say against it; and had it only been distinctly conceived sooner, we should long since have been rid of the thing-in-itself; for it would have been recognized that whatever we may think, we are that which thinks therein, and hence that nothing could ever come to exist independently of us, for everything is necessarily related to our thinking.

9

"For our part," confess other opponents of the Science of Knowledge, "we can conceive nothing under the concept of the self save our own familiar person, in contrast to others. 'I' betokens my own specific person, Caius or Sempronius as my name may be, in contrast to all others who are not so called. If I now abstract from this individual personality, as the Science of Knowledge demands, I am left with nothing whatever that might be characterized as '*I*'; I could equally describe the remnant as '*it*'."

Now what does the objection thus boldly stated really wish to say? Is it referring to the original real synthesis of the concept of individuality (its familiar person and the persons of others),

I, 502 and are the objectors therefore asserting that in this concept nothing is synthesized save the concept of an object in general, the *'it'*, and the distinction from others of its kind, each of which is thus equally an 'it' and nothing more? Or is it relying upon ordinary usage, and do the objectors mean by it that in language the term *'I'* designates nothing more than individuality? As to the first possibility, surely everyone still in possession of his wits is bound to see that by distinction of an object from its peers, that is, from other objects, nothing ensues save a *determinate object*, and certainly not a determinate *person*. The synthesis of the concept of a person is of quite a different kind. *Selfhood* (self-reverting activity, subject-objectivity, or what you will) is initially contrasted to the *it*, to mere objectivity; and the positing of these concepts is absolute, and unconditioned by any other positing; it is thetic, not synthetic. To something posited in this first positing as an it, a mere object or thing outside us, the concept of selfhood discovered within us is transferred, and synthetically united therewith; and through this conditioned synthesis there first arises for us a Thou. The concept of Thou arises through a union of the it and the I. The concept of the I in this opposition, that is, as the concept of the individual, is the synthesis of the I with itself. That which posits itself in the act in question, not in general, but *as a self*, is myself; and that which is posited as a self in the same act, *by me*, and not *by itself*, is you. Now from this product of a synthesis to be expounded, it is certainly possible to abstract; for what a man has himself synthesized, he should surely be able to analyze again as well; and what remains over from this abstraction is the self in general, that is, the non-object. Interpreted in this sense, the foregoing objection would be altogether absurd.

Or do our objectors rely upon linguistic usage? If they were correct in this, that in language the word 'I' has hitherto betokened the individual merely, would it then follow from the fact I, 503   that a distinction to be pointed out within the original synthesis has so far gone unremarked and unexpressed in language, that it is never to be noticed and indicated therein? But are they in fact correct even on this point? What usage are they referring to? That of the philosophers, perhaps? That *Kant* takes the concept of the pure self in the same sense as the Science of Knowledge does, I have already demonstrated above. When I say that I am that which thinks in this thinking, do I then merely posit myself over against other persons outside me? Or do I not rather contrast myself with everything that is thought? "This principle of the necessary unity of apperception," says Kant (*C. P. R.,* B 135), "is itself, indeed, an identical, and therefore analytic, proposition." This is equivalent to what I was just saying: the self arises, not through any synthesis whose manifold could be further dissected, but through an absolute thesis. This self, however, is selfhood in general; for the concept of individuality obviously arises through a synthesis, as I have just shown; and the principle thereof is thus a synthetic proposition. —*Reinhold,* in his principle of consciousness, speaks of the subject, or in plain language, of the self; though only, indeed, of the presenting self: but this is nothing to the purpose here. In distinguishing myself from the presented, as that which presents, do I differentiate myself merely from other persons, or from everything presented, as such? Even among those philosophers commended above, who do not, like *Kant* and the Science of Knowledge, make the self prior to the manifold of presentation, but patch it together therefrom—is their one that thinks amid the manifold of thinking, the individual merely, or is it not rather the intellect in general? In a word, is there a single philosopher of any consequence who has preceded them in discovering that 'I' means the individual merely, and that if we abstract from individuality, we are left only with an object in general?

Or is it common usage they are talking of? To settle this, I am obliged to give examples from everyday life. —If you call out

I, 504   to someone in the dark, "Who's there?," and he, assuming that you know his voice, replies "It is I," he is evidently speaking of himself as this particular person, and is to be understood as saying, "It is I who am called so-and-so, and not any of the others who are not so called"; and this because your question, as to *who* is there, already presupposes that it is in general a rational being, and you now wish to know only which particular one of such possible rational beings it may be. But if, say—forgive me this example, which I find particularly apt—you are sewing or trimming some part of the clothes a person is wearing, and happen to nick him unawares, he may call out, "Hey! That's *I*, you are cutting *me!*" Now what does he mean by this? Not that he is this particular person and no other, for that you know quite well; but that what you have struck is not his dead and insensible garment, but his living and feeling self, a thing you did not know. By this self he distinguishes himself, not from other persons, but from things. This distinction is constantly arising in everyday life, and without it we could not move a step or lift a finger.

In brief, selfhood and individuality are very different concepts, and the element of composition in the latter is very plain to see. By the former we contrast ourselves to everything outside us, and not simply to other persons; and under it we include, not merely our specific personality, but our mental nature generally; and so the word is employed in philosophical and common usage alike. The proffered objection therefore displays not only an uncommon want of thought, but also great ignorance and lack of acquaintance with the standard literature of philosophy.

But our critics stand firm on their inability to frame the concept required of them, and we must take their word for this. Not that they have been wholly deprived of the concept of the pure self through mere rational or mental deficiency; for then I, 505   they would have had to abstain from objecting to us, just as a block of wood is obliged to do. It is *the concept of this concept* that they lack and cannot rise to. They certainly have it within them, and are merely unaware of possessing it. The ground of this inability of theirs does not reside in any special weakness of intellect, but rather in a weakness of their whole character. Their self, in the sense they give to the word, that is, their individual person, is the ultimate goal of their action, and so also for them the boundary of intelligible thought. To them it is the one true substance, and reason a mere accident thereof. Their person does not exist as a specific expression of reason; on the contrary— reason exists to help this person along in the world, and if only the latter could get along equally well in its absence, we could do without reason altogether and there would then be no such thing. This is apparent in every claim made throughout the entire system of their concepts; and many among them are honest enough to make no secret of the fact. In declaring their inability, these latter are, for their own part, perfectly correct; only they should not give out as objective truth what is only valid for themselves. In the Science of Knowledge, we have exactly the opposite relationship; there, reason is the only thing-in-itself, and individuality merely accidental; reason the end, and personality the means; the latter merely a special way of giving expression to reason, and one which must increasingly merge into the general form thereof. Reason alone is eternal, on our view, while individuality must constantly decay. Anyone who does not first accommodate his will to this order of things will also never obtain a true understanding of the Science of Knowledge.

10

This, that the Science of Knowledge is intelligible only on prior fulfilment of certain conditions, has been so often told to our critics already. They want to hear no more of it, and our open warnings about it give them occasion for a new complaint against us. Every conviction, they argue, must admit of communication by concepts, and not only communication, but actual enforcement as well. It would be an evil example, a piece of hopeless fanaticism, and the like, to make out that our science is for certain privileged spirits only, and that all others will be able to see nothing in it and to understand it not at all.

Let us first see what has actually been claimed for the Science of Knowledge on this point. We do not maintain that there is an original and native difference among men, whereby some have been gifted with an ability to think and learn a thing which the rest are by nature absolutely unable to conceive. Reason is common to all, and in all rational beings is exactly the same. A capacity inherent in one such being is present in every one. Indeed, as we have already often averred in this very essay, the concepts at issue in the Science of Knowledge are really operative in every rational being, and operative with a rational necessity; for upon their efficacy the possibility of all consciousness depends. The pure *self,* which our critics profess to find

I, 506

unthinkable, is basic to all their thinking and is present throughout it, in that all thinking comes about only with its aid. So far,
everything proceeds mechanically. But insight into the necessity
just claimed, the thinking upon this thinking, is not a mechanical
affair; it requires an elevation by freedom to an entirely different
sphere, into mastery of which we are not thrust immediately by
the mere fact of our existence. If this capacity for freedom is not
already present and employed, the Science of Knowledge can
make no headway with a person. This capacity alone provides the
premises on which further construction is effected. —This at least
they will not wish to deny, that every science and every art takes
some prior information for granted, which one is obliged to pos-

I, 507   sess before being able to enter upon the science or art in question.
—If, they may reply, it is merely prior information we lack, then
bring it before us. Set it out for once, in a definite and systematic
manner. Is it not your own fault, that you promptly march into
the subject, and expect the public to understand you, before
giving them the preliminary information of which nobody knows
anything except yourself? We answer: The very reason why these
prior notions do not lend themselves to systematic presentation,
do not arise of themselves and cannot be made to do so, is, in a
word, that they are intimations which we can only generate from
within ourselves, thanks to a readiness previously attained. Everything depends upon having become really intimately aware of
one's freedom, through constant exercise thereof *with clear consciousness,* so that it has come to be dear to us beyond all else.
Once education from earliest youth makes it the chief aim and
intended object merely to develop the internal powers of the
pupil, without prescribing their direction; once people start to
cultivate the individual for his own purposes and as an instrument
for his own will, and not as a soulless implement for others, the
Science of Knowledge will then become generally intelligible and
easily understood. Education of the whole man from his earliest
years onwards: that is the only means to the dissemination of
philosophy. This education must first resign itself to being more
negative than positive; interaction *with* the pupil merely, not
action *upon* him—the first so far as may be, that is, it must

always keep that in view, if only as a goal, and should become the second only where it cannot be the first. So long as education consciously or otherwise adopts the opposing aim, and works merely for usefulness to others without considering that the principle of using also has its seat in the individual, it roots out in first youth the sources of self-activity, and accustoms a man never to set himself in motion, but to expect the first push to come from without. And so long as it does this, it will always remain a special grace of nature, beyond accounting for, and described therefore by the vague term 'philosophical genius', when amid the general debility a few persons still elevate themselves to the level of this great idea.

I, 508

The main source of all these critics' errors may well consist in this, that they have never attained a really clear conception of what *proof* is, and have therefore failed to realize that all demonstration is based on something absolutely indemonstrable. On this too they could have learnt from *Jacobi,* by whom this point, like so many others of which they are equally ignorant, has been fully brought to light. —Demonstration achieves only a conditioned, mediate certainty; a thing becomes certain thereby, if something else be certain. If doubt arises as to the certainty of this latter, it must be linked to the certainty of some third thing, and so on continually. Now is this backward reference prolonged to infinity, or is there anywhere a final term? I am aware that some are attached to the former view; but they have not considered that, if they were correct, they would never even have been capable of the idea of certainty, and could not set out to pursue it; for they only know what it is to be certain through being themselves certain of something or other; but if everything is certain only conditionally, then nothing is certain, and is not even certain under conditions. But if there is some final term, not subject to further inquisition as to why it is certain, then there is something indemonstrable, on which all demonstration depends.

They seem not to have considered what it is to prove a thing to *somebody*. This one does by showing him that a certain putative truth is already contained in some other, which he himself acknowledges, according to laws of thought which he is equally

I, 509

prepared to grant us; and that in conceding his acceptance of the second, he necessarily also accepts the first. All imparting of conviction by proof presupposes, therefore, that both parties are agreed at least on something. How could the Science of Knowledge be imparted to the dogmatist, seeing that *on no point whatever does it agree* with him in regard to the *material* of our knowledge;[13] so that they lack the common ground from which they could set out together?

Finally, they seem also to have overlooked that, even where there is such a point in common, neither party can penetrate into the mind of the other without himself being that other; that each must reckon upon the other's self-activity, and can give him, not the particular thought in question, but only the inducement to think this particular thought for himself. The relationship between free beings is interaction through freedom, and not causality through mechanically operative force. So this dispute, like all the others that divide us, comes down to the main point in contention: *they* presuppose throughout the causal relation, since in fact they know nothing higher; and this, too, forms the basis for their demand, that this conviction be implanted in their minds, without preparation on their part, and without their having to make the slightest effort on their own. *We* start from freedom, and in

I, 510

fairness presuppose it also in them. —In thus presupposing the thorough-going validity of the mechanism of cause and effect, they actually contradict themselves from the start; there is contradiction between what they say and what they do. For, in *presupposing* mechanism, they rise above it; their thought of it is already

---

[13]I have already said this a number of times. I have asserted that with certain philosophers I have absolutely nothing in common, and that they never stand, nor could stand, where I do. People seem to have taken this more for an extravagant expression of scorn than for real earnest, since they do not cease from repeating their demands, that I prove my theory *to them*. I must solemnly declare that this statement means exactly what it says, that it is uttered in all seriousness, and expresses my most unqualified conviction. Dogmatism sets out from an *existent* as its *absolute;* and its system therefore never rises above existence. Idealism recognizes no existent whatever, as a thing standing on its own. The former, in other words, proceeds from necessity, the latter from freedom. They therefore find themselves in two worlds, that are entirely sundered from each other.

extraneous thereto. Mechanism is unable to apprehend itself, precisely because it is mechanism. Only the free consciousness can apprehend itself. So here we should have a means of converting them on the spot. But it promptly encounters the difficulty, that this observation lies altogether beyond their purview, and that, in thinking of an object, they lack the agility and dexterity of mind to think simultaneously, not only of the object, but also of their own thinking thereof; and hence this whole statement, which is necessarily beyond them, is made, not for their benefit, but for the sake of others who are attentive and awake.

We revert, therefore, to our oft-repeated assurance: we have no wish to persuade them, since one cannot desire the impossible; we have no wish to refute their system for them, since this we cannot do. *For ourselves,* indeed, we can refute it; it is there for refutation, and very easy to refute; a mere puff from a free man blows it over; it is only *for them* that we cannot lay it low. Our writing, speaking, and teaching is not *for* them, since there is absolutely no point from which we might approach them. If we speak *about* them, it is not for their sake, but for that of others, to warn them against such errors, and to turn them away from such empty and meaningless chatter. Now this explanation is not to be regarded as a disparagement. Our opponents do but expose their own evil consciousness, and openly demean themselves beneath us, if they feel that our observations disparage them. For they, on their own part, are similarly placed towards us; they too can neither refute, nor persuade, nor advance anything calculated to have an effect upon us. We say this ourselves; and we should not be in the least offended, if they were to say the same to us. We tell them what we do out of no malicious intention of causing them annoyance; but merely to spare us both unprofitable trouble. It would really rejoice us if they did not give way to vexation. —Nor is there anything of disparagement in the situation as such. Everyone who today reproaches his brother for this inability, was necessarily once in the same condition himself. For we are all born into it, and it takes time to overcome it. At the very moment when our opponents allow this allegation they dislike so much to provoke them, not to irritation, but to wondering whether there

I, 511

might not be truth in it, they will be likely to have overcome the
defect charged upon them. From that hour they will be like
ourselves, and all objections will cease. We should thus be able to
live most amiably at peace with them, if they so allowed; and the
fault is not ours, if at times we become embroiled in heavy
fighting with them.

From this, however, it at once follows—what in passing I
think it highly pertinent to remark—that whether a philosophy be
scientific does not depend upon its *general acceptance;* as seems
to be assumed by some philosophers, whose very estimable labors
are primarily directed at bringing enlightenment to all. These
philosophers are asking for the impossible. What could it be for a
philosophy to be really generally accepted? Who are the "all" with
whom it is to gain acceptance? Surely not everyone who wears a
human face; for then it would have to hold also for the common
man, to whom thinking is never an end, but always a mere means
to the business at hand, and even for small children. The philosophers, perhaps? But who, then, are the philosophers? Surely not
all who have obtained the doctorate from a faculty of philosophy;
or who have got something printed which they term philosophical;
or who are actually themselves members of some philosophical
faculty? Let anyone try to give us a definite concept of the
philosopher, without first having given us a definition of philoso-
I, 512   phy, that is, a definite philosophy itself! It is all-too-predictable
that those who may think themselves to possess a scientific philosophy will utterly deny the title of philosopher to any who refuse
to acknowledge this philosophy of theirs, and hence will again
transform the acceptance of their philosophy into a criterion of
philosophy in general. So, indeed, they are bound to behave, if
they go about it consistently; for philosophy can only be one. The
present author, for example, has already long since given this as
his own personal opinion, insofar as the Science of Knowledge be
referred to, not as *an individual presentation,* susceptible of in-
definite improvement, but rather as a system of *transcendental
idealism;* and he has not a moment's hesitation in reiterating it
here in so many words. But in so saying we lapse into an obvious
circularity. For that "*my* philosophy is truly acceptable to all who

are philosophers" may then be said with perfect right by anyone, so long as he is himself persuaded; admittedly, his conclusions are accepted by no mortal being other than himself; but then, so he adds, the people who reject them are not philosophers.

My opinion on this point is as follows: If even a single person is completely convinced of his philosophy, and at all hours alike; if he is utterly at one with himself about it; if his free judgment in philosophizing, and what life obtrudes upon him, are perfectly in accord; then in this person philosophy has completed its circuit and attained its goal. For it has assuredly set him down again at the point whence he started with all the rest of mankind: and now philosophy, as a science, is genuinely present in the world, even if no man but this one should grasp or accept it, and even if this one should be quite unable to give it outward expression. Let us not be confronted here with the trivial retort that the system-builders of old were invariably convinced of the truth of their systems. This claim is radically false, and rests solely on ignorance of what conviction is. What it is can be experienced only if one has the fullness of conviction in oneself. The system-builders in question were convinced not of the whole, but only of this or that occult point in their systems, of which they themselves were perhaps but dimly aware; only in certain moods were they convinced. That is not conviction. Conviction is that alone which has no dependence on time or change or situation; which is not something merely contingent to the mind, but is the mind itself. One can be convinced only of the unchanging and eternally true: conviction of error is utterly impossible. In the history of philosophy there can have been few cases of such conviction, perhaps scarcely one, and perhaps not even this one. I am not speaking of ancient writers. Whether these even consciously raised the true problem of philosophy is itself open to doubt. I shall take account only of the greatest thinkers of modern times. —*Spinoza* could not have been in a state of conviction; he could only *think* his philosophy, not *believe* it, for it stood in the most immediate contradiction to his necessary conviction in daily life, whereby he was bound to regard himself as free and independent. He could only be convinced of it insofar as it contained truth, that is, a

I, 513

portion of philosophy considered as a science. That purely objective reasoning necessarily led to his system, was something he was convinced of; for in this he was correct; it did not occur to him to reflect in thought upon his own thinking, and in this he was mistaken, and thereby set his speculation in contradiction to his life. *Kant* could have been convinced; but, if I rightly understand him, he was not so when he wrote his *Critique*. He speaks *of a deception which constantly recurs, even though one knows it to be a deception.* How can Kant know that it always recurs, especially since he was the first to bring this alleged deception to light; and for whom could it recur, when he was writing his *Critique*, except for himself? He could have had this experience only in his own person. To know that one is deceived, and yet to be deceived, is not the state of conviction and agreement with oneself, but rather that of an unstable inner conflict. In my experience, there is no recurrence of deception; for in reason generally there is no deception present. What, then, is this deception supposed to be? This, to be sure, that things-in-themselves are externally present independently of us. But who says so? Surely not ordinary consciousness; for this, since it merely speaks *of itself,* can assert nothing whatever save that things are present for it (for us, from this commonsense viewpoint); and this is no deception that can or should be obviated by philosophy: it is our only truth. The ordinary consciousness knows nothing of a thing-in-itself, precisely because it *is* the ordinary consciousness, of which it is to be hoped that it does not overleap itself. It is a false philosophy which first implants therein this concept fabricated in its own domain. This all-too-avoidable deception, to be radically extirpated by a true philosophy, has thus been created solely by yourself and as soon as you come to be clear about your philosophy, it falls from your eyes like scales, and the deception never returns. You will then claim to know no more in life than that you are finite, and finite in *this particular* way, which you are obliged to account for by the presence of *that sort of world* outside you; and you will no more be minded to overstep these bounds than you are to cease being yourself. *Leibniz,* too, could have been convinced; for, properly understood—and why should he not have properly understood himself?—he is correct. If supreme

I, 514

facility and freedom of mind are evidence of conviction; if
I, 515   dexterity in adapting his conceptions to every form, in applying
them spontaneously to every portion of human knowledge, in
readily allaying every doubt that arises, and in employing his
system, in general, more as an instrument than an object; if
candor, cheerfulness and good humor in life are evidence of unity
with oneself: then Leibniz perhaps had conviction, and was the
only example of it in the history of philosophy.[14]

11

I take another word or two to note a peculiar confusion. It is
that of the self as intellectual intuition, from which the Science of
Knowledge sets out, and of the self as Idea, with which it ends. As
intellectual intuition, the self comprises only the form of selfhood,
the self-reverting act which also, in fact, itself becomes the content thereof; and this intuition has been sufficiently described in
what precedes. In this guise, the self exists only *for the philoso-*
pher, and in apprehending it thus one ascends to the level of
philosophy. The self as Idea is present *for that very self* which the
philosopher observes; and is posited thereby, not as its own, but
as the Idea of the natural, albeit fully cultivated man; just as a
true existent comes about, not for the philosopher, but only for
the self he investigates. The latter is located, therefore, in a
sequence of thought entirely different from that of the former.

The self as Idea is the rational being, partly insofar as it has
exhibited universal reason perfectly within itself, is indeed ration-
I, 516   al throughout, and nothing else but rational: and has thus also
ceased to be an individual, which it was through sensory restriction alone; partly insofar as it has also fully realized reason
outside it in the world, which thus equally continues to be founded in this Idea. The world in this Idea remains a world in general,
a substrate governed by these particular mechanical and organic
laws: yet these laws are adapted throughout to present the ultimate aim of reason. With the self as intuition, the Idea of the self

[14] A vivid sketch of the nature of Leibniz's philosophy, as compared with
that of Spinoza, will be found in *Schelling's* most recent work *Ideen zu einer*
Philosophie der Natur (Leipzig 1797); cf. Introduction, pp. XXIV f. and
XLI ff. [*Werke* (Leipzig 1907), vol. I., pp. 115 ff. and 131 ff.].

has merely this in common, that in neither of them is the self viewed as an individual; in the former, because selfhood there has not yet been particularized into individuality; in the latter, by contrast, because individuality has vanished through cultivation according to general laws. The two are opposed, however, in that the self as intuition comprises only the form of the self, and takes no account at all of any material proper thereto, which is thinkable only through its thinking of a world; whereas in the other, conversely, the complete material of selfhood is envisaged. The former is the starting-point of all philosophy, and is its fundamental concept; to the latter it does not aspire; only in the context of practice can this Idea be postulated as the supreme goal of the striving of reason. The former, as stated, is a primordial intuition, and becomes a concept in the manner already adequately described; the latter is merely an Idea; it cannot be determinately conceived, and will never be actualized, for we are merely to approximate ourselves to this Idea *ad infinitum*.

12

These, so far as I am aware, are the misunderstandings that have to be attended to, and to whose rectification one may hope to contribute something by clear discussion. For certain other modes of opposition to the new system there is no remedy, nor any need of one.

I, 517   If, for example, a system whose beginning and end and whole nature is concerned with forgetting individuality in theory, and rejecting it in practice, is given out as egoism; and given out as such by people who cannot attain understanding of this system, precisely because they themselves are covert theoretical egoists and overt egoists in practice; if it is concluded from the system that its originator is a blackguard,[15] and from this blackguardry of

---

[15]"Is this style of argument not yet out of fashion?" —some well-meaning person may ask, who is not fully acquainted with recent events on the literary scene. I answer: No, it is commoner than ever, and is chiefly directed against myself; though at one time still merely verbal, from professorial chairs and the like, it has lately been employed in writing as well. Its inception may be found in the reply given by the reviewer of Schelling's work *On the Self*, in the *Allgem. Lit. Zeitung* to Herr *Schelling's* counter-critique; to which latter there was not, indeed, much other reply to be made, save that of defaming the author and his system.

his it is further concluded that the system is false, then reasoned arguments can be of no avail; for those who say this are themselves but too well aware of its untruth, and have quite other causes for saying it than that of believing it themselves. The system itself is the very least of their concerns; but the author may elsewhere perhaps have said this or that to displease them and—God knows how or where—may somehow stand in their way. These people, for their part, act perfectly in accordance with their interests and mode of thought; and it would be a foolish undertaking to counsel them to mend their ways. But when thousands upon thousands who know not a word of the Science of Knowledge, nor are fit to know anything of it, and are neither Jews nor their allies, neither aristocrats nor democrats, neither Kantians of the old school nor of any newer school, and not even men of brains, whom the author of the Science of Knowledge has

I, 518 dispossessed or distracted from the important discovery they were just about to bring before the public—when these take up the claim with enthusiasm, and repeat and reiterate it, without any concern for its merits, so long as they too shall be thereby held learned and well-instructed in the mysteries of modern literature: then from them one may hope that for their own sakes they will give a hearing to our request, that they bethink themselves better of what they are saying, and the reasons why they say it.

FOUNDATIONS OF THE ENTIRE
SCIENCE OF KNOWLEDGE (1794)

I, 86   In a book such as this, which was not really intended for the public, I should have had nothing to say to them beforehand, had it not been brought before a part of them, though yet unfinished, in the most indiscreet fashion. This only, then, upon such matters as are now before us.

I thought and still think myself to have discovered the way in which philosophy must raise itself to the level of a manifest science. I modestly announced this,[1] setting forth the manner in which I should have gone to work upon the idea in question, and how, under altered circumstances, I was now obliged to pursue it; and began to put the plan into effect. This was natural. And it was equally natural that other philosophers and workers in the field should have examined, tested and passed judgement on my idea, and that, whether they had internal or extraneous reasons to be displeased at the path on which I wished to put knowledge, they should have sought to refute me. There is, however, no seeing the point of rejecting my claim, without any examination whatever, and at best going to the trouble of distorting it, using every opportunity to vilify and decry it as furiously as possible. But what can have provoked these judges to such total loss of composure? Was I to speak with respect of sequacity and shallowness, though I have no respect for them at all? How could I have been obliged to do so, especially when I had better things to do, and might have left every bungler to go blithely on ahead of me, had he not compelled me to make room for myself by exposure of his bungling?

[1] In *Über den Begriff der Wissenschaftslehre, oder der sogenannten Philosophie,* Weimar 1794; 2nd Ed., Jena and Leipzig 1798.

I, 87   Or is there yet another reason for their hostility? —To men of honor—to whom alone it makes sense—I address myself as follows. —Whatever my views may be, whether true philosophy or gush and nonsense, it affects me personally not at all, if I have honestly sought the truth. I should no more think my personal merits enhanced by the luck of having discovered the true philosophy than I should consider them diminished by the misfortune of having piled new errors on the errors of the past. For my personal position I have no regard whatever: but I am hot for truth, and whatever I think true, I shall continue to proclaim with all the force and decision at my command.

In the present work, together with my *Grundriss des Eigentümlichen der Wissenschaftslehre in Rücksicht auf das theoretische Vermögen,* I think I have carried my system to the point where any intelligent reader may have a complete view, not only of its foundation and extent, but also of the manner in which further construction must be erected upon it. My situation does not permit any definite promise as to *when* and *how* I shall continue to extend it further.

The presentation I freely admit to be most imperfect and defective; in part, because it had to be issued in separate sections, as my lectures required it, for an audience that I could assist by verbal explanation; in part, because I have sought so far as possible to avoid a fixed terminology—the easiest way for literalists to deprive a system of life, and make dry bones of it. I shall adhere to the same maxim in future expositions of the system, until it is finally presented in full. But I shall add nothing more to it at present, since I merely wish to induce the public to join me in surveying its eventual plan. It will be necessary first to obtain a view of the whole before any single proposition therein can be accurately defined, for it is their interconnection that throws light

I, 88   on the parts; a method which certainly assumes willingness to do the system justice, and not the intention of merely finding fault with it.

I have heard many complaints about the obscure and unintelligible character of that part of this book which has so far become generally known, as also of my *Über den Begriff der Wissenschaftslehre.*

So far as the complaints of the latter work relate especially to its §8, I may certainly have been at fault, in that I there gave the principles that my system as a whole determines, without giving the system; and demanded of my readers and critics the indulgence of leaving everything as indeterminate as I had left it myself. So far as the work as a whole is complained of, I confess from the start that in the field of speculation I shall never be able to write anything intelligible to those who have found it beyond them. If the work in question marks the limit of their intelligence, it also marks the limit of my intelligibility; our minds are divided from one another by this boundary, and I entreat them not to waste time in reading my works. —If this failure to understand has a reason, whatever it may be, the Science of Knowledge itself contains a reason why to certain readers it must forever pass their understanding: namely, that it assumes them to possess the freedom of inner intuition. —For every philosophical author may justly demand that his reader should retain the thread of the argument, and not have forgotten what preceded when he comes to what follows. If, on such terms, there is anything in these works that a person could fail to understand, and has not necessarily been compelled to understand rightly, I at least am not aware of it; and I think, after all, that the author of a book himself has some say in the answering of such a question. Anything that has been thought out with complete clarity is intelligible; and I am conscious of having thought everything out with such perfect clarity, that if time and space were granted me, I should be willing to make everything I say as clear as anyone could desire.

I, 89   It is particularly necessary to recall, I think, that I do not tell the reader everything, but have also wished to leave him something to think about. There are numerous misunderstandings that I certainly anticipate, and that a few words of mine could have rectified. Yet I have not said these few words, because I wished to encourage independent thought. The Science of Knowledge should in no way *force* itself upon the reader, but should *become a necessity* for him, as it has for the author himself.

I request the future judges of this work to consider it as a whole, and to view every single thought in it from the standpoint of the whole. The Halle reviewer [J. S. Beck] gives it as his opinion that I have been writing merely in jest; the other judges of my *Über den Begriff der Wissenschaftslehre* appear to have taken a similar view; so lightly do they treat the matter, and so facetious are their objections, as though it was their duty to answer one joke with another.

Having found, after three revisions of this system, that each time my thoughts about individual parts of it were altered, I may expect that on further consideration they will continue to change and renew themselves. For myself, I shall work most diligently to that end, and every usable suggestion from others will be welcome to me. —More, indeed; for however complete my conviction that the foundations of this whole system are unassailable, and however strongly I have here and there expressed this conviction—as I was quite entitled to—it remains nonetheless a possibility (though to be sure I cannot as yet imagine it), that they might after all be overthrown. Even this I should welcome, since truth would be the gainer thereby. Let my critics go to work on these foundations, and try to bring them down.

I, 90   As to the true nature of my system, and the possible modes of classifying it, whether as the truly thorough-going criticism which *I* believe it to be, or as whatever else one wants to call it, that is nothing to the purpose. I have no doubt that many names will be found for it, and that a variety of mutually contradictory heresies will be imputed to it. The world may do this; only let them not rebuke me with old refutations, but refute me themselves.

Jena
Eastertide 1795.

Part I

FUNDAMENTAL PRINCIPLES OF THE ENTIRE
SCIENCE OF KNOWLEDGE

§ 1. FIRST, ABSOLUTELY UNCONDITIONED PRINCIPLE.

I, 91   Our task is to *discover* the primordial, absolutely unconditioned first principle of all human knowledge. This can be neither *proved* nor *defined*, if it is to be an absolutely primary principle.

It is intended to express that *Act* which does not and cannot appear among the empirical states of our consciousness, but rather lies at the basis of all consciousness and alone makes it possible.[1] In describing this Act, there is less risk that anyone will perhaps thereby *fail* to think what he should—the nature of our mind has already taken care of that—than that he will thereby think what he should not. This makes it necessary to *reflect* on what one might at first sight take it to be, and to *abstract* from everything that does not really belong to it.

Not even by means of this abstracting reflection can anything
I, 92   become a fact of consciousness which is inherently no such fact; but it will be recognized thereby that we must necessarily *think* this Act as the basis of all consciousness.

The laws (of common logic) whereby one must straightway think this Act as the foundation of human knowledge, or—what amounts to the same thing—the rules whereby this reflection is initiated, have not yet been proved to be valid, but are tacitly assumed to be familiar and established. Only at a later point will they be derived from that proposition whose assertion is warranted only if they are warranted also. This is a circle, though an

[1]This has been overlooked by all who insist at this point, either that what the first proposition asserts is *not included* among the facts of consciousness, or that it *contradicts* them.

93

unavoidable one. (cf. *Über den Begriff der Wissenschaftslehre,* § 7). But since it is unavoidable, and openly acknowledged, we may appeal to all the laws of common logic even in establishing the highest fundamental principle.

In proceeding to the required reflection, we must set out from some proposition that everyone will grant us without dispute. And there should doubtless be many such. Reflection is free; and it matters not from whence it starts. We choose that which offers us the shortest road to our goal.

So soon as this proposition is conceded, we must simultaneously be granted, as an Act, what we seek to set at the basis of the whole Science of Knowledge. And reflection must confirm *that* this Act is granted as such *along with the proposition.* Let any fact of empirical consciousness be proposed; and let one empirical feature after another be detached from it, until all that remains is what cannot any longer be dismissed, and from which nothing further can be detached.

I, 93

1.   The proposition <u>*A is A*</u> (or A = A, since that is the meaning of the logical copula) is accepted by everyone and that without a moment's thought: it is admitted to be perfectly certain and established.

Yet if anyone were to demand a proof of this proposition, we should certainly not embark on anything of the kind, but would insist that it is *absolutely* certain, that is, *without any other ground:* and in so saying—doubtless with general approval—we should be ascribing to ourselves the power of *asserting something absolutely.*
2.   In insisting that the above proposition is intrinsically certain we are *not* asserting that A *is the case.* The proposition *A is A* is by no means equivalent to *A exists,* or *there is an A.* (*To be,* without a predicate attached, means something quite different from 'to be' with a predicate; of which more anon.) If we suppose that A signifies a space enclosed by two straight lines, the first proposition still remains perfectly true; though the proposition that *A exists* would obviously be false.

On the contrary, what we are saying is: *If* A exists, *then* A exists. Hence there is simply no question here as to *whether* A actually exists or not. It is a matter, not of the *content* of the proposition, but simply of its *form;* not of that *about which* you know something, but of *what* you know about anything at all, whatever it may be.

Thus in claiming that the above proposition is absolutely certain, what is established is that between that *if* and this *then* there is a necessary connection; and it is the *necessary connection between the two* that is posited *absolutely,* and *without any other ground*. To this necessary connection I give the preliminary designation X.

3.   But with respect to A itself we have thereby said nothing, as yet, as to *whether* it exists or not. Hence the question arises: Under what condition, then, *does* A exist?

a)   X is at least *in* the self, and posited *by* the self, for it is the self which judges in the above proposition, and indeed judges according to X, as a law; which law must therefore be given to the self, and since it is posited absolutely and without any other ground, must be given to the self by itself alone.

I, 94

b)   *Whether,* and *how,* A is actually posited we do not know: but since X is supposed to designate a connection between an unknown positing of A and an absolute assertion of that same A, on the strength of the first positing, then *at least so far as this connection is posited,* A is *in* the self and posited *by* the self, just as X is. X is possible only in relation to an A; now X is really present in the self: and so A must also be present in the self, insofar as X is related to it.

c)   X is related to that A which occupies the logical position of subject in the foregoing proposition, just as it also is to that which stands as predicate; for both are united by X. Both, therefore, so far as they are posited, are posited in the self; and given that the A in the subject position is asserted, that in the predicate is asserted absolutely; hence the above proposition can also be expressed as follows: if A is posited *in the self,* it is thereby *posited,* or, it thereby *is.*

4.   Thus the self asserts, by means of X, that *A exists absolutely for the judging self, and that simply in virtue of its being posited in the self as such;* which is to say, it is asserted that within the

self—whether it be specifically positing, or judging, or whatever it may be—there is something that is permanently uniform, forever one and the same; and hence the X that is absolutely posited can also be expressed as $I = I$; I am I.

5.   By this operation we have already arrived unnoticed at the proposition: *I am* (as the expression, not of an *Act,* to be sure, but nonetheless of a *fact*).

For X is posited absolutely; that is a *fact* of empirical consciousness. But now X is equivalent to the proposition 'I am I'; hence this, too, is asserted absolutely.

But the proposition 'I am I' has a meaning wholly different from that of 'A is A'. For the latter has content only under a certain condition. *If* A is posited, it is naturally posited *as* A, as having the predicate A. But this proposition still tells us nothing as to *whether* it actually is posited, and hence whether it is posited with any particular predicate. Yet the proposition 'I am I' is unconditionally and absolutely valid, since it is equivalent to the proposition X^2; it is valid not merely in form but also in content. In it the I is posited, not conditionally, but absolutely, with the predicate of equivalence to itself; hence it really *is* posited, and the proposition can also be expressed as *I am.*

This proposition, 'I am', has so far been founded merely on a fact and has no more than factual validity. Should the proposition $A = A$ be certain (or, more precisely, what is absolutely posited therein, namely X), then the proposition 'I am' must also be certain. Now it is a fact of empirical consciousness that we are constrained to regard X as absolutely certain; and so too with the proposition 'I am', on which X is founded. Hence it is a ground of explanation of all the facts of empirical consciousness, that prior to all postulation in the self, the self itself is posited.   —(I say of *all* the facts: and this depends on proof of the proposition, that X is the highest fact of empirical consciousness, underlying and contained in all others; which might well be conceded without any

---

[2] i.e., in plain language: I, who posit A in the predicate position, necessarily know, because *the same was posited in the subject position,* about my positing of the subject, and hence know myself, again contemplate myself, am the same with myself.

proof, even though the whole Science of Knowledge is occupied in proving it).

6.   We return to the point from which we started.

a)   The proposition 'A = A' constitutes a *judgment*. But all judgment, so empirical consciousness tells us, is an activity of the human mind; for in empirical self-consciousness it has all the conditions of activity which must be presupposed as known and established for purposes of reflection.

b)   Now this activity is based on something that rests on no more ultimate ground, namely X = I am.

c)   Hence what is *absolutely posited, and founded on itself,* is the ground of *one particular* activity (and, as the whole Science of Knowledge will show, of *all* activity) of the human mind, and thus of its pure character; the pure character of activity as such, in abstraction from its specific empirical conditions.

The self's own positing of itself is thus its own pure activity. The *self posits itself,* and by virtue of this mere self-assertion it *exists;* and conversely, the self *exists* and *posits* its own existence by virtue of merely existing. It is at once the agent and the product of action; the active, and what the activity brings about; action and deed are one and the same, and hence the 'I am' expresses an Act, and the only one possible, as will inevitably appear from the Science of Knowledge as a whole.

7.   Now let us consider once more the proposition *'I am I'*.

a)   The I is posited absolutely. Let it be assumed that what is *absolutely posited* is the I occupying the place of formal subject[3] in the above proposition; while that in the predicate position represents that which *exists;* hence, the absolutely valid judgment that

---

[3]This, at all events, is what the logical form of every proposition tells us. In the proposition 'A = A', the first A is that which is posited in the self, either absolutely, like the self itself, or on some other ground, like any given not-self. In this matter the self behaves as absolute subject; and hence the first A is called the subject. The second A designates what the self, reflecting upon itself, discovers to be present in itself, because it has first set this within itself. The judging self predicates something, not really of A, but of itself, namely that there is an A in it; and hence the second A is called the predicate. —Thus in the proposition 'A = B', A designates what is now being posited; B what is already encountered as posited. —*Is* expresses the passage of the *self* from positing to reflection on what has been posited.

both are completely identical, states, or absolutely asserts, that the *self* exists *because* it has posited itself.

b)   The self in the first sense, and that in the second, are supposed to be absolutely equivalent. Hence one can also reverse the above proposition and say: the self posits itself simply *because* it exists. It *posits* itself by merely existing and *exists* by merely being posited.

And this now makes it perfectly clear in what sense we are using the word 'I' in this context, and leads us to an exact account of the self as absolute subject. *That whose being or essence consists simply in the fact that it posits itself as existing,* is the self as absolute subject. As it *posits* itself, so it *is;* and as it *is,* so it *posits* itself; and hence the self is absolute and necessary for the self. What does not exist for itself is not a self.

(To explain: one certainly hears the question proposed: *What* was I, then, before I came to self-consciousness? The natural reply is: *I* did not exist at all; for I was not a self. The self exists only insofar as it is conscious of itself. The possibility of this question is based on a confusion between the self as *subject,* and the self as *object* of reflection for an absolute subject, and is in itself utterly improper. The self presents itself to itself, to that extent imposes on itself the form of a presentation, and is now for the first time a *something,* namely an object; in this form consciousness acquires a substrate, which *exists,* even though without real consciousness, and thought of, moreover, in bodily form. People conceive of some such situation as this, and ask: *What* was the self at that time, *i.e.,* what is the substrate of consciousness? But in so doing they think unawares of the *absolute subject as well,* as contemplating this substrate; and thus they unwittingly subjoin in thought the very thing from which they have allegedly abstracted, and contradict themselves. You cannot think at all without subjoining in thought your self, as conscious of itself; from your self-consciousness you can never abstract; hence all questions of the above type call for no answer, for a real understanding of oneself would preclude their being asked.)

8.   If the self exists only insofar as it posits itself, then it exists only *for* that which posits, and posits only for that which exists.

The self exists for the self—but if it posits itself absolutely, as it is, then it posits itself as necessary, and is necessary for the self. *I exist only for myself; but for myself I am necessary* (in saying '*for my-self*', I already posit my existence).

9.   *To posit oneself* and *to be* are, as applied to the self, perfectly identical. Thus the proposition, 'I am, because I have posited my-self' can also be stated as: '*I am absolutely, because I am*'.

Furthermore, the self-positing self and the existing self are perfectly identical, one and the same. The self is that *which* it posits itself to be; and it posits itself as *that* which it is. Hence *I am absolutely what I am.*

10.   The Act now unfolded may be given immediate expression in the following formula: *I am absolutely,* i.e., *I am absolutely* BECAUSE *I am; and am absolutely* WHAT *I am; both* FOR THE SELF.

If the account of this Act is to be viewed as standing at the forefront of a Science of Knowledge, it will have to be expressed somewhat as follows: *The self begins by an absolute positing of its own existence.*[4]

We started from the proposition A = A; not as if the proposition 'I am' could be deduced therefrom, but because we had to start from something given with *certainty* in empirical consciousness. But it actually appeared in our discussion that it is not the 'I am' that is based on 'A = A' but rather that the latter proposition is based on the former.

If we abstract from 'I am' the specific content, namely the self, and are left with the mere form that is given with this content, *the form of an inference from being posited to being,* as for purposes of logic we are compelled to do (cf. *Begriff der Wissenschaftslehre,* § 6), we then obtain 'A = A' as *the basic proposition of logic,* which can be demonstrated and determined only through the Science of Knowledge. *Demonstrated,* in that A

---

[4]To put all this in other words, which I have elsewhere employed: *the self* is a necessary identity of subject and object: a subject-object; and is so absolutely, without further mediation. This, I say, is what it means; though this proposition has not been so readily understood as one might have thought, or weighed according to its high importance, which, prior to the Science of Knowledge, has been treated with utter neglect; so that the preceding discussion of it cannot be dispensed with. [Note of 1802, Tr.]

is A, because the self that has posited A is identical with that in which A has been posited; *determined*, in that everything that exists does so only insofar as it is posited in the self, and apart from the self there is nothing. No possible A in the above proposition (no *thing*) can be anything other than something posited in the self.

By making a further abstraction from judging, as a specific activity, and having regard only to the general *mode* of action of the human mind that this form presents, we obtain the *category of reality*. Everything to which the proposition 'A = A' is applicable, has reality, *insofar as that proposition is applicable to it*. Whatever is posited in virtue of the simple positing of some thing (an item posited in the self) is the reality, or essence, of that thing.

(The scepticism of Maimon is ultimately based on the question of our right to apply the category of reality. This right can be derived from no other—we are absolutely entitled thereto. The fact is, rather, that all other possible rights must be derived from this; and even Maimon's scepticism inadvertently presupposes it, in that he acknowledges the correctness of ordinary logic. —But we can point out something from which every category is itself derived: the self, as absolute subject. Of every other possible thing to which it may be applied, it has to be shown that reality is transferred to it *from the self:* —that it would have to exist, provided that the self exists.)

That our proposition is the absolutely basic principle of all knowledge, was pointed out by *Kant*, in his deduction of the categories; but he never laid it down specifically *as* the basic

principle. *Descartes*, before him, put forward a similar proposition: *cogito, ergo sum*—which need not have been merely the minor premise and conclusion of a syllogism, with the major premise: *quodcumque cogitat est;* for he may very well have regarded it as an immediate datum of consciousness. It would then amount to *cogitans sum, ergo sum* (or as we should say, *sum, ergo sum*). But in that case the addition of *cogitans* is entirely superfluous; we do not necessarily think when we exist, but we necessarily exist whenever we think. Thinking is by no means the essence, but merely a specific determination of existence; and our existence has many other determinations besides this. —*Reinhold* put forward the principle of representation, and in Cartesian form his basic proposition would run: *repraesento, ergo sum*, or more properly: *repraesentans sum, ergo sum*. He makes a notable advance over Descartes; but if his intention is to establish simply knowledge itself, and not merely a propaedeutic to the same, it is not enough; for even representation is not the essence of existence, but a specific determination thereof; and our existence has still other determinations besides this, *even though they must pass through the medium of representation, in order to attain to empirical consciousness.*

Our principle has been overstepped, in the sense ascribed to it, by *Spinoza*. He does not deny the unity of empirical consciousness, but pure consciousness he completely rejects. On his view, the whole series of presentations in an empirical subject is related to the one pure subject as a single presentation is to a series. For him the self (what he calls *his* self, or what I call *mine*) does not exist absolutely *because* it exists; but because *something else* exists. —The self is certainly a self *for* itself, in his theory, but he goes on to ask what it would be for something other than the self. Such an 'other' would equally be a self, of which the posited self (e.g. *mine*) and all other selves that might be posited would be modifications. He separates *pure* and *empirical* consciousness. The first he attributes to God, who is never conscious of himself,

since pure consciousness never attains to consciousness; the second he locates in the specific modifications of the Deity. So established, his system is perfectly consistent and irrefutable, since he takes his stand in a territory where reason can no longer follow him; but it is also groundless; for what right did he have to go beyond the pure consciousness given in empirical consciousness? —It is easy enough to see what impelled him to his system, namely the necessary endeavor to bring about the highest unity in human cognition. This unity is present in his system, and the error of it is merely that he thought to deduce on grounds of theoretical reason what he was driven to merely by a practical need; that he claimed to have established something as truly given, when he was merely setting up an appointed, but never attainable, ideal.

We shall encounter his highest unity again in the Science of Knowledge; though not as something that *exists*, but as something that we *ought to*, and yet *cannot*, achieve. —I further observe, that if we go beyond the *I am*, we necessarily arrive at Spinózism (that, when fully thought out, the system of Leibniz is nothing other than Spinozism, is shown in a valuable essay by Solomon Maimon: *Über die Progressen der Philosophie, etc.*); and that there are only two completely consistent systems: the *critical*, which recognizes this boundary, and the *Spinozistic*, which over-steps it.

§ 2.   SECOND PRINCIPLE, CONDITIONED AS TO CONTENT.

The same reason which made it impossible either to prove or derive the first principle also applies to the second. Here then, as before, we proceed from a fact of empirical consciousness, and deal with it, on the same terms, in a similar fashion.

1.   The proposition that '$\sim$A is not equal to A' will undoubtedly be accepted by everyone as perfectly certain and established, and it is hardly to be expected that anyone should demand proof of it.

I, 102   2.   Yet, if such a proof were possible, it could not be derived in our system (whose inherent correctness still remains problematic, indeed, until the science is completed) from anything else but the proposition that '$A = A$'.

3.   No such proof is in fact possible. For assuming, at the utmost, that the above proposition were equivalent to '$\sim A = \sim A$' (and hence that $\sim$A is identical with some Y posited in the self), and that it were now to amount to: '*if* the opposite of A is posited, *then* it is posited', we should then be asserting absolutely the same connection ($= X$) as before; and it would in no sense be a proposition derived from and proved by means of '$A = A$', but just that very proposition itself . . . (And hence, too, the form of this proposition, so far as it is a purely logical proposition, is really comprehended under the highest of forms, the condition of *having form* at all, namely, the unity of consciousness).

4. But this has no bearing whatsover on the question: *Is* the opposite of A posited, and under what condition of the *form of mere action* is it posited as such? It is this condition which would have had to be derived from 'A = A', if the foregoing proposition were itself to be considered a derived one. But such a condition simply cannot be obtained from 'A = A', since the form of counter-positing is so far from being contained in that of positing, that in fact it is flatly opposed to this. Hence it is an absolute and uncon-ditional opposition. $\sim$A is posited absolutely, *as* such, just *because* it is posited.

As certainly, therefore, as the proposition '$\sim$A is not equal to A' occurs among the facts of empirical consciousness, there is thus an opposition included among the acts of the self; and this opposition is, as to its mere *form,* an absolutely possible and un-conditional act based on no higher ground.

(The *logical* form of the proposition *as* such (if stated in the form '$\sim$A = $\sim$A') presupposes the identity of subject and predi-cate (i.e., of the *presenting* self, and the self *presented as* present-ing: cf. note p. 99). But even the possibility of counterpositing itself presupposes the identity of consciousness; and the proce-dure of the self in acting thus is properly as follows: A (absolutely posited) = A (the object of reflection). By an absolute act this A, as object of reflection, is opposed to $\sim$A, and this latter is judged to be also opposed to the absolutely posited A, since both A's are the same: a likeness based (§ 1) on the identity of the positing and the reflecting self.   —It is further presupposed that the self which acts in *both* cases, and judges in both, is the same. If it could be opposed to itself in the two acts, $\sim$A would be equal to A. Hence even the transition from positing to counterpositing is possible only through the identity of the self).

I, 103

5. By means, therefore, and only by means, of this absolute act, the opposite is posited, so far as it is *op*posed (as a mere contrary in general). Every opposite, so far as it is so, is so absolutely, by virtue of an act of the self, and for no other reason. Opposition in general is posited absolutely by the self.

6. If any $\sim$A is to be posited, an A must be posited. Hence the act of opposing is also conditioned in another respect. Whether such an act is possible at all, depends on another act; hence the act is

materially conditioned, as being an act at all; it is an act in relation to some other act. That we act *so,* and not otherwise, is unconditioned; *formally* (as to its *how)* the act is unconditioned.

(Opposition is possible only on the assumption of a unity of consciousness between the self that posits and the self that opposes. For if consciousness of the first act were not connected with that of the second, the latter would be, not a *counter*positing, but an absolute positing. It is only in relation to a positing that it becomes a counterpositing).

7.   So far we have spoken of the act as a mere act, of the *kind* of act it is. We now proceed to its outcome = ∽A.

Again we can distinguish two aspects in ∽A, its *form* and its *matter.* The form determines that it is in general an opposite (of some X). So far as it is opposed to a specific A, it has *matter;* it is not some specific thing.

8.   The *form* of ∽A is determined absolutely by the act; it is an opposite, because it is the product of an opposition. Its *matter* is governed by A; it is not what A is, and its whole essence consists in that fact.   —I know of ∽A *that* it is the opposite of some A. But *what* that thing may or may not be, *of* which I know this, can be known to me only on the assumption that I am acquainted with A.

9.   Nothing is posited to begin with, except the self; and this alone is asserted absolutely (§1). Hence there can be an absolute opposition only to the self. But that which is opposed to the self = the *not-self.*

10.   As surely as the absolute certainty of the proposition '∽A is not equal to A' is unconditionally admitted among the facts of empirical consciousness, *so surely is a not-self opposed absolutely to the self.* Now all that we have just said concerning opposition in general is derived from this original opposition, and thus holds good of it from the start; it is thus absolutely unconditioned in form, but conditioned as to matter. And with this we have also discovered the second basic principle of all human knowledge.

11.   Whatsoever attaches to the self, the mere fact of opposition necessitates that its opposite attaches to the not-self.

(The concept of the not-self is commonly taken to be no more than a discursive or general concept, obtained by abstraction from everything presented. But the shallowness of this explanation can easily be demonstrated. If I am to present anything at all, I must oppose it to the presenting self. Now within the object of presentation there can and must be an X of some sort, whereby it discloses itself as something to be presented, and not as that which presents. But *that* everything, wherein this X may be, is not that which presents, but an item to be presented, is something that no object can teach me; for merely in order to set up something as an *object,* I have to know this already; hence it must lie initially in myself, the presenter, in advance of any possible experience. —And this is an observation so striking, that anyone who fails to grasp it, and is not thereby uplifted into transcendental idealism, must unquestionably be suffering from mental blindness).

By abstraction from the content of the material proposition *I am,* we obtained the purely formal and logical proposition 'A = A'. By a similar abstraction from the assertions set forth in the preceding paragraphs, we obtain the logical proposition '~A is not equal to A', which I should like to call the *principle of opposition.* We are not yet in a position to define it, or express it in verbal form; the reason for this will appear in the paragraphs that follow. If now, we finally abstract entirely from the specific act of judgment, and look merely to the form of the inference from counterposition to nonexistence, we obtain the *category of negation.* But of this, too, a clear conception can only be gathered from the next section.

§ 3. THIRD PRINCIPLE, CONDITIONED AS TO FORM.

With every step that we advance in our science, we approach the area in which everything can be proved. In our first principle it was neither possible nor incumbent on us to prove anything at all; it was unconditioned as to both form and content, and certain without recourse to any higher ground. In our second, the *act of counterpositing* was admittedly unprovable; but though unconditionally asserted in respect of its mere form, it could be rigorously demonstrated that *what was counterposited* must = the not-self. Our third propositon is susceptible of proof almost throughout, because, unlike the second, it is determined, not as to content, but rather as to form, and not by one proposition only, but by two.

In describing it as determinate in form and unconditioned only as to content, we have in mind the following: The *task* which it poses *for action* is determinately given by the two propositions preceding, but not the resolution of the same. The latter is achieved unconditionally and absolutely by a decree of reason.

I, 106

We begin, therefore, with a deduction leading to the task, and proceed with it as far as we can. The impossibility of carrying it further will undoubtedly show us the point at which we have to break off and appeal to that unconditioned decree of reason which will emerge from the task in question.

A)

1.   Insofar as the not-self is posited, the self is not posited; for the not-self completely nullifies the self.

Now the not-self is posited in the *self;* for it is counterposited; but all such counterpositing presupposes the identity of the self, in which something is posited and then something set in opposition thereto.

Thus the self is not posited in the self, insofar as the not-self is posited therein.

2.   But the not-self can be posited only insofar as a self *is* posited in the self (in the identical consciousness), to which it (the not-self) can be opposed.

Now the not-self is to be posited in the identical consciousness

Thus, insofar as the not-self is to be posited in this consciousness, the self must also be posited therein.

3.   The two conclusions are opposed to each other: both have been evolved by analysis from the second principle, and both are thus implicit therein. Hence the second principle is opposed to itself and nullifies itself.

4.   But it nullifies itself only insofar as the posited is annulled by the counterposited, which is to say, insofar as it is itself valid.

Now it is supposed to have annulled itself, and to have no validity.
Thus it does not annul itself.

The second principle annuls itself; and it also does not annul
itself.

I, 107   5.   If this is how things stand with the second principle, it
cannot be otherwise with the first as well. It annuls itself and also
does not annul itself.

.   [For, if I = I, everything is posited that is posited in the self.
But now the second principle is supposed to be posited in the
self, and also not to be posited therein.

Thus I does not = I, but rather <u>self = not-self</u>, and <u>not-self =
self.</u>]

B)   All these conclusions have been derived from the principles
already set forth, according to laws of reflection that we have presupposed as valid; so they must be correct. But if so, the identity
of consciousness, the sole absolute foundation of our knowledge,
is itself eliminated. And hereby our task is now determined. For we
have to discover some X, by means of which all these conclusions
can be granted as correct, without doing away with the identity
of consciousness.

1.   The opposites to be unified lie in the self, as consciousness. So X, too, must exist in consciousness.

2.   Both self and not-self are alike products of original acts
of the self, and consciousness itself is similarly a product of the
self's first original act, its own positing of itself.

3.   Yet, according to our previous arguments, the act of
counterpositing that results in the not-self is quite impossible
without X. So X itself must be a product, and of an original act of
the self at that. Hence there is an act of the human mind = Y, whose
product is X.

4.   The form of this act is completely determined by the task
referred to above. The opposed self and not-self are to be unified
I, 108   thereby, to be posited together, without mutual elimination. The
opposites in question must be taken up into the identity of the one
consciousness.

5.   But it is thereby left quite open *how* this is to happen,
and in what fashion it is to be possible; the task itself provides no

answer, nor is there any way of evolving one from it. Hence, as
before, we must make an experiment and ask: How can A and
—A, being and nonbeing, reality and negation, be thought together
without mutual elimination and destruction?

6.   We need not expect anyone to answer the question other
than as follows: They will mutually *limit* one another. And if this
be the right answer, the act Y will be a *limiting* of each opposite by
the other; and X will denote the *limits*.

(I must not be understood to maintain that the idea of a
limit is an analytical concept, inherent in the combination of reality
and negation, and capable of being evolved from this. To be sure,
the opposed concepts have been given by our two first fundamental
principles, while the demand for their unification is contained in the
first. But the manner of their possible unification is by no means
implicit in these principles, being governed, rather, by a *special*
law of our mind, which the foregoing experiment was designed to
bring to consciousness).

7.   But the concept of a limit contains more than the required
X; for it also involves the concepts of reality and negation, as requiring to be united. So in order to obtain X alone, we must make
a further abstraction.

8.   To *limit* something is to abolish its reality, not *wholly*
but in *part* only, by negation. Thus, apart from reality and negation,
the notion of a limit also contains that of *divisibility* (the *capacity
for quantity* in general, not any *determinate* quantity). This idea is
the required X, and hence by the act Y *both the self and the not-
self are absolutely posited as divisible.*

9.   *Both self and not-self are posited as divisible;* for the act
Y cannot *succeed* the act of counterpositing, cannot, that is, be considered as if it was only this latter act that made it possible; for, by
the foregoing argument, mere opposition alone destroys itself and
thus becomes impossible. But the act Y cannot *precede* either; for
it is undertaken simply to make opposition possible, and divisibility
is nothing without something to divide. Hence it occurs immediately, within and alongside the act of opposition; both are one and the
same, and are distinguished only in reflection. Just as a not-self is

opposed to the self, so the self which is opposed, and the not-self which opposes it, are posited as divisible.

C)   It now remains only to inquire whether the supposed act represents a genuine resolution of the problem, and unites all the opposites in question.

1.   The first conclusion is now established as follows: The self is *not* posited in the self to the extent, i.e., with that measure of reality, wherewith the not-self *is* posited. A measure of reality, i.e., that attributed to the not-self, is abolished within the self. This proposition is not contradicted by the second. Insofar as the not-self is posited, so must the self be also; for both in general are posited as divisible in respect of their reality.

Only now, in virtue of the concept thus established, can it be said of both that they are *something*. The absolute self of the first principle is not *something* (it has, and can have, no predicate); it is simply *what* it is, and this can be explained no further. But now, by means of this concept, consciousness contains the *whole* of reality; and to the not-self is allotted that part of it which does not attach to the self, and *vice versa*. Both are something; the not-self is what the self is not, and *vice versa*. As opposed to the absolute self (though—as will be shown in due course—it can only be opposed insofar as it is presented, not as it is in itself), the not-self is *absolutely nothing;* as opposed to the limitable self it is a *negative quantity*.

2.   The self is to be equated with, and yet opposed to, itself. But in regard to consciousness it is equal to itself, for consciousness is one: but in this consciousness the absolute self is posited as indivisible; whereas the self to which the not-self is opposed is posited as divisible. Hence, insofar as there is a not-self opposed to it, the self is itself in opposition to the absolute self.

And so all these oppositions are thus united, without detriment to the unity of consciousness; and this, in effect, is proof that the concept we proposed was the correct one.

D)   Since, according to our presupposition, which only the completion of a Science of Knowledge can demonstrate, there can be no more than one absolutely unconditioned principle, one condi-

I, 110

tioned as to content, and one conditioned as to form, no other principle is possible apart from those established. The resources of the unconditioned and absolutely certain are now exhausted; and I would wish to express the outcome in the following formula: *In the self I oppose a divisible not-self to the divisible self.*

No philosophy goes further in knowledge than this; but every thorough-going philosophy should go back to this point; and so far as it does so, it becomes a Science of Knowledge. Everything that is to emerge hereafter in the system of the human mind must be derivable from what we have established here.

1.   We have unified the opposing self and not-self through the concept of divisibility. If we abstract from the specific content of self and not-self, leaving only the *mere form of the union of opposites through the concept of divisibility,* we obtain the logical proposition known hitherto as the *grounding* principle: A in part = $\sim$A, and *vice versa*. Every opposite is like its opponent in one respect, = X; and every like is opposed to its like in one respect, = X. Such a respect, = X, is called the ground, in the first case of *conjunction,* and in the second of *distinction:* for to liken or compare opposites is to *conjoin* them; and to set like things in opposition is to *distinguish* them. This logical proposition is *demonstrated* and *determined* by the material principle we have established.

Demonstrated, for

a)   Every counterposited $\sim$A is posited counter to an A, and this A is posited. By positing of a $\sim$A, A is both annulled and yet not annulled. Hence it is annulled only in part; and in place of the X in A, which is not annulled, we posit in $\sim$A, not $\sim$X, but X itself: and thus A = $\sim$A in respect of X. Which was our first point.

b)   Everything equated (= A = B) is equal to itself, in virtue of its being posited in the self. A = A. B = B.

Now B is posited equal to A, and thus B is not posited through A; for if it was posited thereby, it would = A and not = B. (There would not be two posits, but only one).

But if B is not posited through the positing of A, it to that extent = $\sim$A; and by the equation of the two we posit neither A nor B, but an X of some sort, which = X, =A, and = B. Which was our second point. From this it is evident how the proposition A = B can be valid, though as such it contradicts the proposition A = A. X = X, A = X, B = X. Hence A = B to the extent that each = X: but A = ⁓B to the extent that each = ⁓X.

Only in *one* particular are equals opposite, and opposites equal. For if they were opposed in many particulars, i.e., if there were opposing characteristics in the opposites themselves, one of the two would belong to that wherein the equals are alike, and so they would not be opposed; and *vice versa*. Every warranted judgment, therefore, has but one ground of conjunction and one of distinction. If it has more, it is not one judgment but many.

2. The logical grounding principle is *determined* by the above material principle, i.e., its validity is itself restricted; it holds only for a part of our knowledge.

Only on the assumption that different things are in general equated or opposed are they opposed or equated in any particular respect. But this is by no means to assert that everything that may occur in our consciousness must absolutely and unconditionally be set equal to some other, and in opposition to a third. A judgment concerning that to which nothing can be equated or opposed is simply not subject to the grounding principle, for it is not subject to the condition of its validity; it is not grounded, but itself is the ground of all possible judgments; it has no ground, but itself provides the ground for everything that does have a ground. The object of such judgments is the absolute self and all judgments of which it is the subject hold absolutely and without any ground at all; of which we have more to say below.

3. The act of seeking in things equated the respect in which they are *opposed,* is called the *antithetic* procedure; commonly described as the *analytical,* though this expression is less convenient, partly because it allows you to suppose that you might perhaps evolve something out of a concept which was not previously put into it by a synthesis, and partly because the former term indicates more clearly that this process is the opposite of the synthetical. For the *synthetic* procedure consists in discovering in opposites the respect in which they are *alike.* In regard to their mere logical form, whereby we abstract completely from all cognitive content and from the

manner in which it is arrived at, judgments obtained in the first way are called antithetic or negative, and those yielded by the second, synthetic or affirmative judgments.

4. The logical rules governing all antithesis and synthesis are derived from the third principle of the Science of Knowledge, and from this, therefore, all command over antithesis and synthesis is in general derived. But in setting forth that principle we saw that the primordial act it expresses, that of combining opposites in a third thing, was impossible without the act of counterpositing; and that this also was impossible without the act of combination; so that both are in practice inseparably united, and can be distinguished only in reflection. From thence it follows that the logical procedures based on this primary act, and which in fact are but special, more precise determinations of the same, will be equally impossible one without the other. There can be no antithesis without a synthesis; for antithesis consists merely in seeking out the point of opposition between things that are alike; but these like things would not be alike if they had not first been equated in an act of synthesis. In antithesis *per se* we abstract from the fact that they have first been equated by such an act: they are simply taken to be alike, without asking why; reflection dwells solely on the element of opposition between them and thereby raises it to clear and distinct consciousness.   —And conversely, too, there can be no synthesis without an antithesis. Things in opposition are to be united: but they would not be op-

I, 114   posed if they had not been so by an act of the self, which is ignored in the synthesis, so that reflection may bring to consciousness only the ground of connection between them.   —So far as content is concerned, therefore, there are no judgments purely analytic; and by them alone we not only do not get far, as *Kant* says; we do not get anywhere at all.

5. The celebrated question which Kant placed at the head of the *Critique of Pure Reason:* How are synthetic judgments *a priori* possible?—is now answered in the most universal and satisfactory manner. In the third principle we have established a synthesis between the two opposites, self and not-self, by postulating them each to be divisible; there can be no further question as to the possibility of this, nor can any ground for it be given; it is absolutely possible, and we are entitled to it without further grounds of any kind. All

other syntheses, if they are to be valid, must be rooted in this one, and must have been established in and along with it. And once this has been demonstrated, we have the most convincing proof that they are valid as well.

6. *They must all be contained in it:* and this at once indicates to us in the most definite fashion the course that our science has now to pursue. There have to be syntheses, so from now on our whole procedure will be synthetic (at least in the theoretical portion of the Science of Knowledge, for in the practical part it is the other way round, as will appear in due course); every proposition will contain a synthesis. —But no synthesis is possible without a preceding antithesis, from which, however, we abstract, so far as it is an act, and merely seek out the product thereof, the opposite in question. In every proposition, therefore, we must begin by pointing out opposites which are to be reconciled. —All syntheses established must be rooted in the highest synthesis which we have just effected, and be derivable therefrom. In the self and not-self thus I, 115 united, and to the extent that they are united thereby, we have therefore to seek out opposing characteristics that remain, and to unite them through a new ground of conjunction, which again must be contained in the highest conjunctive ground of all. And in the opposites united by this first synthesis, we again have to find new opposites, and to combine them by a new ground of conjunction, contained in that already derived. And this we must continue so far as we can, until we arrive at opposites which can no longer be altogether combined, and are thereby transported into the practical part of this work. Hence our course is fixed and certain, and prescribed by the subject-matter itself; and we can know in advance that, given due attention, we simply cannot stray from our path.

7. Just as there can be no antithesis wthout synthesis, no synthesis without antithesis, so there can be neither without a thesis—an absolute positing, whereby an A (the self) is neither equated nor opposed to any other, but is just absolutely posited. This, as applied to our system, is what gives strength and completeness to the whole; it must be a system, and it must be *one;* the opposites must be united, so long as opposition remains, until absolute unity is effected; a thing, indeed—as will appear in due course—which could be brought about only by a completed approximation to infinity, which

in itself is impossible. —The necessity of opposing and uniting in
the manner prescribed rests directly on the third principle; the necessity of combination in general, on the first, highest, absolutely unconditioned principle. The *form* of the system is based on the
highest synthesis; *that* there should be a system at all, on the
absolute thesis. —So much for the application of the foregoing to
our system in general; but it has yet another and more important
application to the form of judgments, which there are many reasons
for not overlooking at this point. For, just as there were antithetic
and synthetic judgments, so there ought, by analogy, to be thetic
judgments also, which should in some respect be directly opposed
to them. For the propriety of the two former types presupposes
a ground, indeed a double ground, firstly of conjunction, and secondly of distinction, of which both could be exhibited, and both
would *have* to be exhibited, if the judgment is to be warranted sound.
(For example, a bird is an animal: here the ground of conjunction
we reflect upon is the specific concept of an animal, that it consists
of matter, of organic matter, of animate living matter; while the
grounds of distinction, which we disregard, consist of the specific
differences among the various kinds of animal, whether they are
bipeds or quadrupeds, and have feathers, scales or a hairy skin.
Again, a plant is not an animal: here the ground of distinction we
reflect upon is the specific difference between plant and animal;
while the ground of conjunction we disregard is the fact of organization in general.) A thetic judgment, however, would be one
in which something is asserted, not to be like anything else or opposed to anything else, but simply to be identical with itself: thus
it could presuppose no ground of conjunction or distinction at all:
the third thing, rather, which as a matter of logical form, it must still
presuppose, would be simply the *requirement* for a ground. The first
and foremost judgment of this type is 'I am', in which nothing whatever is affirmed of the self, the place of the predicate being left
indefinitely empty for its possible characterization. All judgments
subsumed under this, i.e., under the absolute positing of the self,
are of this type (even if they should not always happen to have the
self for logical subject); for example, man is free. This judgment
can be regarded, on the one hand, as positive (in which case it
would read: man belongs to the class of free beings), and then a

I, 116

ground of conjunction would have to be given between man and free beings, which, as the ground of freedom, would be contained in the concept of free beings generally, and of man in particular; but, far from it being possible to provide such a ground, we cannot even point to a class of free beings. Alternatively, it can be regarded as negative, in which' case man is contrasted to all beings that are subject to the laws of natural necessity; but then we should have to give the ground of distinction between necessary and not necessary, and it would have to be shown that the former is not contained in the concept of man, whereas it is in that of the contrasted beings; and at the same time a respect would have to be pointed out in which they both concurred. But man, insofar as the predicate of freedom is applicable to him, that is, insofar as he is an absolute and not a presented or presentable subject, has nothing whatever in common with natural beings, and hence is not contrasted to them either. For all that, the logical form of the judgment, which is positive, requires that both concepts should be united; yet they cannot be combined in any concept whatever, but only in the Idea of a self whose consciousness has been determined by nothing outside itself, it being rather its own mere consciousness which determines everything outside it. Yet this Idea is itself unthinkable, since for us it contains a contradiction. But it is nevertheless imposed upon us as our highest practical goal. Man must approximate, *ad infinitum,* to a freedom he can never, in principle, attain. —The judgment of taste, A is beautiful (so far as A contains a feature also present in the ideal of beauty), is likewise a thetic judgment; for I cannot compare this feature with the ideal, since the latter is unknown to me. It is, rather, a mental task derived from the absolute positing of myself, to discover this ideal, though one that could only be discharged after a completed approximation to the infinite. —Thus Kant and his followers have very properly described these judgments as *infinite,* though nobody, so far as I know, has explained them in a clear and determinate manner.

8. Hence, for any given thetic judgment, no ground can be supplied; but the procedure of the human mind in such judgments generally is based on the self's own absolute positing of itself. It is useful, and gives the clearest and most definite insight into the peculiar character of the critical system, if we compare this explana-

tion of thetic judgments in general with those of the antithetical and synthetic judgments.

All the opposites contained in any concept which articulates their ground of distinction concur in a *higher* (more general and comprehensive) concept, known as the generic concept: i.e., a synthesis is presupposed in which both contain and, so far as they are alike, are contained in, each other. (For example, gold and silver are alike contained in the concept of metal, which does not contain the concept wherein they differ—in this case, say, their specific color). Hence the logical rule of definition, that it must furnish the generic concept, which contains the ground of conjunction, and the specific difference, which contains the ground of distinction. —As against this, all comparisons are opposed in respect of a *lower* concept, expressing some specific feature from which abstraction is made in the conjunctive judgment, i.e., every synthesis presupposes a prior antithesis. For example, in the concept of body we abstract from differences of color, individual weight, taste, smell, etc., and now everything can be a body which occupies space, is impenetrable, and has some weight or other, however opposed it may be to other bodies in respect of these characteristics. *(Which features are more general or more special, and hence which concepts are higher or lower, is determined by the Science of Knowledge. In general, the fewer the intermediate concepts whereby a given concept is derived from the highest, that of reality, the higher it is; the more intermediaries, the lower it is. Y is assuredly a lower concept than X if, in the course of its derivation from the highest concept, X appears; and vice versa.)*

I, 119

With the absolutely posited, namely the self, things are very different. In the very act of opposing a not-self to it, the latter is simultaneously equated thereto, but not, as with all other comparisons, in a *higher* concept (which would presuppose both contained in it, and a higher synthesis, or at least thesis), but rather in a *lower* one. The self as such is degraded into a lower concept, that of divisibility, so that it can be set equal to the not-self and in the same concept it is also opposed thereto. Here, then, there is no sort of *up*grading, as in every other synthesis, but a *down*grading. Self and not-self, as equated and opposed through the concept of their capacity for mutual limitation, are themselves both something (namely accidents) in the self as divisible substance; posited by the self, as absolute, illimitable subject, to which nothing is either equated or opposed. —Hence all judgments whose logical subject is the limitable or determinable self, or something determining the self, must be limited or determined by something higher: but all judgments whose logical subject is the absolutely indeterminable self can be determined by nothing higher; for nothing higher determines the absolute self, since it absolutely grounds and determines such things on its own account.

Now the essence of the *critical* philosophy consists in this, that an absolute self is postulated as wholly unconditioned and incapable of determination by any higher thing; and if this philosophy is derived in due order from the above principle, it becomes a Science of Knowledge. Any philosophy is, on the other hand, *dogmatic,* when it equates or opposes anything to the self as such; and this it does in appealing to the supposedly higher concept of the *thing (ens),* which is thus quite arbitrarily set up as the absolutely highest conception. In the critical system, a thing is what is posited in the self; in the dogmatic, it is that wherein the self is itself posited: critical philosophy is thus *immanent,* since it posits everything in the self; dogmatism is *transcendent,* since it goes on beyond the self. So far as dogmatism can be consistent, Spinozism is its most logical outcome. If we now proceed with dogmatism according to its own principles, as one ought anyhow to do, we inquire of it why it now assumes its thing-in-itself, without any higher ground, when it demanded such a ground in the case of the self; why *this* should now rank as an absolute, when the self was not admitted to be so. But for this no warrant can be produced, and we are thus quite justified in demanding, on its own principle of assuming nothing without a ground, that it should again furnish a higher genus for the concept of thing-in-itself, and another higher one for that, and so on without end. Hence a thoroughgoing dogmatism either denies that our knowledge has any ground whatever, that there is any kind of system in the human mind; or else it contradicts itself. Thoroughgoing dogmatism is a skepticism which doubts whether it doubts; for it must do away with the unity of consciousness, and thereby with the

I, 120

I, 121   whole of logic; hence it is no dogmatism at all, and contradicts itself in purporting to be one.[5]

(Thus Spinoza grounds the unity of consciousness in a substance wherein its unity is necessarily determined alike as to matter (the determinate series of presentations) and as to form. But I ask him what it is, once more, that contains the ground for the necessity of this substance, both as to content (the various series of presentations it contains), and again as to form (whereby *all possible* series of presentations are alleged to be exhausted in it, and to form a completed *whole*). But for this necessity he offers me no further ground, telling me merely that it is absolutely so; and this he says because he is compelled to assume some absolutely primary, ultimate unity. But if this is what he wants, he ought to have stopped forthwith at the unity given him in consciousness, and should not have felt the need to excogitate a higher one still, which nothing obliged him to do.)

There would, moreover, be absolutely no explaining how any thinker should ever have been able to go beyond the self, or how, having once done so, he could ever have come to a standstill, if we did not encounter a practical datum which completely accounts for this phenomenon. It was a practical datum, not, as seems to have been thought, a theoretical one, which drove the dogmatist on beyond the self; namely the feeling that, insofar as it is practical, our self depends upon a not-self that is absolutely independent of our legislation, and is to that extent free. But again it was a practical datum that compelled him to stop somewhere; namely the feeling of a necessary subordination and unity of the entire not-self under the practical laws of the self; though this subordination is by no

---

[5] There are only two systems, the critical and the dogmatic. Skepticism, as defined above, would be no system at all, since it denies the very possibility of any system. But this it can only do in systematic fashion, so that it contradicts itself and is totally unreasonable. The nature of the human mind has already taken care to ensure that it is also impossible. Never yet, in good earnest, has there been a skeptic of this kind. A critical skepticism, such as that of Hume, Maimon or Aenesidemus, is another matter; for it points out the inadequacy of the grounds so far accepted, and shows in doing so, where better are to be found. And if knowledge gains nothing as to content from this, it certainly does as to form—and the interests of knowledge are but poorly recognized in denying to the sharp-sighted skeptic the respect which is his due.

means anything that exists as the object of a concept, being rather the object of an Idea, viz., something that *ought* to exist, and that we ought to bring about, as will be shown in due course.

And from this it finally becomes evident, that dogmatism in general is not at all what it claims to be, that the conclusions we have drawn from it have done it an injustice, and that it is unjust to itself in inviting them. Its highest unity is indeed no other, and can be no other, than that of consciousness, and its thing is the substrate of divisibility in general, or the ultimate substance in which both self and not-self (Spinoza's intellect and extension) are posited. So far from going beyond the pure absolute self, it never even reaches it. At its utmost limit, as in Spinoza's system, it extends to our second and third principles, but not to the first absolutely unconditioned one. Normally, it never rises to anywhere near this level. It was reserved for the critical philosophy to take this final step, and thereby to consummate our knowledge. The theoretical portion of our Science of Knowledge, which will actually be evolved only from the two latter principles, since here the first has a merely regulative validity, is in fact, as will appear hereafter, Spinozism made systematic; save only that any given self is itself the one ultimate substance. But our system adds to this a practical part, whereby the first is grounded and determined, the whole of knowledge is completed, everything encountered in the human mind is exhausted, and whereby common sense, which all pre–Kantian philosophy affronted, and which our theoretical system would seem to have estranged from philosophy beyond hope of reconciliation, is again perfectly reconciled thereto.

9.   If we abstract entirely from the *determinate* form of the judgment, as a judgment of *comparison* or *contrast,* based on a ground of *conjunction* or *distinction,* we are left merely with what is common to the type of action involved, namely the limiting of one by another. We thus obtain the category of *determination* (bounding, or as Kant calls it, limitation). For a positing of quantity in general, whether it be quantity of reality or of negativity, is called determination.

Part II

FOUNDATION OF THEORETICAL KNOWLEDGE

§ 4. FIRST DISCOURSE

I, 123   Before embarking on our course, let us meditate briefly upon it. —We have established only three logical principles; that of *identity*, which is the foundation of all the others; and then the two which are reciprocally based upon it, the principle of *opposition* and the *grounding* principle. It is the latter two which first make possible the process of synthesis in general, by establishing and grounding its form. We need nothing more, therefore, to assure us of the formal validity of our method of reflection. —In the first synthetic act, the fundamental synthesis (of self and not-self), we have likewise established a content for all possible future syntheses, and from this side also require nothing further. From this basic synthesis it must be possible to develop everything that belongs in the domain of the Science of Knowledge.

    But if anything is to be derived from it, there must be still other concepts contained in those that it unites, which have not yet been established; and our task is to discover them. We now proceed to this, as follows. —According to § 3, all synthetic concepts arise through a unification of opposites. We ought therefore to begin by seeking out such opposed characteristics in the concepts already postulated (the self and the not-self, insofar as they are posited as determining one another); and this is done by reflection, which is a voluntary act of the mind:—'*Seek out*', I

I, 124   said; and this presupposes that they are already present, and not first created or fabricated somehow by reflection (which it is quite incapable of doing); that is, we presuppose a primary and necessary act of antithesis on the part of the self.

    This antithetical activity must be set up by reflection, which is to that extent initially analytical. For to attain by reflection a clear consciousness of the opposing features contained in a given concept A *as indeed* opposed, is to analyze that concept. Here, however, it must be particularly noted that our reflection is engaged in analyzing a concept which has so far not been given to it at all, but is due to be discovered only by analysis; until analysis is completed, the concept analyzed is a mere X. And this raises the question: How can a concept be analyzed when it is unknown?

No act of antithesis, of the kind prerequisite for the possibility of analysis in general, is possible without an act of synthesis; and again, no determinate antithesis is possible without its determinate synthesis (§ 3). Both are internally united, are one and the same act, and can be distinguished only in reflection. Hence, given the antithesis, we can infer the synthesis; and can equally establish the third thing, in which the two opposites are united, not as a product of reflection, but as something discovered thereby. It *is*, however, a product of that original synthetic act of the self, and *as* an act, can thus no more attain to empirical consciousness than can the acts already postulated. From now on, therefore, we encounter purely synthetic acts, though they are no longer absolutely unconditioned, as their predecessors were. Our deduction has shown, however, that they *are* acts, and acts of the self. For this they are as certainly as is the first synthesis, from which they derive, and with which they are identical. And this latter is an act as certainly as is that highest Act of the self, whereby it first posits itself. —The acts thus postulated are *synthetic,* though the reflection which postulates them is *analytic.*

I, 125 These antitheses, however, which are prerequisite for the possibility of a reflective analysis, must be thought of as preestablished, that is, as being of a kind on which the possibility of the forthcoming synthetic concepts depends. Yet no antithesis is possible without a synthesis. Hence a higher synthesis is presupposed as having already taken place, and our first business must be to seek this out and definitely establish it. Now in fact this must already have been accomplished in the preceding section. Yet we may find that, in virtue of the transition to a quite new area of knowledge, we shall need to go back to this in rather greater detail.

A. *Determination of the Synthetic Proposition to be Analyzed.*

Both self and not-self are posited, in and through the self, as capable of *mutually* limiting *one another,* in such a fashion, that is, that the reality of the one destroys that of the other, and *vice versa* (§ 3).

In this principle, the following two others are contained:

1. *The self posits the not-self as limited by the self.* This proposition will be of great importance later, especially in the practical part of our science, but for the present it seems, at least, to be of no use whatever. For till now the not-self has been nothing; it has no reality, and it is thus quite inconceivable how the self could deprive it of a reality that it does not possess; how it could be limited, when it is nothing. So the proposition appears completely useless, at least until the not-self can in some fashion be accorded reality. To be sure, the principle it falls under, that self and not-self mutually limit one another, has already been asserted; but whether what has just been proposed is also asserted and contained therein, is entirely problematic. It may be that the self can be limited in respect of the not-self, simply and solely when it has first limited the latter itself —when the limiting first proceeds from the self. Perhaps the not-self does not limit the self, as such, at all, but merely the limiting activity of that self. In that case, the above principle would continue to hold true, without the need to ascribe any absolute reality to the not-self, and without our problematically established proposition falling under it.

2. The following is also implicit in our principle: *The self posits itself as limited by the not-self.* This can be put to use, and it has to be accepted as certain, since it can be derived from the principle established above.

The self is initially posited as absolute, and then as a limitable reality capable of having quantity, and thus open to limitation by the not-self. But all this is posited by the self, and these, then, are the main points of our principle.

(It will appear, 1) That this second proposition is the basis of the theoretical portion of the Science of Knowledge—but only on completion of the latter, as is bound to be the case with a synthetic

I, 126

mode of exposition. 2) That the first and so far problematic proposition underlies the practical part of our science. But just because it is problematic, the possibility of such a practical part remains correspondingly doubtful. Hence follows 3) The reason why reflection must set out from the theoretical part; though it will appear in the sequel that it is not in fact the theoretical faculty which makes possible the practical, but on the contrary, the practical which first makes possible the theoretical (that reason in itself is purely practical, and only becomes theoretical on application of its laws to a not-self that restricts it).—This is so, because the *thinkability* of the practical principle depends on that of the theoretical. And thinkability is, after all, what we are concerned with in reflec-

tion. 4) From this it follows that the division thus effected in the Science of Knowledge, between the theoretical and the practical, is a purely problematic one (which is also why we have been compelled to make it only in passing, and have been unable to mark out a definite boundary, which is not yet known to us as such). We still have no notion whether we shall complete the theoretical part, or will not perhaps encounter a contradiction that is absolutely beyond resolution; still less can we tell whether we shall be driven on from the theoretical portion to a distinctively practical one.

B. *Synthesis of the Opposites Contained in our Proposed Principle, and in General.*

That *the self posits itself as determined by the not-self* has thus been derived from the third basic principle; if that holds, then this must do so too. But the basic principle must hold, if the unity of consciousness is not to be abolished, and the self to be no longer a self (§ 3). So the principle must hold as surely as the unity of consciousness is not to be abolished.

Our first duty is to analyze it, that is, to see whether and what sort of opposites it contains.

The self posits itself as *determined by the not-self*. Hence the self is not to determine, but to *be determined*, while the not-self is to determine, to set limits to the reality of the self. So the immediate upshot of our principle is as follows:

The not-self (actively) *determines the self* (which is to that extent passive). *The self posits itself* as determined, through an absolute activity. Now all activity, so far as we can see at the moment, anyway, must proceed from the self. The self has posited itself, has posited the not-self, has posited both in terms of quantity. But to say that the self posits itself as determined obviously amounts to saying that *the self determines itself.* Hence the principle in question also implies:

I, 128   *The self determines itself* (by an absolute activity).

As yet we are wholly ignoring the possibility that either of these two principles might contradict itself, might harbor an internal contradiction, and so annul itself. But this much is obvious at once, that they are in conflict with one another; that the self cannot be active if it is supposed to be passive, and *vice versa.*

(To be sure, the concepts of *activity* and *passivity* have yet to be deduced and developed as opposites; but nor is anything further to be derived from the opposition of these concepts; the words are employed here merely in the interests of clarity. It is evident enough that one of the resultant principles affirms what the other denies and *vice versa*, and that is surely a contradiction.)

If two principles, contained in one and the same principle, are in contradiction, they annul one another; and the principle that contains them annuls itself. This is the case with our principle set forth above. So it eliminates itself.

But this it cannot do, if the unity of consciousness is to be kept inviolate; so we must attempt to reconcile the opposites in question. (In the light of the foregoing, this does not mean that in the course of reflection we are to invent for them some artificial point of union. On the contrary, since the unity of consciousness is posited, together with this principle that threatens to overthrow it, the point of union must already be present in consciousness, and the task of reflection is merely to find it. Thus we have analyzed a synthetic concept, X, which is genuinely present, and from the opposites disclosed by analysis we now have to infer what sort of concept the unknown X can be).

We proceed to the solution of our problem.

The one principle affirms what the other denies. It is reality and negation, therefore, which annul one another, and do not annul, but are to be reconciled, and this is to come about (§ 3) by limitation or determination.

In saying that the self determines itself we ascribe to it an absolute totality of the real. The self can only determine itself as a reality, for it is posited as the absolutely real (§ 1), and as containing no negation. Yet it was supposed to be determined by itself. This cannot mean that it abolishes some reality in itself, for then it would at once be thrown into contradiction with itself. The meaning must be: the self determines reality and, by means of that, itself. It posits all reality, as an absolute quantity. Beyond this reality there is no other, and it is attributed to the self. Hence the self is determined, insofar as the reality is so.

It should be noted, further, that this is an absolute act of the self, and the same as that which emerged in § 3, where the self posited itself as quantity; a thing that needed to be clearly and definitely established at this point, in the interests of continuity.

The not-self is opposed to the self; and it contains negation as the self contains reality. If an absolute totality of the real is posited in the self, there must necessarily be posited in the not-self an absolute totality of negation; and negation itself must be posited as an absolute totality.

Both, the absolute totality of the real in the self, and the absolute totality of negation in the not-self, are to be united by way of determination. The self thereby *determines itself in part, and is in part determined*—in other words, the principle is to be taken in *two* senses, which must nonetheless be capable of subsisting together.

Yet both must be thought of as *one and the same*, that is, in the very respect in which the self is determined, it must be self-determining, and must likewise be determined in the very respect in which it determines itself.

That the self *is* determined means that reality is destroyed therein. So if the self thus posits within itself only *a portion* of the absolute totality of the real, it thereby destroys the remainder of this totality within itself. And, by virtue of the counterpositing (§ 2) and equivalence of quantity to itself, it posits a portion of

reality, equal to that destroyed, in the not-self (§ 3). A degree is
I, 130   always a degree, whether it be a degree of reality or of negation.
(Thus if the whole of reality is divided into ten equal parts, and
five of them are posited in the self, then there are necessarily five
portions of negation posited in the self.)

However many portions of negation the self posits in itself, a
corresponding number of parts of reality is posited in the not-self;
and this reality in the opponent actually annuls the reality in the
self. (Thus if five parts of negation are posited in the self, five
parts of reality are posited in the not-self.)

Hence the self posits negation within itself, insofar as it
posits reality in the not-self, and reality in itself, insofar as it
posits negation in the not-self. It thereby posits itself as *self-determining*, insofar as it *is determined,* and as *being* determined,
insofar as it *determines* itself: and the problem, so far as it was
posed above, is thereby solved.

(So far as it was posed; for it still leaves unanswered the
question, how the self could posit negation in itself, or reality in
the not-self; and if this question admits of no answer, virtually
nothing has been accomplished. We insert this reminder, lest
anyone should be deterred by the apparent futility and inadequacy of our solution.)

We have thus embarked on a new synthesis. The concept
established therein is contained under the higher generic concept
of *determination*, for it serves to posit quantity. But if it is really
to be a different concept, and the synthesis it expresses really a
new synthesis, it must be possible to point out its specific difference from the concept of determination in general, the ground of
distinction between the two. —*Determination* in general *establishes* mere *quantity,* no matter how, and in what manner; by the
synthetic concept we have just put forward the quantity *of the one
is posited in terms of that of its opposite,* and *vice versa.* In
determining the reality or negation of the self, we simultaneously
determine the negation or reality of the not-self, and *vice versa.* I
I, 131   can set out from whichever of the opposites I please, and in either
case, by an act of determination, I have simultaneously determined the other. This more determinate determination may con-

veniently be called *interdetermination* (on the analogy of interaction). It is the same as what Kant speaks of as *relation*.

C. *Synthesis by Interdetermination of the Opposites Contained in the First of the Opposing Principles.*

It will soon be evident that, in itself, the synthesis by interdetermination is of no great avail in resolving the main difficulty. But we have gained a firm footing for the method.

If the major principle set forth at the beginning of this section contains all the opposites that are here to be united—as should be the case in virtue of the foregoing reminder about method; and if these opposites have also, in general, called for unification through the concept of interdetermination; then necessarily the opposites contained in the general principles already united must *already have been indirectly united by way of interdetermination.* Just as the specific opposites are contained under the more general ones set forth, so also must the synthetic concept which unites them be contained under the general concept of interdetermination. We thus have to proceed with this concept precisely as we have already done with the concept of *determination* in general. We *determined* this latter itself, that is, we restricted its range of application to a smaller quantity, by adding the condition that the quantity of the one was to be determined by its opposite, and *vice versa;* and thereby obtained the concept of interdetermination. In accordance with the argument just advanced, we now have to determine more narrowly this concept itself, that is, to restrict its range by adding a special condition; and hence we obtain synthetic concepts that are included under the higher concept of interdetermination.

We shall thus be in a position to determine these concepts by
I, 132   their clearcut boundary-lines, so that the risk of confusing them, and of straying from the territory of the one to that of the other, is completely eliminated. Every error will reveal itself at once through the want of precise determination.

The not-self is to determine the self, that is, it is to annul reality therein. But this can only be done if it has in itself that very part of reality which it is to annul in the self. Hence, *the not-self has reality in itself*.

But *all reality is posited in the self*, while the not-self is opposed to the self; hence there is no reality at all in the not-self, but only sheer negation. All that is not-self is negation; and *it thus has no reality in itself*.

The two propositions annul one another. Both are contained in the principle 'the not-self determines the self'. And the latter therefore annuls itself.

But this principle is contained in the major principle already established, and this in the principle of the unity of consciousness; if it is annulled, so is the major principle that contains it and with that in turn the unity of consciousness. So it cannot annul itself, and the opposites it contains must be capable of reconciliation.

1. The contradiction is not to be straightway resolved through the concept of interdetermination. If we assert the absolute totality of the real to be *divisible, i.e.,* capable of increase or diminution (and even the right to do this has still to be justified deductively), then certainly we can remove any parts from it at will, and by the same token must necessarily posit them in the not-self; so much, indeed, has been obtained from the concept of interdetermination. *But how, then, are we able to remove parts of reality from the self?* That is the question we have still not touched; in virtue of the law of inter-
I, 133 determination, reflection assuredly asserts the reality eliminated from the one to be contained in its opposite, and *vice versa; assuming* it has first eliminated reality from somewhere. But what is it, then, that entitles or requires it to effect an interdetermination in any case?

Let us put the matter more precisely. Reality is absolutely posited in the self. In the third basic principle, and quite definitely just now, the not-self was posited as a *quantum:* but every quantum is *something,* and hence also a *reality*. Thus the not-self must be negation, and in some sense a real negation, or negative quantity.

Now so far as the concept of mere relation is concerned, it is all one, which of the two opponents we care to credit with reality, and which with negation. It depends on which of the two objects reflection takes as its starting-point. This is actually the case in mathematics, which disregards quality entirely and looks only to quantity. Whether I choose to count backward or forward steps as positive quantities is in itself a matter of complete indifference, and depends entirely on whether I wish to establish the first or the second total as the final result. So too in the Science of Knowledge. Whatever is negation in the self is reality in the not-self, and *vice versa;* so much, but no more, is laid down by the concept of interdetermination. Whether I now wish to call the content of the self reality, or negation, is left entirely to my choice: we are talking only of a relative[1] reality.

We thus encounter an ambiguity in the concept of reality itself, which is introduced by the very notion of interdetermination. If this ambiguity cannot be removed, the unity of consciousness is destroyed: the self is reality, and the not-self is reality likewise, and the two are no longer in opposition, and the self equals, not the self, but the not-self.

I, 134

2. If the contradiction presented is to be satisfactorily resolved, we must first of all dispose of that ambiguity, behind which the contradiction may lurk, as it were, and be no true contradiction, but only an apparent one.

The source of all reality is the self, for this is what is immediately and absolutely posited. The concept of reality is first given with and by way of the self. But the self *exists* because it *posits itself,* and *posits itself* because it *exists.* Hence *self-positing* and *existence* are one and the same. But the concepts of *self-positing* and of *activity* in general are again one and the same. Hence, all reality is *active;* and everything *active* is reality. Activity is *positive,* absolute (as opposed to merely *relative)* reality.

(It is most necessary to frame the concept of activity here in an absolutely pure fashion. It can designate nothing but what is contained in the self's own absolute assertion of itself; nothing but what is immediately implicit in the proposition '*I am.*' Hence it is clearly necessary to abstract completely, not only from all *temporal conditions*, but also from every *object* of activity. The Act of the self,

---

[1]It is worth nothing that in ordinary usage the word *relative* is always and quite properly used of that which differs only in respect of quantity, and can be distinguished on no other ground; and yet that no definite concept at all is attached to the word *relation,* from which it derives.

whereby it posits its own existence, is not directed to any object, but returns in upon itself. Only when the self presents itself to itself does it become an object. —Imagination finds it difficult to refrain from interpolating into the pure concept of activity this latter feature, that of the object to which activity is directed; but it is sufficient to have been warned of the deception involved, for us at least to abstract in our conclusions from everything that might stem from such interpolation.)

3.   The self is to be determined, that is, reality, or (as this concept has just been defined) *activity* is to be annulled in it. And thereby we posit in it the opposite of activity. But the opposite of activity is called *passivity*. Passivity is *positive*, absolute negation, and to that extent is contrasted to merely *relative* negation.

I, 135
(One could wish that the word passivity had fewer associated meanings. It scarcely needs saying that we are not to think of painful feeling here. But we need a reminder, perhaps, that it is necessary to abstract from all *temporal conditions*, and, so far, at least, *from all activity* in the opposite *that may occasion the passivity*. *Passivity* is the mere negation of the pure concept of activity just established; and yet *quantitative* in character, since the latter is itself quantitive; for mere negation of activity, without regard to its quantity $= 0$, would be *rest*. Everything in the self that is not immediately implicit in the *I am*, not immediately posited through the self's own self-assertion, is *passivity* for it, or affection in general.)

4.   In light of the above, if the absolute totality of the real is to be conserved when the self is in a state of passivity, then, in virtue of the law of interdetermination, a similar degree of activity must necessarily be carried over into the not-self.

And with this the foregoing contradiction is resolved. The *not-self*, as such, *has no reality of its own; but*, by virtue of the law of interdetermination, *it has reality insofar as the self is passive.*

At least so far as we can see at present, *the not-self has reality for the self only to the extent that the self is affected, and in the absence of such affection, it has none whatever;* this proposition is of great importance for what follows.

5.   The synthetic concept thus derived is contained under the higher concept of interdetermination; for in it the quantity of the one, the not-self, is determined by the quantity of its opponent, the self. But it is also specifically distinct. For in the concept of inter-

determination it was a matter of complete indifference which of the two opponents was determined by the other: which of the two was credited with reality, and which with negation. Quantity was deter-

mined, but beyond mere quantity, nothing else. —In the present synthesis, however, the interchange is not a matter of indifference, for it is determined which of the two members of the opposition is credited with reality, not negation, and which with negation, not reality. Hence, in the present synthesis, *activity* is posited, and to the same degree in the one as passivity is asserted in its opposite, and *vice versa*.

This synthesis is called the synthesis of *efficacy* (causality). That which is held to be *active,* and to that extent *not passive,* is called the *cause (Ursache*—the original reality, the positive reality absolutely posited, as the word *Ursache* strikingly brings out). That which is held to be *passive,* and to that extent *not active,* is called the *product* (the effect, and thus something dependent on another, and not an original reality). Both taken together are called *a causal process.* The product should never be spoken of as a process.

(In the concept of efficacy, as just deduced, we have to abstract completely from the empirical *temporal conditions;* and it can indeed be perfectly well thought of without them. For one thing, time has not yet been deduced, and we still have no right at all, at this point, to employ the conception; for another, it is in general simply not true that we are obliged to think of the cause *as such,* i.e., so far as it is active in a given process, as preceding the effect in time—as will later emerge in the schematism. In virtue of their synthetic unity, cause and effect ought, indeed, to be thought of as one and the same. It is not the cause as such, but the substance to which efficacy is attributed, that precedes the causal process in time, for reasons which will appear. But in this respect the substance acted on also takes precedence in time over the effect produced therein.)

D. *Synthesis by Interdetermination of the Opposites Contained in the Second of the Opposing Principles.*

The second principle shown to be contained in our major principle, namely, 'The self posits itself as determined, that is, it

determines itself', itself contains opposites, and thus annuls itself.

But since it cannot do this, without the unity of consciousness being thereby eliminated as well, we have to unite its opposites by a new synthesis.   a) The self determines itself; it is the *determinant* (i.e., the verb is active), and hence it too is active.   b) It determines itself; it is a *determinate,* and hence passive. (In its inner significance, determinacy always betokens passivity, a breakdown of reality.) Thus in one and the same action the self is both active and passive; reality and negation are simultaneously attributed to it, which is undoubtedly a contradiction.

This contradiction is to be resolved through the concept of interdetermination, and it would certainly be resolved completely if the following proposition could be entertained in place of that above: *The self determines its passivity through activity; or its activity through passivity.* In that case it would be both active and passive in one and the same state. The only question is, *whether* and *how* this proposition can be entertained.

If determination (or measurement) of any kind is to be possible, we must establish a scale of measure. Yet this scale can be none other than the self itself, since originally it is the self alone that is absolutely posited.

Now in the self reality is posited. And thereby the self must be posited as an *absolute totality* of the real (which is to say, as a quantum in which all others are contained, and which can serve as a measure for all of them); and this originally and absolutely, if the problematic synthesis just proposed is to be possible, and the contradiction to be satisfactorily resolved. Thus

1.   The self posits absolutely, without ground or condition of any kind, an *absolute totality of the real,* as a quantum which, simply in virtue of this assertion, is unsurpassable by any other; and this absolute maximum of reality it posits *within itself.*   —Everything posited in the self is reality; and all reality that exists is posited in the self (§ 1). Yet this reality in the self is a quantum, and an absolutely posited quantum at that (§ 3).

2.   By reference to this absolutely posited standard, the amount of a want of reality (a passivity) is to be determined. But the want is nothing, and nor is that which wants. (Nonexistence cannot be perceived). So it can be determined only by determining the *re-*

mainder of reality. Hence the self can *determine* only the amount of its own *reality* that is restricted; and by this determination, the amount of *negation* is then also determined at the same time (by means of the concept of interdetermination.)

(We shall take no account whatever here of the determination of negation as the opposite of *reality as such,* in the self: and direct our attention merely to the determination of a quantum of reality smaller than the whole.)

3.   A quantum of reality not equal to the whole is itself a *negation,* namely *negation of totality.* As a limited quantity, it stands in opposition to the whole; but everything in opposition is the negation of what it is opposed to. Every determinate quantity is nontotality.

4.   But if (by the rules of all synthesis and antithesis) it is to be possible for such a quantum to be *opposed,* and thus also *compared,* to the totality, there must be a ground of conjunction between the two; and this, then, is the concept of *divisibility* (§ 3). In absolute totality there are no parts; but it can be compared with parts, and distinguished from them: and in this way the foregoing contradiction can be satisfactorily resolved.

5.   To see this with full clarity, let us consider the concept of reality. The concept of reality is equivalent to the concept of activity. To say that all reality is posited in the self is to say that all activity is posited therein, and conversely: to say that everything in the self is reality, is to say that the self is *solely* active; it is self merely insofar as it is active; and so far as it is not active it is not-self.

I. 139   All passivity is inactivity. Thus there is no other way of determining passivity, save by reference to its connection with activity.

But now this is precisely in accord with the terms of our problem, which was that of determining a passivity by way of activity, through an interdetermination.

6.   Passivity cannot be related to activity, save under the condition that it possess a ground of conjunction therewith. But this can be no other than the general ground of conjunction between reality and negation, namely quantity. To say that passivity can be related to activity by way of quantity is to say that *passivity is a quantum of activity.*

7.   In order to conceive of a quantum of activity, we need a measure of activity, namely, *activity in general* (what we earlier called

the absolute totality of the real). Quantum in general is the measure.

8.   If *all* activity in general is posited in the self, then the positing of a *quantum of activity* represents a diminution of the same; and insofar as it is not the *whole* of activity, such a quantum is a passivity; even though *in itself* it may still be activity.

9.   Hence by positing a quantum of activity we posit a passivity, in opposing it to activity, not *qua activity in general,* but *qua* the *whole* of activity; that is, this quantum of activity *as* such is itself posited as a passivity; and is as such *determined.*

(I say *determined.* All passivity is a negation of activity; a quantum of activity negates the totality of activity. And so far as this occurs, the quantum belongs to the sphere of passivity.   —If it is regarded generally as activity, then it no longer belongs to the sphere of passivity, but is excluded from it.)

10.   We have now pointed to an X which is at once reality and negation, activity and passivity.

a)   X is *activity,* so far as it is related to the not-self, because it is posited in the self, and in the positing, acting self.

I, 140

b)   X is *passivity,* so far as it is related to the totality of action. It is not action in general, but a *determinate* action: a special mode of agency included in the sphere of action in general.

(Describe a circle = A; the whole area enclosed in it, = X, is then opposed to the infinite plane in infinite space which is excluded thereby. Describe within the circumference of A another circle, = B; then the area enclosed in it, = Y, is first of all enclosed within the circumference of A, and at the same time opposed, with it, to the infinite plane excluded by A, and to that extent wholly identical to the surface X. But to the extent that you regard it as enclosed by B, it is opposed both to the infinite excluded plane, and also to that part of the surface X that does not lie within it. Hence the area Y is opposed to itself; for it is either a part of surface X, or it is the independently subsisting surface Y.)

To illustrate: *I think* is from the first an expression of activity; the self is posited as *thinking,* and to that extent as *acting.* It is also an expression of negation, limitation, passivity; for *thinking* is a specific determination of being; and from the concept of this all other modes of being are excluded. The concept of thinking is thus at variance with itself; in relation to the object of thought, it denotes an activity; in relation to being in general it denotes a passivity; for being must be restricted, if thinking is to be possible.

Every possible predicate of the self denotes a limitation thereof. The subject, I, is the absolutely active or existent thing. The predicate (e.g., I present, I strive, etc.) confines this activity within a delimited sphere. (How and whereby this happens, is a question not yet at issue here.)

I, 141

11. We can now see perfectly, how the self should be able to determine its passivity through and by means of its activity, and how it can be at once both active and passive. It is *determinant,* insofar as it posits itself, through absolute spontaneity, in a determinate sphere among all those contained in the absolute totality of its realities; and insofar as we think merely of this absolute positing without regard for the limits of the sphere. It is *determinate,* insofar as it is regarded as posited in this particular sphere, without regard for the spontaneity of the positing as such.

12. We have discovered the original synthetic act of the self, whereby the proposed contradiction is resolved, and have thus lighted on a new synthetic concept, which still requires a closer examination.

Like the previous concept of efficacy, it is a more specific form of interdetermination; and we shall obtain the fullest understanding of both in comparing them with this latter, as well as among themselves.

By the rules of determination in general, both must be a) akin to interdetermination; b) opposed to it; c) akin to one another, to the extent that they are so opposed; d) opposed to one another.

a) They resemble interdetermination, in that in both, as in the latter, activity is determined by passivity, or reality by negation (which is the same thing) and *vice versa.*

b) They are both opposed to it. For in interdetermination an interchange is merely *posited* in general, but not *determined.* It is left entirely open, whether we wish to proceed from reality to negation, or the other way round. But in both the syntheses just derived, the order of interchange is fixed and determined.

I, 142

c) By the very fact that the order in both is fixed, they are alike.

d) In regard to the order of interchange, the two are opposed. In the concept of causality, activity is determined by passivity; in that just derived, passivity is determined by activity.

13.   Insofar as the self is regarded as embracing the whole absolutely determined realm of all realities, it is *substance*. So far as it is posited within a not absolutely determined area of this realm (how and by what determined we do not at present inquire), to that extent it is *accidental*, or *has an accident within it*. The boundary which cuts off this specific region from the whole realm is what makes the accident an accident. It is the ground of distinction between substance and accident. It is in this realm, so that the accident is in, and belongs to, substance: it excludes something from this whole realm, so that the accident is not substance.

14.   No substance is conceivable without relation to an accident: for only by positing possible areas within the absolute realm does the self become a substance; only through possible accidents are *realities* engendered, for otherwise all reality would be absolutely one.   —The realities of the self are its modes of action: it is substance, to the extent that all possible modes of action (ways of being) are posited therein.

No accident is conceivable without substance; for in order to recognize that something is a *determinate* reality, I must relate it to *reality in general*.

Substance is *conceived of as all change in general:* accident is a *determinate that interchanges with some other changing thing*.

There is initially only one substance, the self; within this one substance, all possible accidents, and so all possible realities, are posited. —We shall see in due course, how various accidents of the one substance, *alike in some respect,* can be conceived together and themselves thought of as substances, whose accidents are determined by *the difference of these respects* among themselves, which goes along with their likeness.

I, 143

Note. We have left untouched and in total obscurity, first, that activity of the self whereby it distinguishes and compares itself as substance and accident; and second, what it is that leads the self to engage in such an act. The latter, so far as we may surmise from the first synthesis, could well be an effect of the not-self.

Thus, as commonly happens in every synthesis, we have everything properly joined and tied in the middle, but not at the two extremities.

This observation presents the concern of the Science of Knowledge from a new angle. It will always go on interpolating links between the opposites, yet the contradiction is not completely resolved thereby, but only further extended. If, on closer examination of the elements united, we find that their unity is still not complete, and insert a new link between them, the latest discovered contradiction does indeed disappear; but in order to resolve it, we have had to accept new end-points, which are again in opposition, and must be reconciled anew.

The truly supreme problem which embraces all others is, how can the self operate directly on the not-self, or the not-self on the self, when both are held to be utterly opposed to each other? We interpolate some X in between them, on which both may act, so that they also work indirectly upon one another. But we soon discover that there must again be some point in this X, at which self and not-self are in immediate contact. To prevent this, we interpose between them and replace the sharp boundary by a new link, Y. But it soon appears that here too, as in X, there must be a point at which the two opponents come up against each other directly. And so it would go on forever, if the knot were not cut, rather than loosed, by an absolute decree of reason, which the philosopher does not pronounce, but merely proclaims: Since there is no way of reconciling the not-self with the self, *let there be* no not-self at all!

We may view the matter from still another angle. —Insofar as the self is restricted by the not-self, it is finite; in itself, however, as posited through its own absolute activity, it is infinite. These two, its infinity and its finitude, are to be reconciled. But such a unification is intrinsically impossible. For a time, indeed, the dispute is composed by mediation: the infinite delimits the finite. But at length, once the utter impossibility of the attempted union is apparent, finitude itself must go; all bounds must fall away, and the infinite self must alone remain, as one and as all.

In a boundless space, A, put *light* at a point *m,* and at a point *n, darkness:* then, given that the space is continuous, and there is no *hiatus* between *m* and *n,* there must necessarily be a point *o* somewhere between the two, which is both light and darkness; a contradiction. —Set between the two a middle condition, *twilight.* If it stretch from *p* to *q,* then at *p* the twilight will march with light, and at *q* with darkness. But by this you have gained only a respite; the contradiction has not been satisfactorily resolved. Twilight is a mixture of light and darkness. Now at *p* the daylight can only march with the twilight, in that *p* is at once light and twilight; and thus (since twilight only differs from light in being also darkness) in that it is at once both light and darkness. Similarly at *q.* —Hence, the contradiction is soluble in no other way than this: light and darkness are not opposed in principle, but differ only in degree. Darkness is simply a very minute amount of light. —That is precisely how things stand between the self and the not-self.

I, 145

E. *Synthetic Union of the Opposition between the Two Types of Interdetermination.*

The self posits itself as determined by the not-self; this was our primary principle and point of departure, which could not be eliminated without also abolishing the unity of consciousness. But it harbored contradictions which we have had to resolve. First arose the question: How can the self both *determine* and *be determined* together? To which our answer was: In virtue of the concept of interdetermination, *determination* and *determinacy* are one and the same; just as the self posits a determinate quantum of negation in itself, so it also posits a determinate quantum of reality in the not-self, and *vice versa.* This left open the question: Where, then, is reality to be posited, in the self, or the not-self? On recourse to the concept of efficacy, this was answered as follows: Negation or passivity must be posited in the self, and, by the rule of interdetermination in general, the same quantum of reality or activity in the not-self. —But how, then, can a passivity be posited in the self? was our next question, and the concept of substantiality provided the answer: Passivity and activity in the self are one and the same, for passivity is merely a lesser quantum of activity.

I, 146   But these answers have taken us winging in a circle. *If* the self posits a lesser degree of activity in itself, then it admittedly posits thereby a passivity in itself and an activity in the not-self. But the self can have no power to posit absolutely a lower degree of activity in itself; for in virtue of the concept of substantiality, it posits all activity, and nothing but activity, in itself. Hence the positing of this lower degree of activity in the self would have to be preceded by an activity of the not-self; the latter, indeed, would first have to have abolished some part of the self's activity, before the self could assert some lesser part thereof in itself. But this is impossible, in that, owing to the concept of efficacy, the not-self can be credited with an activity only to the extent that a passivity is asserted in the self.

    Let us now give a clearer, though not yet canonical form to the main point at issue. I must beg permission, in so doing, to presuppose as familiar the concept of time. Assume, as the first case under the pure concept of efficacy, that the limitation of the self arises wholly and solely from the activity of the not-self. Suppose that, at time A, the not-self is not operating on the self, so that all reality and no negation at all is posited in the self, and hence, by the foregoing, that no reality is posited in the not-self. Suppose further, that at time B the not-self operates with three degrees of activity on the self, so that in virtue of the concept of interdetermination, three degrees of reality are abolished in the self, and three degrees of negation posited in their stead. But in this the self merely behaves passively; the degrees of negation are posited, indeed, but they *are* merely *posited—for some intelligent being* external to the self, which observes the self and not-self engaged in this transaction, and judges by the rule of interdetermination; but not *for the self as such.* The latter would require that it should be able to compare its state at time A with that at

I, 147   time B, and to distinguish the different quanta of its activity at both times; and we have not yet shown how this is possible. In the case supposed, the self would certainly be limited, but it would not be aware of its limitation. To put it in terms of our principle, the self would indeed be *determined;* but *it would not posit itself* as determined, for only a being external to it could posit it so.

Or suppose, as the second case under the pure concept of substantiality, that the self should have an absolute power, independent of any influence from the not-self, of positing arbitrarily a diminished quantum of reality in itself; the presupposition of transcendent idealism, and in particular of the preestablished harmony, which is an idealism of this type. Here we abstract entirely from the fact that this presupposition already contradicts our absolute first principle. Grant further that the self has the power of comparing this diminished quantity with absolute totality, and of measuring it thereby. Suppose, on these terms, that at time A the self has two degrees of diminished activity, and at time B, three. It can then be easily understood, how the self could judge itself to be limited at both times, and to be more limited at time B than at time A. But there is no seeing at all how this limitation could be related to anything in the not-self as its cause. For the self would be obliged, rather, to regard itself as the cause thereof. In terms of our principle, the self would then certainly posit itself as determined, but not as determined *by the not-self.* (The justification for this relation to a not-self is, indeed, denied by the dogmatic idealist, and to that extent he is consistent: but he cannot deny the fact of relation, nor has it occurred to anyone to do so. But then he at least has to explain this admitted fact, as distinct from its justification. And on his own presuppositions he cannot do this, so that his philosophy is incomplete. If he simply takes for granted the existence of things outside us, as is done in the preestablished harmony of at least some Leibnizians, he is inconsistent on this point.)

I, 148

Thus both syntheses, employed in isolation, fail to explain what they should, and we still have the contradiction complained of above: if the self posits itself as determined, it is not determined by the not-self; if it is determined by the not-self, it does not posit itself as determined.

I.   We now state this contradiction in precise terms. The self can posit no passivity in itself, without positing activity in the not-self; but this it cannot do without positing a passivity in itself; it can do neither without the other; it can do neither absolutely; so it cannot do either of the two. Hence,

1.   The self posits neither passivity in itself, so far as it posits activity in the not-self, nor activity in the not-self by positing passivity in itself: it posits nothing at all. (It is not the *condition* that is denied, but the *conditioned*—a point to be carefully noted; we are referring, not to the general rule of interdetermination as such, but to the general application of this to the present case.) The above has just been demonstrated.

2.   But the self is to posit passivity in itself, and activity, therefore, in the not-self, and *vice versa:* as follows from the principles absolutely asserted above.

II.   The first proposition denies what the second affirms. Both are related, therefore, as negation and reality. But negation and reality are united by way of quantity. Both propositions must hold good, therefore, but only *in part.*

They are to be thought of as follows:

1.   The self *in part* posits passivity in itself, *insofar* as it posits activity in the not-self; but *in part* it does *not* posit passivity in itself, *insofar* as it posits activity in the not-self; and *vice versa.* (More precisely, the interdetermination is applied and is valid *in a certain respect;* but *in a certain other respect* it is not so applied.)

2.   Insofar as it posits activity in the self, the self posits passivity in the not-self only *in part,* and *in part* does not do so. (To put it more specifically, an activity is posited in the self, which is not opposed to any passivity in the not-self, and an activity in the not-self, which is not opposed to any passivity in the self. Activity of this sort we shall term for the moment *independent* activity, until we are better acquainted with it.)

III.   But such independent activity in self and not-self contradicts the law of opposition, which has now been more accurately determined through the law of interdetermination; hence, in particular, it contradicts the notion of interdetermination which governs our present inquiry.

All activity in the self determines a passivity in the not-self (allows us to infer such a passivity) and *vice versa*. This in virtue of the concept of interdetermination. —But we now have the following proposition established:

A certain activity in the self determines no passivity in the not-self (allows no inference to such a passivity), and a certain activity in the not-self determines no passivity in the self; the latter being related to the former as negation to reality. Hence both must be united by a determination, that is, both can hold good only in part.

The proposition contradicted above is the principle of interdetermination. This, then, can hold good only in part, that is, it must itself be determined; its validity must be confined to a certain area by a rule.

Or, to put the matter otherwise, the independent activity of self and not-self is independent only *in a certain sense*. This will at once become clear. For

I, 150   IV.   In accordance with the above, there must be an activity in the self which determines a passivity in the not-self, and is itself determined thereby; and, conversely, an activity in the not-self which determines a passivity in the self, and is determined thereby. To this activity and passivity the concept of interdetermination is applicable.

Both must simultaneously contain an activity that is not determined by any passivity in the other; as was postulated just now, so that the apparent contradiction could be resolved.

Both propositions should be able to subsist together; so it must be possible to entertain them, through a synthetic concept, as united in one and the same act. But this concept can be no other than that of interdetermination. The principle, in which both would be entertained as united, is as follows:

Independent activity is determined by interaction and passion (action and passion determining one another by interdetermination); *and, conversely, interaction and passion are determined by independent activity.* (What belongs to the sphere of reciprocity, does not belong to that of independent activity, and *vice versa;* so that each sphere can be determined by that opposed to it).

If this principle were tenable, it would be clear 1.) In what sense the independent activities of self and not-self determine one another, and in what sense not. They do not determine one another *directly,* but *through the medium* of their supposedly mutual action and passion. 2.) How the principle of interdetermination could be at once both valid and invalid. It is applicable to reciprocity and independent activity, but not to independent activity and independent activity in itself. Reciprocity and independent activity fall under it, but independent activity and independent activity in itself do not.

We now consider the meaning of the principle laid down above.

I, 151   The following three propositions are contained in it.

1.) An independent activity is determined by interaction and passion.

2.) An interaction and passion are determined by an independent activity.

3.) Each is determined by the other, and it matters not whether we go from interaction and passion to independent activity, or *vice versa.*

I

As regards the first proposition, we must begin by inquiring what it means, in general, to assert that an independent activity is determined by an interaction; and we then have to apply it to the case before us.

1.   Through interaction and passion an independent activity is, *in general,* determined (a determinate quantity thereof is *posited*). —It will be remembered that here we are setting out to determine the concept of interdetermination itself, that is, to *limit* the scope of its validity by a rule. But *determination* occurs by the exhibition of a ground. As soon as the ground of application of this proposition is set forth, the latter is at once limited.

Now, by the principle of interdetermination, the positing of an activity in one thing immediately leads to the positing of a passivity in its opposite, and *vice versa.* And from the principle of opposition it is certainly clear that *if*, in general, a passivity is to be posited, it must be posited in the opposite of what is active. But the question *why in general* a passivity must be posited, instead of letting matters rest with the activity in the first thing, that is, why, in general, there has to be an interdetermination, is not yet answered thereby. —Passivity and activity, *as* such, are opposed; but if passivity is to be immediately posited through activity, and *vice versa*, then by virtue of the principle of determination, they must also concur in a third thing, X (which permits the transition from passivity to activity, and *vice versa*, without interruption of the unity of consciousness, or the occurrence, if I may so put it, of a *hiatus* therein). This third thing is the *ground of conjunction* between action and passion in their interplay (§ 3).

I, 152

This ground of conjunction is not dependent on interdetermination; for the latter is dependent on it. It is not made possible thereby, for only by virtue of it is interdetermination possible. Hence, though in reflection admittedly *posited* through interdetermination, it is posited as independent of the latter, and of that which changes by way thereof.

In reflection, also, it is *determined* by reciprocity, its position conceptually indicated; if, that is, there is a positing of interdetermination, then the ground of relation is posited in that sphere which incorporates the sphere of interdetermination; it describes, as it were, a larger circuit around that of the interdetermination, in order to stabilize the latter thereby. It fills the sphere of determination in general, whereas the interdetermination occupies only a part of it; as is already clear from the foregoing, though it needs to be recalled at this point for purposes of reflection.

This ground is a reality, or, if interdetermination is conceived as a transaction, an activity. —Hence an independent activity is determined by interdetermination in general.

(It is equally apparent from the above, that the ground of all interdetermination is the absolute totality of the real. This may not be annihilated on any account, and hence that quantum of it that is abolished in one thing must be posited in its opposite.)

2. We now apply this general principle to the particular case that falls under it, and is at present before us.

a) By means of the reciprocal concept of *efficacy,* an activity of the not-self is posited through a passivity of the self. This is one of the types of interplay referred to: and by it, an independent activity is to be posited and determined.

The interdetermination proceeds from passivity. Passivity *is* posited, and by means of it activity is posited. The passivity is posited *in the self*. The concept of interdetermination completely accounts for the fact that, *if* an activity is to be opposed to this passivity, it must be posited in the opposite of the self, namely the not-self. —In this transition, however, there is and must be a connecting link; or a ground, which is here a ground of conjunction. This, as we know, is quantity, which is alike in both self and not-self—in passivity and also in activity. This is the ground of relation, though we may conveniently refer to it as the *ideal* ground. Hence the passivity in the self is the ideal ground of the activity of the not-self. —The procedure now examined has been completely justified by the rule of interdetermination.

A question of quite another sort is as follows: Should the rule of interdetermination be applied here, and why then in general should it be? Once passivity has been posited in the self, it will be granted without hesitation that activity is posited in the not-self; but why then, in general, is activity posited? The answer to this question is no longer to be found in the principle of interdetermination, but in the higher grounding principle.

A passivity *is posited* in the self, that is, a quantum of its activity is abolished.

This passivity, or *diminution* of activity, must have *a ground;* for that which is abolished must be a *quantum;* but, by the principle of determination, (§ 3), every quantum is determined by another quantum, in virtue of which it is neither smaller nor greater, but precisely this amount.

The ground of this diminution cannot lie in the self (it cannot proceed directly from the primordial nature of the self); for the self posits only activity in itself, and not passivity; it posits itself simply as existent, but not as nonexistent (§ 1). The ground does not lie in the self; thanks to the opposition whereby the not-self is allotted whatever is not allocated to the self (§ 2), this proposi-

I, 153

I, 154

tion is equivalent to the following: The ground of diminution lies in the not-self.

Here we are no longer talking of mere *quantity*, but of *quality;* insofar as the self exists, passivity is opposed to its nature, and only to that extent could the ground of this be posited, not in the self, but necessarily in the not-self. Passivity is posited as a quality opposed to reality, as negation (not simply as a lesser quantum of activity; cf. B in this section.) But the ground of a quality is called its *real ground*. The real ground of passivity is an activity of the not-self, independent of reciprocity and already presupposed in the possibility thereof; and this activity is posited, so that we may have a real ground for passivity.   —Hence the above reciprocity serves to posit an activity of the not-self, independent of reciprocity and presupposed thereby.

(Here we have arrived at one of the points of vantage from which a view of the whole system can very readily be obtained; partly for this reason, and partly also so as not to allow dogmatic realism, even in the short run, the confirmation that it might extract from the foregoing statements, we again point out expressly that the inference to a real ground in the not-self is based on the fact that the passivity in the self is a *qualitative* affair; (as reflection on the mere principle of efficacy would in any case oblige one to accept). Hence this inference holds no further than the presupposition in question can do.   —Once we examine the second reciprocal concept, that of substantiality, it will appear that, in reflection upon it, passivity cannot be considered as in any way *qualitative,* but can only be thought of as a *quantitative* affair, as a mere diminution of activity; and hence that in this reflection, where the ground disappears, the grounded does also, and the not-self again becomes a merely ideal ground.   —To put it briefly; if the explanation of presentation, that is, the whole of speculative philosophy, proceeds from the premise that the not-self is posited as the cause of presentation, and the latter as an effect thereof, then the not-self is the real ground of everything; it exists absolutely, because it exists and as it exists (Spinoza's fatalism). Even the self is a mere accident thereof, and not a substance at all, and we arrive at materialistic Spinozism, which is a form of dogmatic realism; a system which presupposes

I, 155

failure to achieve the highest possible degree of abstraction—from the not-self—and, since it does not establish the ultimate ground, is totally ungrounded. —If, on the contrary, the explanation of presentation proceeds from the premise that the self is the substance of presentation, and the latter an accident thereof, then the not-self is by no means the real, but merely the ideal ground of presentation; hence it has no sort of reality apart from presentation, is not a substance, is nothing self-subsistent or absolutely posited, but merely an accident of the self. In this system no kind of ground could be given for the limiting of reality in the self (for the affection whereby a presentation arises). Inquiry into the question is here entirely cut off. Such a system would be a form of dogmatic idealism, which has indeed undertaken the highest degree of abstraction, and is thus completely grounded. But for all that, it is incomplete, since it does not explain everything that ought to be explained. Hence the real question at issue between realism and idealism is as to which road is to be taken in explaining presentation. It will become evident that in the theoretical part of our Science of Knowledge this question remains completely unanswered; that is, it is answered by saying: Both roads are correct; under a certain condition we are obliged to take the one, and under the opposite condition we must take the other; and by this, then, all human, that is, all finite reason is thrown into conflict with itself, and embroiled in a circle. A system in which this is demonstrated is a critical idealism, of the kind most fully and coherently set forth by Kant. This conflict of reason with itself must be resolved, even if it should not prove possible within the theoretical Science of Knowledge; and since the absolute existence of the self cannot be given up, the issue must be decided in favor of the second line of argument, just as in dogmatic idealism (but with this difference, that our idealism is not dogmatic but practical; does not determine what *is,* but what *ought* to be). But this must be done in such a way as to explain what needs explaining; which dogmatism could not do. The diminished activity of the self must find an explanation in the self as such; the ultimate ground of it must be posited in the self. This comes about in that the self, which in this respect is practical, is posited as a self that *ought* to contain in itself the ground of exis-

I, 156

tence of the not-self, which diminishes the activity of the intellective self; an infinite idea, which cannot itself be thought, and by which, therefore, we do not so much explain the explicandum as show, rather, *that,* and *why,* it is inexplicable; the knot is not so much loosed as projected into infinity).

I, 157   Through the interplay between passivity of the self and activity of the not-self, an independent activity of the latter was *posited;* through the very same interplay, it is also *determined;* it is posited to provide the ground for a passivity posited in the self; hence also its scope extends no further than the scope of the latter. The not-self has no sort of intrinsic reality or activity for the self, save insofar as the latter is passive. No passivity in the self, no activity in the not-self; and this also holds good when we speak of this activity as an activity independent of the concept of efficacy, which *is* a real ground. Even the thing-in-itself only exists to the extent that at least the possibility of a passivity is posited in the self: a canon which obtains its complete determination, and becomes applicable, only in the practical part of our work.

          b)   By means of the concept of substantiality, activity in the self (accident in the self) leads to the positing and determining of a passivity (negation) therein. Both are conceived in the interplay; their mutual determination is the second type of interdetermination set forth above; and by this reciprocity also, an activity independent thereof, and not coconceived therein, is to be posited and determined.

          Activity and passivity are in themselves opposed; and as seen above, it may indeed happen that through one and the same act whereby a determinate quantum of activity is posited in the one, a similar quantum of passivity may be posited in its opposite, and *vice versa.* But that through one and the same act, activity and passivity should be posited, not in the opposite, but in the very same thing itself, is a contradiction.

          But now already in our earlier deduction of the concept of
I, 158   substantiality this contradiction has in general been removed, in that passivity as such, and in respect of its quality, is to be nothing other than activity; though in respect of quantity it must be a lesser activity than the totality; and hence it could certainly be conceived in general, how a lesser quantity, measured against absolute totality,

and just because it is not equal thereto in quantity, could be posited *as* a lesser.

The ground of conjunction between the two is now activity. Both the totality and the nontotality of the two is activity.

But even in the not-self activity is posited, and an activity, at that, which is not equal to the totality, but restricted. Hence the question arises: How is a restricted activity of the self to be distinguished from a restricted activity of the not-self? Which means nothing less than, how, under these conditions, are self and not-self to be still distinguished at all? For the ground of distinction between self and not-self, whereby the first was supposed to be active and the second passive, has been abolished (—a point which the reader is earnestly requested not to overlook).

If this distinction cannot be made, then the required interdetermination is equally impossible, and so, too, are all the derived determinations in general. The activity of the not-self is determined by the passivity of the self; but the latter is determined by the amount of *its* activity that remains after diminution. For here, of course, the possibility of relation to the absolute totality of the self's activity presupposes that the lessened activity should be an activity *of the self*—and the very same self in which absolute totality is posited.   —Diminished activity is opposed to the totality of activity: but the totality is posited in the self: hence, by the foregoing rule of counterpositing, the opposite of totality, namely lessened activity, should be posited in the not-self. But if it were to be posited there, it would have no ground of conjunction at all to unite it to the absolute totality; the interdetermination would not take place, and everything derived so far would be annihilated.

Hence the diminished activity which, as *activity in general,* would be incapable of relation to totality, must have a further property which could yield the ground of conjunction; a property whereby it would be an activity of the self and could not possibly be an activity of the not-self. This property of the self, however, which cannot possibly be attributed to the not-self, is *to posit and be posited absolutely, without any ground* (§ 1). This diminished activity would therefore have to be *absolute* in character.

To be absolute and ungrounded is, however (§ 3), to be

I, 159

wholly without limitation; and yet this act of the self is required to be a limited one. The answer to this is as follows: Simply insofar as it is an action at all, and nothing more, there must be no ground or condition to restrict it; it may or may not take place; action as such occurs with absolute spontaneity. But insofar as it requires to be directed to an object, it is restricted; there might be no action (notwithstanding an affection from the not-self, if we care to think it possible for a moment, in reflection, that this should occur without inclination from the self); but *once* an action takes place, it *must* be directed to this very object and can relate to no other.

I, 160   Hence, by the interdetermination alluded to, an independent activity is *posited.* For the activity conceived of in the interplay is itself independent, not insofar as it is *therein conceived of,* but insofar as it is *activity.* To the extent that it enters into the interplay, it is restricted, and to that extent a passivity. It is looked at from two points of view.

This independent activity is further determined by the interplay, that is, in pure reflection. To make the reciprocity possible, the activity would have to be regarded as absolute; hence it is postulated—not as *absolute activity in general,* but as *absolute activity that determines a reciprocity.* (Its name is *imagination,* as will appear in due course.) Such an activity is merely posited, however, insofar as a reciprocity is to be determined; and its scope is thus determined by the scope of this interplay itself.

II

An interaction, and passion, are determined by an independent activity: this is the second proposition we have to discuss. We have

1.   To explain this proposition in general, and to distinguish its meaning sharply from that of the foregoing.

In the previous proposition we began from reciprocity; it was presupposed as occurring, hence we were not talking at all about its *form,* as a mere reciprocity (a transition from one to the other), but rather about its *matter,* the components involved in the interplay. If a reciprocity occurs—so it was generally argued above—

then there must be components present that can be exchanged. How are these possible?—and we then pointed to an independent activity as the ground thereof.

I, 161

Here, however, we do not set out from reciprocity, but proceed to it, from that which first makes possible the interplay *as* such, and in its mere form, as a *transition* from one to the other. There we were speaking of what grounds the *matter* of the interplay; here, of what grounds its *form*. This formal ground of reciprocity must also be an independent activity; and this is the claim that we have to establish here.

The ground of distinction between the form and matter of the interplay can be still more clearly set forth, if we are prepared to reflect upon our own course of reflection.

In the first instance, the interplay is presupposed as *occurring;* hence there is complete abstraction from the manner in which it may take place, and reflection is confined merely to the possibility of the components involved in the reciprocity. —The magnet attracts iron: the iron is attracted by the magnet: these are two propositions in reciprocal relation, that is, one of them is posited by way of the other. This is a fact presupposed, and presupposed as *having a ground;* and no question is asked, therefore, as to *which* one is posited *via* the other, or *how* in general it comes about that one proposition is posited through another. The question is merely as to why *just these two* propositions are included within the sphere of propositions, of which one can be posited in place of the other. Something must be implicit in both, which makes them fit to be in reciprocity; this, the material factor which makes them reciprocal propositions, is what needs to be sought out.

In the second instance, we reflect on the *occurrence* of the reciprocity itself, and thus abstract completely from the propositions in reciprocal relation. The question is no longer, by what right are *these* propositions in reciprocity, but *how* there can be reciprocity at all. And here it appears then, that in addition to the iron and the magnet an intelligent being must be present, observing both, uniting the concepts of both in his consciousness, and obliged to attach to the one the opposite predicate (attracting and being attracted) from that of the other.

I, 162

In the first instance, there is simple reflection upon the phenomenon—that of the observer; in the second, there is reflection upon this reflection—that of the philosopher upon the nature of the observation.

Now once it has been established that the independent activity we are in search of is to determine the form of reciprocity, but not its mere matter, nothing prevents us from proceeding in our reflection from the interplay, by a heuristic method, since the inquiry is greatly facilitated thereby.

2.   Having thus explained the proposition in general, we now apply it to the individual cases contained under it.

a)   In the reciprocal relation of *efficacy,* an activity is posited in the not-self by means of a passivity in the self, that is, a certain activity is *not* posited in the self, or removed therefrom, and posited instead in the not-self. In order simply to obtain the pure form of this reciprocity, we must abstract alike from *that which* is posited, namely the activity, and from the components in which positing and nonpositing occurs, namely the self and not-self: and we are then left with the pure form, namely a *positing by means of a nonpositing,* (a conferring in consequence of a deprivation), or a *transference.* This, then, is the formal character of reciprocity in the synthesis of efficacy, and thus the material character of the *activity reciprocated* (or, in the active sense, which brings about the interplay itself).

This activity is independent of the interplay made possible and completed thereby, nor is it the latter that first makes it possible.

It is independent of the parties to the interplay *as such;* for they become reciprocating factors only by means of it; it is this activity which effects an interplay between them. In themselves, both may continue to exist without it; it is sufficient that they are isolated and not interconnected in any way.

I, 163   But all positing is the prerogative of the self; hence this activity of transference, to make possible a determination through the concept of efficacy, is attributable *to the self.* The self transfers activity from itself into the not-self, and thus to that extent abolishes activity in itself; and this, by the foregoing, means that through activity it posits a passivity in itself. Insofar as the self is active in transferring activity to the not-self, the not-self is passive; activity *gets* transferred to it.

(There is no need for premature alarm at the fact that this proposition expressly contradicts the first principle, from which, upon application of the immediately preceding proposition, we now deduce a reality of the not-self independent of all reciprocity (p. 146). It is sufficient that this conclusion follows by correct inferences from established premises, no less than that which it contradicts. The ground of their unity will emerge in due time, without any arbitrary assistance from us.

It should not go unnoticed, what we have observed above, that this activity is independent of *the particular* reciprocity *made possible thereby*. Thus there might be another such, which is not first made possible by this activity.

Despite all the restrictions to which our proposition is liable, we have gained at least this much from it, that the self, insofar as it is passive, must *also* be active, even though it be not *merely* active; and this may very well prove to be a most important advance, and a rich reward for all the pains of our inquiry.)

b) In the interplay of *substantiality,* activity is to be posited as limited by means of absolute totality; that is, the portion of absolute totality that is excluded by the limit is posited as *not* posited in the positing of the limited activity, as missing therefrom. Thus the purely formal character of this reciprocity is a *nonpositing* by way of a positing. The missing portion is posited in the absolute totality; it is *not* posited in the limited activity; it is posited *as* not posited in the interplay. We set out from an absolute positing, and a positing, indeed, of the absolute totality; this in virtue of the concept of substantiality already set forth above.

I, 164

The material character of the act which itself posits this interplay must therefore equally be a nonpositing through a positing, and indeed through an absolute positing. As to where it comes from, this not-*being*-posited in the limited activity, which is then regarded as already given, and as to what it may be that grounds it—these are questions entirely disregarded here. The limited activity occurs; that is presupposed; and we are asking, not how it may come to occur as such, but merely how it may enter into reciprocal relation with nonlimitation.

All positing in general, and absolute positing in particular, is attributable to the self: the act which posits the present interplay itself proceeds from an absolute positing, and is thus an act of the self.

This action or activity of the self is wholly independent of the interplay that is first posited thereby. It first posits absolutely one component of the interplay, namely absolute totality, and by means of this then posits the other, *as diminished* activity; as being less than the totality. Where the activity as such may come from, is not the question here, for *as such* it is not a party to the interplay; it is so, merely as *diminished* activity, and this it becomes only through the positing of absolute totality, and through its relation thereto.

I, 165

The independent activity in question proceeds from the act of positing; but it is nonpositing that we actually arrive at: hence we may to that extent entitle the latter *an alienation*. A determinate quantum of absolute totality is excluded from the activity posited as diminished; is regarded as not in the latter, but located outside it.

The characteristic difference between this *alienation,* and the *transference* just previously referred to, should not go unremarked. In the latter, to be sure, there is also something eliminated from the self, but we abstract from this, and simply confine our attention to the fact that it is posited in the opposite.   —Here, by contrast, there is simple exclusion. In this context, at least, it is nothing to the purpose, whether the excluded item be posited in some other thing, or what this other may be.

The activity of alienation, thus described, must have a passivity opposed to it; and such there is, indeed, in that a portion of absolute totality *is* alienated; *is* posited as not posited. The activity has an object, and this object is part of the totality. What substratum of reality this lessening of activity, or passivity, belongs to, whether to self or not-self, is not the question here; and it is of much importance that one should infer no further than is to be inferred from the proposition as stated, and should grasp the form of the interplay in all its purity.

(Every thing is what it is; it has those realities that are posited, just as it is posited. A = A (§ 1). If anything be an accident of this thing, this is to say in the first place that it is not posited in the positing of the thing; it does not belong to the nature thereof, and

is to be excluded from its primary conception. It is this characterization of the accident that we have now explained. But in a certain
sense again, the accident is attributed to the thing, and posited
therein. The state of affairs in that connection we shall also see in
due course.)

III

Both the reciprocity and the activity independent of it must
mutually determine one another. Just as before, we have first to
inquire what this proposition may signify in general, and then to
apply it to the particular cases falling under it.

1. In the independent activity, as also in the reciprocity, we have
again made a double distinction; we have distinguished the form
of reciprocity from its matter, and, on the strength of this, we have
further differentiated between an independent activity determining
the former, and another which is determined, in reflection, by the
latter. Hence we cannot proceed to examine the proposition in
question precisely as it is here set forth; for if we now speak of
reciprocity, it is uncertain whether we are referring to its form or its
matter; and so too with independent activity. So first, in each of
them, the two must be unified: but this can only be accomplished
through the synthesis of interdetermination. Hence, in our present
proposition, the following three must again be contained: α) The
activity independent of the form of the interplay determines the
activity independent of its matter, and *vice versa;* that is, they both
determine one another, and are synthetically united. β) The form
of the interplay determines its matter, and *vice versa;* that is, they
both determine one another and are synthetically united. And only
now can our proposiiton be understood and discussed: γ) The
interplay (as synthetic unity) determines the independent activity
(as synthetic unity) and *vice versa;* that is, they both determine one
another, and are themselves synthetically united. α) The activity

which is to determine the *form* of the interplay, or reciprocity *as*
such, but be quite independent thereof, is a *transition* from one
component of the interplay to the other, *qua* transition (and not as
an action in general). The activity which determines the *matter* of

the interplay is one which posits in the components that which enables a transition to be made from one to the other. —This second
activity provides the above-sought X (p. 144), contained in both
components, and containable *only in both,* not in either alone;
the X which makes it impossible to be content with the positing
simply of one component (reality or negation), but compels us at
once to posit its counterpart, since it demonstrates the insufficiency
of either without the other; —the X to which the unity of consciousness aspires, and must aspire, if no *hiatus* is to arise in it; and so,
as it were, its *guide*. The first activity is consciousness itself, insofar
as it aspires, beyond the components, to this X—is one, though it
brings its objects, these components, into reciprocity, and must
necessarily do so, if it is to be one.

That the first activity should determine the second would
mean that the transition itself is the ground of that to which transition is made; by the mere transition, the transit becomes possible
(an idealist claim). That the second activity should determine the
first would mean that the transition, as an action, is grounded on
that to which transition is made; insofar as the latter is posited, the
transition itself is immediately posited (a dogmatic claim). That
each should determine the other would mean, therefore, that by
the mere transition there is posited in the components that whereby
transition can be made; and that by the positing of them as components, there is an immediate interplay between them. The transition is made possible by the fact of its occurrence; and it is possible
only to the extent that it really does occur. It is grounded upon
itself; it occurs absolutely because it occurs, and is an absolute act
without any determining ground or condition beyond itself.   —In
consciousness itself, and nowhere else, lies the ground of transition
from one component to the other. Consciousness, simply because
it is consciousness, must make the transition; and there would be a
hiatus in it if it did not do so, simply because it would then be no
consciousness at all.

β)   The form of the interplay, and its matter, are each to
determine the other.

The *interplay,* as we lately recalled, differs from the *activity
it presupposes,* in that we abstract from this activity (e.g. from that
of an observing intelligence who posits in his mind the components,

I, 168

as due to be set in reciprocity). The components are thought of as reciprocally related on their own; we project upon the things what may perhaps be located only in ourselves. To what extent this abstraction may or may not be valid, will appear in due course.

In this context, then, the components reciprocate among themselves. The mutual *intrusion* of each upon the other is the *form;* the *activity and passivity* that at once emerges in both, through intrusion and being intruded upon, is the *matter* of the interplay. For brevity's sake, we shall call it the mutual *relation* of the components to one another. The intrusion is to determine the relation of the components, that is, the latter is to be determined immediately, without any other determination, and through the mere intrusion *as such:* and *vice versa;* the relation of the components is to determine their intrusion, that is, through their mere relation without any other determination, it is posited that they intrude upon each other. Through their mere relation, here thought of as determinant

I, 169   *prior* to interplay, their intrusion is already posited (it is not just an accident in them, which they could still exist without): and through their intrusion, here thought of as determinant prior to relation, their relation is simultaneously posited. Intrusion and relation are one and the same.

1)   They are so related to one another that they reciprocate; and apart from this they have no sort of mutual relation to each other. If they are not posited as reciprocating, they are not posited at all.

2)   Since, in mere *form,* a reciprocity *in general* is posited between them, the matter of this interplay, i.e., its nature, the *amount* of action and passion, etc., posited thereby, is simultaneously *determined* completely without any further ado.   —They necessarily *reciprocate,* and do so only in one possible way, determined absolutely by the fact *that* they reciprocate. If *they* are posited, then a determinate interplay is posited; and if a determinate interplay is posited, then *they* are posited. They and a determinate interplay are one and the same.

γ)   The independent activity (as synthetic unity) determines the interplay (as synthetic unity) and *vice versa;* that is, both determine one another and are themselves synthetically united.

The activity, as synthetic unity, is an absolute *transition;* the

interplay, an absolute and completely self-determined *intrusion.*
That the former should determine the latter would mean that, merely through the occurrence of transition, the intrusion of the components is posited. That the latter should determine the former
would mean that, just as the components intrude, so the activity
must necessarily go over from one to the other. That both should
determine one another means that, just as the one is posited, so is
the other, and *vice versa;* from either term of the comparison, one
can and must go over to the other. Everything is one and the same.
—But the whole is absolutely posited; it is grounded upon itself.

I, 170   To render this principle more illuminating, and to bring out its
importance, we apply it to the propositions falling under it.

The activity determining the form of the interplay determines
everything that emerges therein; and conversely, everything that
emerges in the interplay determines it. In form the mere interplay, that is, the intrusion of the components upon one another,
is impossible without the act of transition; indeed, the intrusion of
the components is posited through the transition. Conversely, the
transition is posited through the intrusion of the components; in that
they are posited as intruding, transition necessarily takes place. No
intrusion, no transition; no transition, no intrusion: both are one
and the same, and to be distinguished only in reflection. Furthermore, the same activity determines the matter of the interplay; only
through the necessary transition are the components posited *as such,*
and, since they are posited *merely* as such, first posited at all; and
conversely, just as the components are posited as such, so also is
there posited the activity which does and should make the transition. Thus one can start from whichever one wishes of the elements
discriminated; as soon as one of them is posited, the other three
are also. The activity determining the matter of the interplay determines the whole interplay; it posits that to which transition can,
and therefore must, be made, and so posits the activity of the form,
and thereby everything else.

Thus the activity returns into itself by way of the interplay;
and the interplay returns into itself by way of the activity. Everything reproduces itself, and there can be no *hiatus* therein; from
every component one is driven to all the others. The activity of the

I, 171   form determines that of the matter, this the matter of the interplay, and this in turn its form; the form of the interplay determines the activity of the form and so on. They are all one and the same synthetic affair. The act returns into itself by way of a circle. But the whole circle is absolutely posited. It is because it is, and no higher ground can be given for the same.

The application of this principle will only become apparent in what follows.

2. The principle that the interplay, and the activity hitherto regarded as independent thereof, are each to determine the other, must now be applied to the specific cases falling under it; and first a) to *the concept of efficacy*. We investigate the synthesis postulated thereby, according to the schema just established: α) in the interplay of efficacy, the activity of the form determines that of the matter, and *vice versa;* β) in it, the form of the interplay determines the matter thereof, and *vice versa;* γ) the synthetically united activity determines the synthetically united interplay, and *vice versa:* that is, they are themselves synthetically united.

α) In its mere form, the activity prerequisite for the interplay postulated in the concept of efficacy is a *transference, a positing by way of a nonpositing:* by the fact that, in one respect, we do *not* posit, in another respect we *do.* Through this activity *of the form,* the activity *of the matter* of the interplay is to be determined. This was an independent activity of the not-self, whereby was first made possible the component from which the interplay started, namely a passivity in the self. To say that the latter is determined, grounded or posited by the former is obviously to say that it is this very activity of the not-self which is posited through the former, in virtue of its positing function; and is posited merely *insofar* as something is

I, 172   *not* posited. (We have no need to inquire here, what this unposited thing may be.) —A limited sphere is thus prescribed to the activity of the not-self; and this sphere is the activity of the form. The not-self is active only insofar as it is posited as active by the self (to which the activity of the form belongs) by means of a nonpositing. —No positing by a nonpositing—no activity of the not-self. Conversely, the activity of the matter, that is, the independent activity of the not-self, must ground and determine the activity of the form, that is, the transference, the positing through a nonpositing. Now according to all that has gone before, this obviously means that it must determine the transition, as a *trans*ition; it must posit that X which indicates the insufficiency of the one component, and so compels us to posit it as a *com*ponent, and thereby to posit a second, with which it reciprocates. This component is passivity *as* such. Thus the not-self is the ground of *non*positing; and thereby determines and conditions the activity of the form. The latter posits by way of a nonpositing and in absolutely no other way; but the nonpositing is conditional upon an activity of the not-self, and thus the whole act postulated is so as well. The positing by a nonpositing falls within the sphere of an activity of the not-self. —No activity of the not-self—no positing by means of a nonpositing.

(Here then the conflict deplored above is close upon us, in an only slightly mitigated form. The outcome of the first mode of reflection provides the basis for a dogmatic idealism: *all reality of the not-self is simply a transference out of the self*. The outcome of the second mode of reflection provides the basis for a dogmatic realism: *there can be no transference, unless an independent reality of the not-self, a thing-in-itself, is already presupposed*. The synthesis now to be established must therefore do no less than to re-

I, 173   solve the conflict and point out the middle road between idealism and realism.)

Both propositions are to be synthetically united, that is, they are to be regarded as one and the same. This comes about as follows: That which is activity in the not-self is passivity in the self (in virtue of the principle of opposition); we can therefore posit *passivity of the self* in place of activity of the not-self. Hence—by virtue of the postulated synthesis—in the concept of efficacy, the passivity of the self and its activity, its nonpositing and its positing, are completely one and the same. In this concept, the propositions: the self does not posit something in itself—and—the self posits something in the not-self—say exactly the same thing: they designate, not different acts, but one and the same act. Neither grounds the other, nor is either grounded by the other: for the twain are one.

Let us give further thought to this proposition. Its content is as follows: a)   The self does not posit something in itself, that is, it posits the same in the not-self. b) What is thereby posited in the not-self is *precisely what* that which is unposited in the self *does not* posit, or negates. The act returns upon itself; insofar as the self is not to posit something in itself, it is itself not-self. Yet since it must, after all, exist, it must posit: and since it is not to posit in the self, it must do so in the not-self. But however precisely this proposition may now be demonstrated, ordinary common sense still continues to resist it. We wish to discover the ground of this resistance, in order to still the demands of common sense, at least until we have been genuinely able to satisfy them by pointing out the area in which they hold sway.

I, 174   In the two propositions just established there is obviously an ambiguity in the meaning of the word *posit*. Common sense perceives this, and hence its resistance. —That the not-self *does not* posit something in the self, or negates it, means that, for the self, the not-self does not posit at all, but merely annuls; to that extent, therefore, it is *qualitatively* opposed to the self, and is the *real ground* of a determination of the latter. —But that the self does not posit something in the self does not mean that the self does not posit at all; it certainly posits, in that it does not posit something, or posits it as negation; what the proposition means, rather, is that the self does not posit only *in part*. Hence the self is not *qualitatively* opposed to itself, but only *quantitatively;* it is thus merely the *ideal ground* of a determination in itself. That it *does not* posit something in itself, and that it posits this in the not-self, are one and the same: thus the self is in no other sense a ground of the reality of the not-self than it is of determination in itself, or of its own passivity: it is merely an *ideal ground.*

What is now merely posited *idealiter* in the not-self must become *realiter* the ground of a passivity in the self; the ideal ground must become a real one; and this the dogmatic tendency in man is unable to grasp. —We can throw it into great perplexity if, in the sense that dogmatism demands, we allow the not-self to be a real ground, to operate upon the self without the latter's cooperation, to yield a matter of some kind, which ought really to be first created; and now ask how, then, the real ground is to become an ideal one; —which it must in fact become, if ever a passivity is to be posited in the self and brought to consciousness *via* presentation.

I, 175

—A question, this, whose answer, like that of its predecessor, presupposes the direct encounter of self and not-self, and to which dogmatism and all its defenders will never give us a thoroughgoing answer. —Both questions are answered by means of our synthesis; and they can only be answered thus, that is, one can only be answered through the other, and *vice-versa.*

Hence the deeper significance of the above synthesis is as follows: *In the concept of efficacy* (and so everywhere, since in this concept alone is a real ground present) *ideal and real ground are one and the same.* This principle, which is the basis of critical idealism, and by which idealism and realism are united, will never be intelligible to mankind; and their failure to grasp it lies in the want of abstraction.

For if different things outside us are related to one another by the concept of efficacy—how rightly or wrongly, will appear in due course—a distinction is drawn between the real and ideal grounds of their possibility of relation. In things-in-themselves there must be something independent of our presentation, whereby they intrude upon one another without intervention on our part; but that *we* relate them together must have its ground in ourselves, for instance, in sensation. So we then also posit our self outside us, who are *doing the positing,* as a *self-in-itself,* as a thing existing without our cooperation, and who knows how; and now, without any cooperation from us, some other thing is supposed to act upon it, as the magnet does on a piece of iron.[2]

[2]Less for my auditors than for other learned and philosophical readers into whose hands this book may fall, we make the following observation. —The majority of men could sooner be brought to believe themselves a piece of lava in the moon than to take themselves for a *self.* Hence they have never understood Kant, or read his mind; hence, too, they will not understand this exposition, though the condition for all philosophizing lies at its head. Anyone who is not yet at one with himself on this point has no understanding of any fundamental philosophy, and needs none. Nature, whose machine he is, will lead him, even without his own cooperation, into all the occupations that are his to pursue. Philosophizing calls for independence, and this one can only confer on oneself. Without eyes, we ought not to wish to see; but nor ought we to maintain that it is the eye that sees. (Note to 1st Ed.)

On the first appearance of this note, it was variously ridiculed by persons known to the author, who felt themselves assailed thereby. I should now be willing to cancel it; but I am mindful, alas, that it is not yet out of date.

I, 176   But the self is nothing outside the self, for it is simply the self. Now if the nature of the self consists simply and solely in the fact that it posits itself, then for it *self-positing* and *existence* are one and the same. Real ground and ideal ground are here at one. —Conversely, *non-self-positing* and *nonexistence* are equally one, for the self; the real and ideal grounds of negation are also one. If this is spelled out in part, the propositions: the self *does not posit* some thing in itself, and: the self *is* not some thing, are likewise one and the same.

Obviously, therefore, to say that something *is* not *posited* in the self *(realiter),* means that the self *posits* it not in itself *(idealiter),* and *vice versa;* the self *posits* something not in itself, means, it is not posited in the self.

That the not-self is to operate on the self, to annul something therein, clearly means that it is to annul a positing therein; it must bring it about that the self posits something not in itself. If only what is acted upon be really a *self,* then no other action upon it is possible save that of effecting a nonpositing therein.

Conversely, that there has to be a not-self for the self, can only mean that the self has to posit reality in the not-self; for there is and can be no other reality for the self, save one that is posited thereby.

That activity of the self and not-self are one and the same,
I, 177   means that the self can only *not* posit something in itself by positing it in the not-self; and only posit something in itself by *not* positing it in the not-self. Posit in general it must, so long as it is a self; but it need not posit in *itself.* —Passivity of the self, and of the not-self are also one and the same. That the self posits something not in itself, means that the same is posited in the not-self. Activity and passivity of the self are one and the same. For insofar as it posits something *not* in itself, it posits the same in the not-self. —Activity and passivity of the not-self are one and the same. Insofar as the not-self is to operate on the self, to annul something therein, the same is posited in the not-self by the self. And with this, the complete synthetic union is clearly accomplished. Not one of all the elements mentioned is the ground of any other; for they are all one and the same.

Hence the question, what is the ground of passivity in the self?

is in general without an answer, and is least of all to be answered by presupposing an activity of the not-self, as a thing-in-itself; for there is no mere passivity in the self. But another question is certainly left standing, namely this: what, then, is the ground of the whole interplay just established? To say that it is in general posited absolutely and without any ground, and that the judgment which asserts its existence is a thetic judgment, is not permissible; for only the self is posited absolutely, and in the self as such there is no such interplay. But it is straightway clear that, in the theoretical Science of Knowledge, such a ground is incomprehensible, since it is not included under the basic principle thereof, viz. that the self posits itself as determined by the not-self; on the contrary, it is presupposed by that principle. Hence a ground of this kind, if it is to be identified at all, would have to lie outside the boundaries of the theoretical Science of Knowledge.

I, 178   And thus the critical idealism prevailing in our theory is definitely established. It runs dogmatically counter to dogmatic idealism and realism, in that it shows how neither does the mere activity of the self provide the ground of the reality of the not-self, nor the mere activity of the not-self the ground of passivity in the self; but, confronted with the question it is called upon to answer, namely, what then may be the ground of the interplay assumed between the two, it is resigned to its own ignorance, and shows us that investigation of this point lies beyond the bounds of theory. In its account of presentation, it proceeds neither from an absolute activity of the self, nor of the not-self, but rather from a determinacy which is at the same time a determining, since nothing else either is, or can be, immediately contained in consciousness. As to what this determination may again determine, the theory offers no decision at all; and in virtue of this incompleteness, we are thus driven on beyond theory into a practical part of the Science of Knowledge.

At the same time, the oft-used expressions, *diminished, restricted* and *limited* activity of the self are made perfectly clear. They designate an activity directed to something in the not-self, to an *object;* hence, an objective act. The acts of the self in general, or the positing thereof, are not, and cannot be, limited at all; but its positing *of the self* is limited, in that it must posit a not-self.

β) In the concept of efficacy, the form of mere reciprocity, and the matter thereof, each determine one another.

We have found in what precedes that mere reciprocity in general can be distinguished only by means of reflection from the activity independent thereof. If the interplay is posited in the reciprocating components themselves, we then abstract from the activity, and consider the reciprocity merely in itself and *as* such. Which point of view is correct, or whether perhaps neither is, if applied by itself, will appear in due course.

In reciprocity as such, the form can at all events be distinguished from its matter. The form of reciprocity is no more than the mutual intrusion, as such, of the components upon each other. The matter is that in the components which ensures that they can, and must, so intrude. —The characteristic form of reciprocity in the relation of efficacy is a *coming-to-be through a passing-away* (a becoming through a disappearance). (Here, be it noted, we must abstract altogether from the substance that is acted upon, from the substrate of passing away, and hence from all *temporal conditions*. If this substance is posited, then *in relation thereto* the incoming change is certainly posited in time. But this we must abstract from, however hard the imagination may find it to do so, for the substance does not enter into the reciprocity; only the *incoming* factor, and what is thereby *suppressed* and *abolished*, take part in the interplay; and we are only concerned with what does take part therein, insofar as it does so. For example, X destroys —X: —X was certainly there *previously, before* it was destroyed; if it is to be regarded as existing, then it must certainly be posited in the time preceding, and X, by contrast, in the time following. However, it is supposed to be thought of, not as existing, but as *not existing*. But the existence of X and nonexistence of —X are by no means occurrent at different times, but rather at the *very same moment*. Hence, if there is nothing else that obliges us to locate this moment in a *series* of moments, they are simply not in time). The matter of the interplay to be examined is *essential opposition* (qualitative incompatibility).

That the form of this interplay is to determine its matter, means that, because and insofar as the reciprocating components

I, 179

I, 180

mutually annihilate one another, they are essentially opposed. The (actual) mutual annihilation determines the scope of the essential opposition. If they do not annul one another, they are not essentially opposed *(essentialiter opposita)*. This is a paradox, against which the above-mentioned misunderstanding is again brought forward. For it will be thought at first sight that here we are inferring from a contingency to something essential; from the current annihilation one could indeed infer the essential opposition; but we cannot go in reverse from the essential opposition to the current annihilation: for this a further condition would have to be added, namely, the immediate influence of each upon the other (for example, in bodies, their presence in the same space). Both the essential opposites could be perfectly isolated and devoid of all connection; in that case they would be no less opposed, and yet would therefore fail to annihilate each other.   —The source of this misunderstanding, and the means of removing it, will be shown forthwith.

That the matter of this interplay is to determine its form, means that the essential opposition determines the mutual annihilation; only on condition that the components are essentially opposed, and insofar as they are, can they mutually abolish one another.   —If the current elimination is posited, indeed, in the sphere of opposition in general, yet without, so to speak, filling this sphere, but merely a smaller one, whose boundary determines the required condition for actual influence, then everyone will accept this proposition without demur, and the only paradox involved could be that we should expressly have stated the proposition in the first place. But

I, 181   Matter and form of the interplay are to determine one another, that is, the mutual annulment, and hence also the intrusion, the immediate influence, are to follow from the mere opposition; and the opposition is to follow from the mutual elimination. Both are one and the same; they are in themselves set counter to each other, or —they mutually annihilate each other. Their influence and their essential opposition are one and the same.

We now give further reflection to this result. That which has actually been posited between the components, by the synthesis we have undertaken, is the necessity of their conjunction: that X which indicates the incompleteness of either, and can only be contained in both. The possibility of separating existence in itself from existence in reciprocity is denied: both are posited as components, and apart from their interplay are not posited at all.   —From real opposition we infer to counterpositing, or ideal opposition, and *vice versa*. Real and ideal opposition are one and the same.   —The shock that common sense feels at this is removed as soon as we remember, that one component of the interplay is the self, to which nothing *is* opposed, but what it *posits* counter to itself; and which *is* not itself opposed to anything that it does not *posit* itself counter to. Thus the present result is precisely that previously arrived at, in another form.

  γ)   In the relation of efficacy, the activity, considered as a synthetic unity, and the reciprocity, similarly conceived, are mutually determinant of each other and themselves form a synthetic unity.

  The activity, as a synthetic unity, may be described as a *mediate positing* (a mediated attribution), (using the word *positing* in an affirmative sense—a positing of reality by way of a nonpositing thereof); the mere reciprocity, as a synthetic unity, consists in the *identity of essential opposition and real annihilation.*

  1.   That the activity determines the reciprocity, means that the *mediacy* of the positing (which is all that is really involved here) is the condition and ground of the fact that essential opposition and real annihilation are completely one and the same; because and insofar as the positing is mediate, opposition and annulment are identical.   —a) If we had an *immediate* positing of the reciprocating components, then opposition and annihilation would be distinct. Suppose the components to be A and B. Suppose that at first A = A and B = B, but that afterwards, after a certain interval, that is, A is also equal to $\sim$B, and B to $\sim$A: then both could perfectly well have been posited according to their first interpretation, without thereby eliminating one another. We should have abstracted from that wherein they were opposed; they would thus no longer be posited as essentially opposed (their essence consisting in the mere fact of opposition), and as mutually annihilating one another, since they would be posited *immediately,* as each independent of the other. But then, too, they would not be posited as mere reciprocal components, but as realities in themselves (A = A.

§1). Such components can only be posited *mediately;* A is equal to
—B and absolutely nothing more; and B is equal to —A and absolutely nothing more; and from this mediacy of positing there follows
the essential opposition and the mutual annihilation, and the identity
of both. For b)   Suppose A is posited merely as the counterpart of
B, and is susceptible of no other predicate whatever, and B merely
as the counterpart of A, and equally susceptible of no other predicate (not even that of *a thing,* which an imagination still unaccus-
tomed to strict abstraction is constantly ready to interpose); in that

I, 183

case A cannot be posited as real, save in that B is not posited—and
B cannot, save in that A is not: if so, their common essence obviously consists in the fact that each is posited through the nonpositing of the other, and hence in the *fact of opposition;* and—if we
abstract from an active intelligence that posits, and reflect merely
on the components—in the fact that they mutually annul one another. Their essential opposition and mutual annihilation are thus
identical, to the extent that each component is posited merely
through the nonpositing of the other, and in absolutely no other
way.

Now this, by our preceding argument, is the case with the self
and the not-self. The self (here regarded as absolutely active) can
transfer reality to the not-self only by *not* positing reality in itself;
and conversely, can only transfer reality into itself by not positing
it in the not-self. (That the last point is in no contradiction to the
previously established absolute reality of the self, will appear when
it is more exactly specified; and is partially clear here already: we
are speaking of a *transferred* reality, and not of any *absolute* reality). The essential nature of these components, insofar as they are
to reciprocate, consists then, simply in the fact that they are in
opposition to, and mutually annihilate, one another.

The *mediacy* of positing, and it alone (as will subsequently
appear, it is the law of consciousness: *no subject, no object; no object, no subject*), is thus the ground of the essential opposition of
self and not-self, and thereby of all reality, either of the not-self or
the self—insofar as the latter is to be a reality merely posited *as*
posited, an ideal reality; for absolute reality is not lost thereby; it
lies in *what posits.* So far as we have progressed in our synthesis,
this mediacy cannot again be grounded in what is grounded thereby;

nor can it legitimately be grounded by way of the grounding principle. So the ground thereof does not lie in the elements established, in the reality of the not-self or the ideal reality of the self. It must be located, therefore, in the absolute self; and this mediacy must thus itself be absolute, that is, grounded in and through itself.

I, 184

The above line of argument, perfectly correct in this context, leads to a new form of idealism, still more abstract than its predecessor. In the earlier version, an activity, posited as such, was annulled through the nature and essence of the self. The said activity, perfectly possible in itself, was abolished absolutely and without any further ground; and thereby an object, a subject, etc., were made possible. According to this earlier idealism, presentations *as* such were evolved, in a manner quite unknown and inaccessible to us, from out of the self; as if in a coherent, that is, purely idealist, preestablished harmony.

In our present form of idealism, the activity in general has its law immediately in itself; it is a mediate activity and absolutely nothing else, absolute because it is so. Hence there is no sort of activity eliminated in the self; the mediate activity occurs, and there simply cannot be an immediate one. But from the mediacy of this activity, everything else—the reality of the not-self and corresponding negation of the self, the negation of the not-self and corresponding reality of the self—can be fully accounted for. Here the presentations are evolved from the self according to a determinate and knowable law of its nature. For *them* a ground can be provided, albeit not for the *law* itself.

This second form of idealism necessarily eliminates the first, since it genuinely explains from a higher ground what to the first was inexplicable. The first form of idealism can actually be refuted in idealistic fashion. The basic principle of such a system would run: *the self is finite, simply because it is finite.*

But now whether or not such idealism makes a higher ascent, it does not ascend so high as one should; to the absolutely posited and unconditioned. To be sure, a finitude is to be absolutely posited; but everything finite is limited, in virtue of its concept, by what is counterposited thereto: and absolute finitude is a self-contradictory concept.

I, 185

In order to distinguish them, I call this first form of idealism, which abolishes something intrinsically posited, the *qualitative* form; the second, which starts by ascribing a restricted quantity to itself, I call the *quantitative* form.

2. The mediacy of positing is determined by the fact that the essence of the components consists in mere opposition; it is possible only on this condition. If the essence of the components consists in something other than mere opposition, it is evident at once that by the nonpositing of one of them in its entire essence, the other is by no means posited in its entire essence, and *vice versa.* But if their essence consists in nothing else, then if they are to be posited, they can be posited only mediately; as is apparent from what has just been said.

But here we have essential opposition, opposition as such, established as the ground of the mediacy of positing. The former is an absolute in this system and cannot be further explained; the latter is grounded upon the former.

Just as our earlier line of argument set up a quantitative idealism, so this one establishes a quantitative realism, which must certainly be distinguished from the qualitative realism postulated above. In the latter, a not-self, having reality in itself independently of the self, gives rise to an impression on the self, whereby the latter's activity is to some extent repressed; the merely quantitative realist confesses his ignorance about this, and acknowledges that the positing of reality in the not-self first takes place for the self according to the grounding law; but he insists on *the real presence of a limitation of the self,* without any contribution on the part of the self as such, either through absolute activity, as the qualitative idealist maintains, or in virtue of a law inherent in its nature, as is held by the quantitative idealist. The qualitative realist proclaims the reality, independent of the self, of a *determinant;* the quantitative, the reality, independent of the self, of a mere *determination.* There is a determination present in the self, whose ground is not to be posited in the self; that, for him, is a fact: as to its ground *as such,* he is cut off from inquiring into it, that is, it is absolutely and ungroundedly present for him. To be sure, he must relate it to something in the not-self, as real ground, in accordance with the grounding law inherent in himself; but he knows that this law lies merely in himself, and is not deceived thereby. It will at once be apparent

I, 186

to everybody that this realism is nothing other than what was set forth above under the name of critical idealism; just as even Kant established nothing other than this, nor was able or willing, at the level of reflection on which he had placed himself, to establish anything else.[3]

The present realism differs from the quantitative idealism previously described in that, although both assume the self to be finite, the latter is committed to a finitude absolutely posited, whereas the former opts for a contingent one, which cannot, however, be further accounted for. Quantitative realism eliminates the qualitative form thereof as ungrounded and superfluous, in that without it, albeit with the same error, it completely accounts for what it is called upon to explain: the presence of an object in consciousness. With the same error, I say: for it is absolutely unable to explain how a real determination can become an ideal one; how a determination present *as such* can become a determination *for the positing self.* —Certainly, it has now been shown how the mediacy of positing is determined and grounded through essential opposition; but what, then serves as the ground of *positing* in general? *If* there is to be positing, then it can indeed only be mediate; but positing, as such, is still an absolute act of the self, which in this capacity is absolutely undetermined and indeterminable. This system is therefore troubled by the impossibility often pointed out already, of passing from the limited to the unlimited. Quantitative idealism does not have to contend with this difficulty, since it eliminates the transition altogether;

I, 187

---

[3]Kant demonstrates the ideality of objects from the presupposed ideality of space and time: we, on the contrary, shall prove the ideality of space and time from the demonstrated ideality of objects. He required ideal objects to fill up space and time; we require space and time in order to locate the ideal objects. Hence our idealism, though critical and by no means dogmatic, goes a step or two further than his.

This is not the place to show, what can manifestly be shown nonetheless, that Kant also *knew* very well what he *did not say.* Nor is it in place to give the reasons why he neither could nor would say everything that he knew. The principles established and yet to be established here are obviously the basis of his own, as anyone can convince himself who is willing to make a study of the *spirit* of Kant's philosophy (which should not indeed be lacking therein). He has said on several occasions that in his *Critiques* he was not seeking to establish science, but only the propaedeutic thereof; and it is hard to see why this is the only thing his devotees have not wanted to believe in him.

but it is then annihilated, on the other hand, by an obvious contradiction, in that it absolutely posits what is finite.   —We may expect our investigation to take exactly the same course as before; and by synthetic union of both syntheses to arrive at a *critical* quantitative idealism, as a middle road between these two modes of explanation.

I, 188

3.   Mediacy of positing and essential opposition each determine the other; both occupy one and the same sphere to its full extent, and are one. It is clear right away how this must be conceived of, in order for it to be conceived of as possible; *being* and *being posited,* ideal and real relationship, opposing and being opposed, must be one and the same. It is also clear, moreover, under what condition this is possible: namely, if what posits and what is correlatively posited are one and the same, that is, if what is posited in relation is the self. —The self has to stand to some X, which must necessarily to that extent be a not-self, in a relationship such that it can only be posited through the non-positing of the other, and *vice versa.* Now the self, as surely as it is such, stands in a certain relationship only to the extent that it posits itself as standing in this relation. Thus in application to the self, it is all one, whether we say that it *is posited* in this relation, or that it *posits itself* therein. It can be transposed into it *(realiter)* only insofar as it posits itself therein *(idealiter);* and can posit itself therein only to the extent that it is transposed; for no such relation is posited by the mere absolutely posited self—indeed, it is even contradictory thereto.

We shall set out more precisely the significant content of our synthesis. Presupposing always the principle laid down at the outset of this section, the principle of all theoretical procedure, from which everything hitherto has been developed; but presupposing nothing else—it is, we maintain, a law for the self, that both self and not-self can only be posited mediately: that is, the self can be posited only through the nonpositing of the not-self, and the not-self only through the nonpositing of the self. (The self is in every case, and so absolutely, *that which posits,* though in our present inquiry we abstract from this; it is *that which is posited* only under the condition that the not-self is posited as not posited; or is negated).   —To put it in plainer language: the self, as at present conceived, is simply the counterpart of the not-self, and nothing more; and the not-self

I, 189   simply the counterpart of the self and nothing more. No Thou, no I:

no I, no Thou. Henceforth, for clarity's sake, we shall refer to the not-self—in *this* context but no other—as *object,* and to the self as *subject;* though the fitness of these designations is something we cannot yet demonstrate here. The not-self independent of this interplay is not to be called an object, nor the self independent of it a subject. Thus the subject is that which is not an object, and so far has no other predicate than this; and the object is that which is not a subject, and so far, too, has no other predicate.

If, while seeking no further ground for it, we employ this law as a basis for the explanation of presentation, we have no need in the first place of that influence of the not-self, which the qualitative realist postulates, to account for the passivity present in the self; —nor do we even need this passivity (affection, determination), which the quantitative realist postulates for the purpose of his explanation. —Assume that the self must in general posit, in virtue of its essential nature; a proposition that we shall prove in the major synthesis that follows. Now all it can posit is either the subject or the object, and both only mediately. It is to posit the object; —then it necessarily eliminates the subject, and there arises in it a passivity, which it necessarily refers to a real ground in the not-self, and hence arises the presentation of a reality of the not-self independent of the self. —Alternatively, it posits the subject, and so necessarily eliminates the posited object, and there again arises a passivity, which, however, is referred to an activity of the subject, and evokes the presentation of a reality of the self independent of the not-self (the presentation of a freedom in the self, though in our present line of argument it is a freedom *merely in idea*).
—Hence, as should happen anyway according to the law of synthesis, the intermediate factor provides a complete ground and explanation for the (ideal) passivity of the self, and the (ideal) independent activity of self and not-self alike.

I, 190

But since the postulated law is obviously a *determination* (of the activity of the self *as* such), it must have a *ground,* and this ground the Science of Knowledge is called upon to display. Now if we do not insert an intermediary through a new synthesis, as we ought to, the ground can be sought only in the factors *immediately limiting this determination,* namely the *positing* or the *passivity* of the self. The first is adopted as the ground of determination by the quantitative idealist, who makes this law into the law of positing in general; the second is the choice of the quantitative realist, who derives it from the passivity of the self. On the first view, the law is a subjective and ideal principle, having its ground merely in the self; on the second, it is an objective and real principle, whose ground is not in the self.   —Where such a law may have its ground, or whether it has one at all, is a topic precluded from further inquiry. The supposedly inexplicable affection of the self must admittedly be referred to a reality in the not-self that brings it about; but this happens merely in consequence of a law in the self, which can be, and is in fact explained by the affection itself.

It is the outcome of the synthesis we have just set forth, that both these views are wrong; that the law in question is neither merely subjective and ideal, nor merely objective and real, but that its ground must lie in both object and subject at once. But as to how it may lie in both, inquiry is precluded from the outset, and we confess our ignorance on this topic; and this, then, is the critical quantitative idealism that we promised above to establish. Since, however, the problem proposed to us is not yet fully resolved, and we still have a number of syntheses ahead of us, it should certainly be possible in the future to say something more specific about the type of grounding involved.

I, 191   b)   Having dealt with the concept of efficacy, we now go on in the same manner to treat of the concept of substantiality; we make a synthetic union of the activity of the form with that of the matter; then of the form of mere reciprocity with the matter thereof; and finally, of the resultant synthetic unities, one with another.

α)   First, the activity of the form and of the matter (the sense in which these expressions are used here is presumed to be familiar from the foregoing).

The main point at issue with these factors, as with all that follow, is to gain a correct and precise grasp of the *characteristic* nature of substantiality (in respect of the contrast with efficacy).

The activity of the form in this particular interplay is, by the foregoing, a nonpositing through an absolute positing; —the positing of something as *not posited,* through the positing of something else as *posited:* negation through affirmation. —Thus the non-posited still has to be posited—to be posited, that is, as not posited. Hence it must not be altogether *annihilated,* as in the interplay of efficacy, but merely excluded from a determinate sphere. Thus it is negated, not by *positing in general,* but only by a *determinate* positing. Through this positing that is determined in its function, and hence as objective activity is also determinant, the *posited* (as posited) must likewise be determined, that is, posited in a determinate sphere as completely filling it. And thus we may see how, through such a positing, something else can be posited as *not* posited; it is not posited *in this sphere* merely, and not posited therein, or excluded therefrom, precisely because what *is* posited therein is to *fill up* this sphere.   —Now by this act, the excluded is still far from being posited in a determinate sphere; its sphere acquires absolutely no other predicate thereby, save a negative one: it is *not this sphere.* Of what kind it may be, or whether it is a determinate sphere at all, remains quite unsettled by this alone. —Hence, *the determinate character of formal activity in the interdetermination through substantiality is an exclusion from a sphere determinate, filled up, and to that extent having totality* (of what it contains).

I, 192

The difficulty here is obviously this, that the excluded item, B, is posited anyway, and *not* posited merely in the sphere of A; whereas the sphere of A has to be posited as an absolute totality, from which it would follow that there could be no positing of B whatever. Hence the sphere of A must be posited as both totality and nontotality at once. It is posited as a totality in relation to A; and as a nontotality in relation to the excluded B. But now the sphere of B is itself indeterminate; it is determined merely negatively, as the sphere of not-A. Taking all this into account, A would thus be posited as the determinate, and to that extent total, complete part of an indeterminate, and to that extent incomplete, whole. The positing of such a *higher sphere, incorporating both, the determinate and the indeterminate,* would be the very activity whereby the previously postulated formal activity would become possible; and is hence the activity *of the matter* that we are looking for.

(Suppose a determinate piece of iron = C, that moves. You posit the iron absolutely, as an absolute totality, as it is posited through its mere concept = A (in virtue of the principle A = A,

§1), and in the sphere of this you fail to find the movement = B; hence, by the positing of A, you exclude B from its sphere. Yet you do not eliminate the motion of the iron = C, you have no wish to deny absolutely the possibility of this: so you posit it outside the sphere of A, in an *indeterminate* sphere, because you simply *do not know on what condition, and for what reason, the piece of iron =*

C may move. Sphere A is the totality of the iron, and yet is also not so, for the motion of C, which is also iron, after all, is not included therein. Hence you must describe a higher sphere around them both, which shall include both the iron in motion and the iron at rest. To the extent that the iron occupies this higher sphere, it is substance (not to the extent that it occupies sphere A as such, as is commonly yet mistakenly supposed; in this aspect it is a thing-in-itself, determined by its mere concept, according to the principle A = A); motion and absence of motion are accidents of the iron. We shall see in due course that lack of motion attaches to it in a sense different from motion, and also the reason for this).

That activity of the form determines that of the matter would mean that, simply insofar as something is excluded from the absolute totality, and posited as not contained therein, a more comprehensive yet indeterminate sphere is posited; only on the premise of actual exclusion is a higher sphere possible; no exclusion, no higher sphere; that is, no accident in the self, no not-self. The sense of this proposition is clear right away, and we merely append a few words concerning its application. —The self is originally posited as *positing itself;* and this *self-positing* to that extent fills out the sphere of its absolute reality. If it posits an object, this objective positing must be excluded from that sphere, and *posited* in the opposite one of *non-self-positing.* Positing an object is the same thing as—not positing oneself. Our present argument proceeds from this act; it runs as follows: The self posits an object, or excludes something from itself, simply because it excludes, and on no higher ground: by means of this exclusion, the higher sphere of *positing in general* (regardless of whether the self or a not-self is posited) now first becomes possible.   —It will be evident that this is an idealist line

of argument, and coincides with the quantitative idealism previously established, whereby the self posits something as a not-self, absolutely because it posits the latter. In such a system, therefore, the concept of substantiality would have to be explained exactly as we have just explained it. —It will further be evident here in general, that *self-positing* appears in a twofold relation of quantity; first, as absolute totality; second, as the determinate part of an indeterminate whole. This proposition should have highly important consequences in the future. —It is further clear that by substance we designate, not the *enduring,* but the *all-comprehending.* The attribute of duration only attaches to substance in a very derived sense.

That activity of the matter determines and conditions that of the form would mean that the more comprehensive sphere, as a more embracing one (including therefore its subordinate spheres of self and not-self) is absolutely posited; and hence (under a condition yet to be appended) the exclusion first becomes possible as a genuine act of the self. —It will be evident that this line of argument leads to a realism, and of the qualitative variety at that. Self and not-self are posited as opposed: the self is in general *that which posits;* that under a certain condition, namely when it does *not* posit the not-self, it *posits itself,* is a contingent matter, and determined by the ground of positing in general, which does not lie in the self. —In this line of argument, the self is a presenting entity, which must accommodate itself to the constitution of things-in-themselves.

But neither of these two lines of argument can hold, for each must be mutually modified by the other. Because the self has to exclude something from itself, a higher sphere must exist and be posited, and because a higher sphere exists and is posited, the self must exclude something from itself. More briefly, a not-self exists, because the self opposes something to itself; and the self opposes something to itself, because a not-self exists and is posited. Neither is ground of the other, for both are one and the same act of the self, which can be distinguished only in reflection. —It will be evident at once, that this result is identical with the principle established earlier, viz., that the ideal and the real ground are one and the same, and can be elucidated therefrom; and hence that critical idealism is established by our present result, no less than by the principle in question.

β) The form and the matter of the interplay in substantiality must mutually determine one another.

I, 195

The *form of the interplay* consists in the components mutually excluding and being excluded by each other. If A is posited, as absolute totality, then B is excluded from its sphere and posited in the indeterminate but determinable sphere B.   —Conversely, if B is posited (if we reflect on B as posited), A is excluded *from the absolute totality,* that is, no longer subsumed under the concept thereof, and the sphere of A is now no longer that of absolute totality, but is conjoined with B as part of an indeterminate but determinable sphere. —The last point should be carefully noted and correctly grasped, for everything depends upon it. —Hence, the form of the interplay is a mutual exclusion of the components from the absolute totality.

(Posit iron in general and in itself; you then have a determinate complete concept which wholly occupies its sphere. Posit the iron as moving; you then have a feature not contained in this concept, and thus excluded from it. But as you still ascribe this movement to the· iron, the previously determinate concept thereof no longer ranks as determined, but merely as determinable; it lacks a determination that you will determine in due course as the capacity for magnetic attraction).

As regards the *matter of the interplay,* it will be clear at once I, 196 that, in the form of it just expounded, it remains undetermined what the actual totality may be. If B is to be excluded, then the totality is occupied by the sphere of A; if B on the other hand is to be posited, then the spheres of both B and A together occupy the still indeterminate, but determinable, totality. (We are here abstracting entirely from the fact that even these latter spheres of A and B have still to be determined). This indeterminacy cannot persist. The totality in both its aspects is a totality. Now if neither has an additional feature beyond this, whereby they can be distinguished, then the entire postulated interplay is impossible; for the totality is then a unity, and there is only one component; and so no interplay at all. (To put it more intelligibly, if with less stringency: Fancy yourself a spectator of this reciprocal exclusion. If you cannot distinguish the twofold totality between which the reciprocity plays, then there is for you no interplay. But you cannot distinguish them, if there is not some X lying outside them both, insofar as they constitute nothing but a totality, whereby you orientate yourself). Hence the *determinability* of the totality, as such, is presupposed in order to make the postulated interplay possible; it is presupposed that both totalities should be distinguishable in some particular; and this determinability is *the matter of the interplay,* the point to which the interplay progresses and the one and only thing that fixes it.

(Take the iron, as presented, say, to ordinary experience, without technical acquaintance with scientific law, and posit it in itself, that is, as isolated and lacking any discernible connection with anything outside itself, and amongst other things as having *fixity of position;* then motion has no part in the concept thereof, and if it is given to you in appearance as moving, you are quite right in referring this motion to something outside it. But if, as you are also right in doing, you nonetheless attribute the motion to the iron, then your former concept is no longer complete, and you have to determine it further in this respect, and posit, for example, the capacity for magnetic attraction as falling within its scope. —This creates a distinction. If you set out from the first concept, then *fixity of position* is *essential* to the iron, and only the *movement* in it is *contingent;* but if you proceed from the second concept, then the *fixity is no less contingent* than the movement; for the first is no less conditional upon the absence of a magnet than the second is upon its presence. You are thus disorientated if you cannot give a reason why you should proceed from the first concept and not the second, or *vice versa;* that is, in general, if there is no way of determining which totality needs to be reflected on—either the absolutely posited and determinate totality, or the determinable one arising from this and the excluded factor, or both).

That *the form of the interplay determines its matter* would mean that it is the mutual exclusion which determines the totality in the sense just established, that is, which indicates which of the two possible totalities is the absolute one, and from which it is necessary to proceed. That which excludes some other thing from the totality is, insofar it excludes, the totality in question; and conversely; and beyond this it has no ground of determination whatever. —If B is excluded by the absolutely posited A, then A is *to that extent* the totality; and if we reflect on B, and thus no longer regard A as totality, then *to that extent* A + B, which in itself is indeterminate, is the determinable totality. Determinate or determinable is totality, according as we happen to take it. —What emerges in this result is admittedly nothing new, but precisely what we al-

ready knew to have been said beforehand, prior to the synthesis; but previously we still had hopes of finding some ground of determination. By the present result, however, these hopes are completely extinguished; its significance is negative, and it tells us: there is absolutely no possible ground of determination, except through relation.

(In the previous example, one may set out from the absolutely posited concept of the iron, in which case its fixity of position is *of the essence;* or from the determinable concept thereof, in which case it is an *accident.* Either is correct, according as one takes it, and no sort of determining rule can be given on the point. The distinction is purely relative).

That *the matter of the interplay determines its form* would mean that the determinability of the totality, in the sense explained, *which is posited in virtue of the fact* that it is to determine something else (that is, the determination is really possible, and there is an X whereby it occurs, though we are not concerned with its discovery here), determines the mutual exclusion. One of the two, either the determinate or the determinable, is absolute totality, and the other is therefore not; and hence there is also something absolutely excluded, which this totality rules out. If, for example, the determinate is absolute totality, then what it excludes is the absolutely excluded factor. Hence—and this is the result of our present synthesis—there is an absolute ground of totality, and this is not purely relative.

(In the above example—it is not a matter of indifference, whether one seeks to proceed from the determinate concept of the iron or the determinable concept thereof, and whether one wishes to treat fixity of position as an essential or contingent feature. Once

it is posited that we must, for some reason, have proceeded from the determinate concept of the iron, then only its motion is an absolute accident, but not, however, its fixity).

Neither of the two is to determine the other, but both are to determine each other mutually means—to come to the point without further ado—that the absolute and relative grounds for determination of the totality must be one and the same; the relation must be absolute, and the absolute must be nothing more than a relation.

We now attempt to clarify this highly important result. —By determination of the totality, the factor to be excluded is simultaneously determined, and *vice versa:* this too is a relation, but no question arises concerning it. The question is: Which of the two possible modes of determination is to be adopted and established? On the first alternative, the answer is as follows: Neither of the two; we have no sort of determinate rule here, such that, if we adopt the one, we can to that extent refuse to adopt the other, and *vice versa;* which of the two we ought to adopt is an issue about which nothing can be settled. On the other alternative, the answer runs: One of the two must be adopted, and there must be a rule about this. But what this rule may be must naturally remain undecided, since *determinability,* rather than *determination,* was to be the ground for determining the factor to be excluded.

These two propositions are unified by our present principle; for what it maintains is that there certainly is a rule, though not one which sets up either of the two modes of determination, but rather both, *as mutually determinant by way of each other.* —No single one of the totalities hitherto considered as such is the one we are in search of; the latter is first constituted by both totalities mutually determined by one another. Thus what we are speaking of is *a relation of the two modes of determination,* the relational and the absolute; and by this relation the desired totality is first established. The absolute totality is to be neither A, nor A + B, but A determined by A + B. The determinable is to be determined by the determinate, and the determinate by the determinable; and the resultant unity is the totality we seek. —It is evident that this must be the outcome of our synthesis; but it is somewhat harder to understand what its import may be.

That the determinate and the determinable should mutually determine one another, obviously means that the determination of the thing to be determined consists in the fact that the latter is a determinable. It is *a determinable,* and nothing else; its whole essence consists in that. —Now this determinability is the totality

I, 200

we were in search of, that is, the determinability is a determinate quantum; it has its limits, beyond which no further determination occurs; and within these limits all possible determinability lies.

If we apply this result to the case before us, everything will at once become clear. —The self posits *itself*. Its absolutely posited reality consists in this; the sphere of this reality is exhausted, and therefore contains absolute totality (the absolutely posited reality of the self). The self posits *an object*. This objective positing must necessarily be excluded from the sphere of the self-positing of the self. Yet this objective positing must be attributed to the self; and we thereby obtain the sphere A + B as the (so far unlimited) totality of acts of the self. —According to the present synthesis, both spheres must mutually determine each other: A supplies what it possesses, namely absolute limits; A + B supplies what it possesses, namely content. And now the self in positing is either an object, and so not a subject, or the subject, and so not an object—

I, 201 insofar as it *posits itself* as positing according to this rule. And the two spheres thus fall within each other, and only in combination first fill out a single *limited* sphere; and to that extent the determination of the self consists in its determinability by subject and object.

Determinate determinability is the totality we were looking for, and this is what we call a *substance*. No substance is possible as such, unless it has first proceeded from the absolutely posited, in this case the self, which posits *only itself;* that is, unless something is excluded therefrom, in this case a posited not-self, or an object. —But then substance, which as such is to be no more than determinability, albeit of a determinate, fixed and established kind, remains undetermined and is no substance (no *all*-comprehending thing), if it is not again determined by the absolutely posited, in this case by *self-positing.* The self *posits itself,* either as *positing itself* by exclusion of the not-self, or as *positing the not-self* by exclusion of itself. *Self-positing* appears twice over here; but in very different guises. The first designates an *unconditioned* positing; the second, a positing *conditioned* and determinable by an exclusion of the not-self.

(If the determination of the iron as such be *fixity of position,* then change of position is excluded thereby; and to that extent the iron is *not substance,* for it is *not determinable.* But now change of position is to be attributed to the iron. This is not possible on the supposition that fixity of position should be wholly eliminated thereby, for then the iron itself, as posited, would be eliminated as well; and then change of position would not be attributed to the iron, which is in contradiction to what we proposed. Hence fixity can only be abolished in part, and the change of position is determined and bounded by the fixity; that is, the change only takes place within the sphere of a certain condition (say, the presence of a magnet), and does not occur outside this sphere. Beyond it, fixity again continues to prevail. —Can anyone fail to see that in this case fixity presents itself in two very different interpretations, in the first instance as *unconditioned,* and in the second as *conditioned by the absence of a magnet?*).

To proceed with our application of the principle set forth above—just as A + B is determined by A, so B too is determined, for it falls within the scope of the determinable now determined; and A itself, as has just been shown, is now a determinable. Now to the extent that B itself is determined, A + B can also be determined thereby, and an absolute relation established—since it alone can fill out the desired totality, it *must* be determined thereby. *Hence,* if A + B is posited, and to that extent A is set within the sphere of the determinable, A + B *is determined in return by B.*

This proposition will at once become clear if we apply it to the case before us. —The self is to exclude something from itself; this is the action hitherto regarded as the first element in the entire interplay currently under investigation. I further infer—and being here in the realm of grounds, I have the right to do so—that if the self is to exclude that something from itself, then it must be in the self prior to its exclusion, that is, be posited *independently* of the exclusion; hence, since we can propose no higher ground, it is posited absolutely. If we proceed from this point, then *the excluding on the part of the self* is something not posited in the absolutely posited, insofar as it is such, and must be excluded from the latter's sphere; it is not intrinsic thereto. (Given that the object is simply posited in the self (for possible exclusion) in a manner quite incomprehensible to us, and to that extent must at all events be an object, it is *contingent* thereto that it *be excluded,* and—as will subsequently appear—that it be *presented* in consequence of this exclusion.

I, 202

I, 203

In itself, that is, not outside but in the self, it would be present without this exclusion. The object in general (here B) is the determinate: the fact of exclusion by the subject (here B + A) is the determinable. The object can be excluded or not, as the case may be, and still remains in the above sense an object. —Here the positing of the object occurs twice over; but anyone can see in what different senses: once *unconditioned* and absolutely; and once *conditionally upon an exclusion on the part of the self*).

(Motion is to be excluded from the iron posited as stationary. In terms of its concept, motion was not posited in the iron, and is now to be excluded therefrom; hence it must be posited independently of this exclusion, and posited, indeed, absolutely, in virtue of not having been posited through the iron itself. [To restate this more comprehensibly, if with some loss of rigor: If the motion is to be opposed to the iron, it must already be *known* to us. But it cannot be known *by way of the iron.* Hence it is known from some *other* quarter; and since we are here taking no account of anything whatever except iron and motion—it must be known absolutely.] If we proceed from *this* conception of motion, it is contingent thereto that it should also attach, among other things, to the iron. *It* is of the essence, and *the iron,* for it, is the contingent thing. It is the motion that is posited absolutely. The iron is excluded from its sphere, as fixed in its own place. Now the fixity is eliminated, and motion is attributed to the iron. —Here the concept of motion occurs twice over: once unconditionally, and the second time as conditioned by the removal of fixity in the iron).

Hence—and this was the synthetic proposition set forth above
I, 204 —the totality consists simply in the complete relation, and there is nothing else of an intrinsically stable kind that determines this. The totality consists in the completeness of a *relationship,* but not of a *reality.*

(The terms of the relationship, taken individually, are the *accidents,* while their totality is *substance,* as already observed above. —Here it merely needs stating expressly, for those who cannot draw so simple a conclusion on their own, that in substance we are not to think of anything fixed at all, but simply of an interplay. —If a substance is to be *determined*—a topic already discussed at length—or if something *determinate is to be considered as a substance,* then certainly the interplay must proceed *from one of the components,* which is *to that extent* fixed, insofar as the interplay is to be determined. But it is not fixed *absolutely;* for I can equally well set out from the opposing term; and then the very component that was previously established, fixed, essential—becomes contingent; as is evident from the examples given above. The accidents, synthetically united, yield the substance; and the latter contains nothing whatsover beyond the accidents: the substance, on analysis, yields the accidents, and after a complete analysis, there remains nothing at all of substance beyond the accidents. We must not think of an enduring substratum, or of some sort of bearer of accidents; any accident you care to choose is in every case the bearer of *its own* and *the opposing* accident, without the need of any special bearer for the purpose. —The positing self, through the most wondrous of its powers, which we shall examine more closely in due course, holds fast the perishing accident long enough to compare it with that which supplants it. This power it is—almost always misunderstood—which from inveterate opposites knits together a unity; which intervenes between elements that would mutually abolish each other, and thereby preserves them both; it is that which alone makes possible life and consciousness, and consciousness, especially, as a progressive sequence in time; and all this it does simply by carrying forward, in and by itself, accidents which have no *common* bearer, and *could* have none, since they would mutually destroy each other).

I, 205

γ) The activity, as synthetic unity, and the interplay, as synthetic unity, are to mutually determine one another, and themselves form a synthetic unity.

The activity, as synthetic unity, is most briefly described *as an absolute conjoining and holding fast of opposites,* a subjective and an objective, *in the concept of determinability,* in which, however, they are also opposed. (To elucidate and establish a higher and more comprehensive viewpoint, the synthesis here outlined should be compared with the above-effected unification (§ 3) of self and not-self in general by means of quantity. Just as there the self was first absolutely posited, in its *quality,* as an absolute reality, so here *something,* namely a *quantitatively* determined thing, is absolutely posited in the self; or, the self is absolutely posited, as *determinate quantity.* A subjective *something* is posited, as absolutely subjective; and this procedure is a *thesis,* and a quantitative thesis at that, in contrast to the qualitative thesis above. But all modes of action of the self must originate from a thetic procedure. [In the theoretical part of the Science of Knowledge, that is, and within the limits we have here prescribed for ourselves by our basic principle, it is a thesis, since we can proceed no further on account of that limitation; though once we break through these limits, it may appear that it

is equally a synthesis to be derived from the highest thesis.] Just as, previously, a not-self was opposed to the self in general, as an opposite *quality,* so here, an objective is opposed to the subjective, by the mere exclusion of the former from the sphere of the subjective, and thus simply by and by means of *quantity* (of limitation or determination); and this procedure is a quantitative antithesis, just as the earlier procedure was a qualitative one. But now the subjective is neither to be destroyed by the objective, nor the objective by the subjective, any more than the self in general was formerly to be annulled by the not-self, or *vice versa;* both, on the contrary, are to subsist alongside each other. Hence they must be synthetically united, and are so by the third thing, in respect of which they are both alike, namely determinability. Both of them—not subject and object as such, but the subjective and objective posited through thesis and antithesis—are mutually determinable by each other, and, merely to the extent that they are so, can be brought together and fixed and held fast by that power of the self (imagination) which is active in the synthesis.   —Yet, just as before, the antithesis is impossible without a thesis, since only to the posited can there be a counterpositing; and not only so, but the thesis here required is impossible, as to its matter, without the matter of the antithesis; for before a thing can be absolutely determined, *i.e.,* the concept of quantity applied to it, it must be present in respect of its quality. Hence something must in general be present, wherein the active self traces out a boundary for the subjective, and consigns the remainder to the objective.   —In form, however—just as before—the antithesis is impossible without the synthesis; for otherwise the posited would be abolished by the antithesis, so that the latter would be no antithesis, but itself a thesis; thus all three actions are but one and the same action; and only in reflection upon them can the individual constituents of this one action be distinguished).

As to the mere interplay—if its form, the mutual exclusion of the components, and its matter, the embracing sphere in which both, as excluding each other, are contained, are synthetically united, then the mutual exclusion is itself the embracing sphere, and the embracing sphere is itself the mutual exclusion; the interplay, that is, consists in the mere relation; nothing at all is present beyond the mutual exclusion, the determinability just referred to.   —It is easy to see that this must be the synthetic intermediary, but, given a mere determinability, a mere relation without anything to relate (here and throughout the theoretical part of the Science of Knowledge we have utterly to abstract from this thing), it is rather harder to imagine anything that would not be an absolute nullity. Let us guide the imagination as best we can.   —A and B (it is already known that A + B is actually determined by A, and shown thereby that the same A + B is determined by B, but for our purpose we can neglect this and simply call them A and B); A and B, then, are opposed, and if the one is posited, the other cannot be: and yet they have to stand together, and that not merely *in part*, as has hitherto been required, but *in toto*, and *as* opposed, without mutually abolishing each other; and the problem is, to conceive of this. But they can be thought of together in no sort of fashion, and under no possible predicate, save merely *insofar as they mutually destroy each other*. We are not to think of A, and not to think of B; but the *clash*—the *incursion* of each upon the other is what we are to think of, and this alone is the point of union between them.

(At the physical point X, posit light at instant A, and darkness at the immediately subsequent instant B: light and darkness are thereby sharply distinguished, as they should be. But instants A and B immediately bound one another, and there is no interval between them. Picture to yourself the sharp boundary between the two instants = Z. What is there at Z? Not light, for that is at instant A, and Z is not identical with A; and not darkness either, for that is at instant B. So it is neither of the two.   —But I might equally well say that both are present, for if there is no interval between A and B, there is none between light and darkness either, and so both are in immediate contact at Z.   —It might be said that in this latter argument Z itself, which was to be only a boundary, is extended into an instant by my own imagination; and *so in fact it is.* [The instants A and B have themselves arisen no otherwise than through such extension by means of the imagination]. So by mere imagination I *can* extend Z; and *must* do so, if I wish to conceive of the immediate bounding of instants A and B.   —And here at once we have begun an experiment with the wonderful power of productive imagination in ourselves, which will shortly be explained, without which nothing at all in the human mind is capable of explanation— and on which the entire mechanism of that mind may very well be based).

a)   That the above-explained activity determines the interplay already discussed, is to say that the clash of the components, as such, is conditioned by an absolute activity of the self, whereby it opposes an objective and a subjective, and unites them both. Only in the self, and by virtue of this act of the self, do they become components; only in the self, and by virtue of this its act, do they come together.

I, 209   It will be evident that the principle established is an idealist one. If the proposed activity be taken as exhausting the nature of the self, so far as it is an intelligence—as it must indeed be taken, albeit with certain limitations—then presentation consists in the fact that the self posits a subjective and counterposits another thing thereto as an objective, and so on; and thus we see the beginning to a series of presentations in empirical consciousness. We earlier proposed a law of the mediacy of positing, whereby—as also holds good in the present case—no objective could be posited without elimination of a subjective, and no subjective without elimination of an objective; and from this it would then have been possible to explain the interplay of presentations. Here we add the determination, that both are synthetically united, that both are to be posited through one and the same act of the self; and from this we may then explain the unity of that wherein the interplay consists, when the components are in opposition, which the law of mere mediacy was not able to do. And hence we should obtain an intelligence, with all its possible determinations, simply and solely through absolute spontaneity. The self would be constituted *as* it so posited, as it posited itself, and *because* it posited itself as so constituted.   —But however far back we go in the series, we must still eventually arrive at a situation already present in the self, in which one thing is determined as subjective, and another opposed to it as objective. The presence of what is to be subjective could indeed be explained by the self's own absolute positing of itself, but not the presence of what is to be objective; for that is something not posited in the absolute positing of the self. —So the proposed principle is not a full explanation of what needs to be explained.

I, 210   b)   That the interplay determines the activity, is to say that the opposing and conjoining through the self's activity becomes possible, not indeed through the actual presence of opposites, but—as just explained—through their mere clash or self-contact in consciousness: the encounter is the condition of the activity. It is merely a matter of understanding this correctly.

Against the proposed idealist mode of explanation it was immediately pointed out, that if something is to be determined as a subjective within the self, and something else by that determination to be excluded from its sphere as objective, then it needs to be explained how this latter element, that is to be excluded, could come to be present in the self; and this the former line of argument was unable to account for. Our present principle yields an answer to this objection, as follows: The objective to be excluded has no need at all to be present; all that is required—if I may so put it—is the presence of a check on the self, that is, for some reason that lies merely outside the self's activity, the subjective must be extensible no further. Such an impossibility of further extension would then delimit—the mere interplay we have described, or the mere incursion; it would not set bounds to the activity of the self; but would give it the task of setting bounds to itself. But all delimitation occurs through an opposite; hence the self, simply to do justice to this task, would have to oppose something objective to the subjective that calls for limitation, and then synthetically unite them both, as has just been shown; and thus the entire presentation could then be derived. It will at once be apparent that this mode of explanation is a realistic one; only it rests upon a realism far more abstract than any put forward earlier; for it presupposes neither a not-self

I, 211   present apart from the self, nor even a determination present within the self, but merely the requirement for a determination to be undertaken within it by the self as such, or the *mere determinability* of the self.

One might think for a moment that this task of determination was indeed itself a determination, and that the present train of argument was in no way different from the quantitative realism outlined above, in which the presence of a determination was presupposed. But it is very illuminating to set forth the difference between them. There, the determination was given; here, it is only to be accomplished through the spontaneity of the active self. (If we may be permitted to glance ahead a little, the distinction can be presented more precisely still. For it will appear in the practical part of our work, that the determinability here referred to is a feeling. Now a feeling is certainly a determination of the self, but not of the self as an intelligence, that is, of that self which posits itself as determined by the not-self; and yet that is all we are at present referring to. Hence this requirement for determination is not the determination itself).

Our present line of argument suffers from the error of all realism, namely that it regards the self merely as a not-self, and so fails to explain what required explaining, the transition from the not-self to the self. If we grant what is asked, then the determinability of the self, or the requirement that the self should be determined, is certainly posited, but without any assistance from the self; and from this we could certainly explain how the self *could be determinable* through and *for something external to itself* but not—though this latter was demanded—how it *could be determinable* through and *for the self* (how this need for determination could ever come to its knowledge, so that it should now knowingly determine itself thereby). The self is by nature determinable only insofar as it posits itself as determinable, and only so far can it determine itself; but how this may be possible, the proposed line of reasoning fails to explain.

I, 212   c) Both types of argument are to be synthetically united; the activity and the interplay must mutually determine each other.

We could not assume that the interplay, or a mere check occurring without any concurrence from the positing self, could impose on the self the task of self-limitation, since the ground of explanation did not include what was to be explained; hence it became necessary to suppose that this check did not occur without concurrence of the self, but took place, rather, in consequence of the latter's own activity in positing itself; that its outward-striving activity was, as it were, thrown back (or reflected) into itself, from which the self-limitation, and thence every thing else that was called for, would then very naturally follow.

By this the interplay and the activity would then really be mutually determined and synthetically united, as the course of our investigation has required. The check (unposited by the positing self) occurs to the self insofar as it is active, and is thus only a check insofar as there is activity in the self; its possibility is conditional upon the self's activity: no activity of the self, no check. Conversely, the activity of the self's own self-determining would be conditioned by the check: no check, no self-determination.—Moreover, no self-determination, no objective, etc.

We now seek further light upon the very important and terminal result that we have here arrived at. The activity (of the self) in conjoining opposites, and the clash of these opposites (as such, and apart from the self's activity), are to be united and become one and the same.   —The main difference lies between the *conjoining* and the *clashing;* so we shall penetrate most deeply into the spirit of the proposed principle if we meditate upon the possibility of uniting these two.

I, 213   That the clash, as such, is and must be conditional upon a conjoining, is easy enough to see. The opposites, as such, are completely opposed; they have nothing whatever in common; if one is posited the other cannot be: they clash only insofar as the boundary between them is posited, and this boundary is posited by the positing neither of the one nor of the other; it must be posited on its own. —But the boundary is then nothing other than what is common to both; and to posit their boundaries—is to bring them together, though this conjunction of the two is likewise possible only through the positing of their bounds. They clash only if they are conjoined, for and through what brings them together.

The conjoining, or, as we can now more definitely call it, the positing of a boundary, is conditional upon a clash; or, since (in virtue of the above) what is active in bounding must itself, and simply *as* active, be one of the parties to the encounter, it is conditional upon a check to its activity. This is possible only if the activity in question, in and by itself, and left to its own devices, reaches out into the unbounded, the indeterminate and the indeterminable, that is, into the infinite. If it did not extend to infinity, it would follow not at all from a bounding thereof, that a check to its activity would have occurred; it could well be the boundary set by its own mere concept (as would have to be assumed in a system, wherein a finite self was absolutely postulated). In that case, there might well be new boundaries, within the limits set to it by its own concept, from which a check from without could be inferred; and this would have to be determined from elsewhere. But from bounding in general, as deduction is here to be made from it, no such conclusion could be drawn.

I, 214   [The opposites here referred to must be absolutely opposed; there must be no point of union whatever between them. No finite things, however, are absolutely opposed to each other; they are alike in respect of determinability; they are determinable throughout by one another. That is the common characteristic of every finite thing. And so too is every infinite thing (so far as there can be more than one) alike in respect of indeterminability. Hence there are no things whatever that are flatly opposed and alike in no respect at all, save the finite and the infinite, and these must therefore be the opposites that are alluded to here.]

Both are to be one and the same; this signifies, in brief: *no infinity, no bounding; no bounding, no infinity; infinity and bounding are united in one and the same synthetic component.* —If the self's activity did not extend into the infinite, it could not itself set limits to this activity; it could posit no bounds thereto, though this it is obliged to do. The activity of the self consists in unbounded self-assertion: to this there occurs a resistance. If it yielded to this obstacle, then the activity lying beyond the bounds of resistance would be utterly abolished and destroyed; to that extent the self would not posit at all. But for all that, it must also posit beyond this line. It must limit itself, that is, it must posit itself to that extent as not positing itself; it must set the indeterminate, unbounded, infinite limit ($= B$ above) within this sphere; and if it is to do this, it must be infinite. —Moreover, if the self did not bound itself, it would not be infinite. —The self is only what it posits itself to be. That it is infinite, is to say that it posits itself as infinite; it *determines* itself by the predicate of infinitude: hence it bounds itself (the self) as substratum of in-

finitude; it differentiates itself from its infinite activity (both of which, as such, are one and the same); and so it was obliged to behave, if the self was to be infinite.   —This infinitely outreaching activity that it differentiates from itself must be *its* activity; must be attributed to itself: so that simultaneously, in one and the same undivided and indistinguishable act, the self must again receive this activity into itself (determine A + B by A). But in thus being received, the activity is determined, and so not infinite; yet it must be infinite, and so must be posited outside the self.

This interplay of the self, in and with itself, whereby it posits itself at once as finite and infinite—an interplay that consists, as it were, in self-conflict, and is self-reproducing, in that the self endeavors to unite the irreconcilable, now attempting to receive the infinite in the form of the finite, now, baffled, positing it again outside the latter, and in that very moment seeking once more to entertain it under the form of finitude—this is the power of *imagination*.

But by this the clash and the conjuncture are now perfectly united. The clash, or boundary, is itself a product of the apprehending self, in and for purposes of apprehension (absolute thesis of imagination, which is to that extent absolutely productive). Insofar as the self and this product of its activity are opposed, the clashing elements are themselves opposed, and at the boundary neither of them is posited (antithesis of imagination). But insofar as both are again united—the productive activity in question is to be attributed to the self—the bounding elements are themselves brought together in the boundary. (Synthesis of imagination; which in these its antithetic and synthetic capacities is reproductive—all of which we shall perceive more clearly in due course.)

The opposites are to be conjoined in the concept of mere *determinability* (not that of determination). This was a major point in the required unification, and on this too we need to reflect; by which reflection the foregoing observations will be rendered perfectly determinate and clear. For if the boundary posited between the opponents (of which one is itself the counterpositor, whereas the other lies intrinsically quite outside consciousness, and is posited merely for purposes of the bounding required), is posited as a stable, fixed, unchangeable boundary, then both are united by *determination,* but not by *determinability:* but then, too, the totality required in the interplay of substantiality would not be completed (A + B would be determined merely by the determinate A, and not simultaneously by the indeterminate B). Hence the boundary in question must not be taken as a fixed one. And nor indeed it is, according to the account just given of the power of imagination active in this bounding process. In order to determine the subject, it posits an infinite boundary, as product of its endlessly outreaching activity. It attempts to ascribe this activity to itself (to determine A + B by A), yet were it actually to do so, it would no longer be *this* activity, but, as posited in a determinate subject, would be itself determined, and so not infinite; the imagination is thus thrown back, as if into infinity (it is left to determine A + B by B). Hence all that we have is determinability, the hereby unattainable idea of determination, but not determination itself.   —The imagination posits no sort of fixed boundary; for it has no fixed standpoint of its own; reason alone posits anything fixed, in that it first gives fixity to imagination itself. Imagination is a faculty that wavers in the middle between determination and nondetermination, between finite and infinite; and hence it does indeed determine A + B, *both* through the determinate A, and *also* through the indeterminate B, which is that very synthesis of imagination of which we were speaking just now.   —This wavering is characteristic of imagination even in its product; in the course of its wavering, so to speak, and by means thereof it brings the latter to birth.

I, 217

[It is this wavering of imagination between irreconcilables, this conflict with itself, which—as will later appear—extends the condition of the self therein to a moment of *time:* (For reason pure and simple, everything is simultaneous; only for imagination is there such a thing as time). The imagination does not sustain this long— no longer, that is, than a moment (except in the feeling of the sublime, where there comes upon us an *amazement,* a suspension of the interplay in time); reason enters the scene (whereby a reflection ensues) and determines imagination to receive B into the determinate A (the subject): but now the A posited as determinate must again be bounded by an infinite B, and imagination proceeds with this, precisely as above; and so it goes on, to the point where the (here theoretical) reason is completely determined by itself, where no limiting B other than reason is needed in the imagination, to the point, that is, *where the presenting self is presented.* In the practical sphere, imagination goes on into the infinite, to the absolutely indeterminable idea of the highest unity, that would be possible only after a completed infinity, which is itself impossible.]

—————

I, 218

1.   Without infinitude of the self—without an absolute productive power thereof, extending into the unlimited and the illimitable, we cannot even account for the possibility of presentation. From the postulate that a presentation must exist, which is contained in the principle: the self posits itself as determined by the not-self, this absolute power of production is hereafter synthetically derived and demonstrated. But we may notice beforehand, that in the practical part of our science, this power will be traced back to a still higher source.

2.   All the difficulties that obstructed our path have been satisfactorily overcome. The task was that of uniting the opposites, self and not-self. By the power of imagination, which reconciles contradictions, they can be perfectly united.   —The not-self is itself a product of the self-determining self, and nothing at all absolute, or posited outside the self. A self that posits itself *as* self-positing, or a *subject,* is impossible without an object brought forth in the manner described (the determination of the self, its reflection upon itself as a determinate, is possible only on the condition that it bounds itself by an opposite).   —As to the question, how and by what means there occurs that check to the self that is prerequisite for explaining presentation, this alone is not to be answered here: for it lies beyond the bounds of the theoretical part of the Science of Knowledge.

3.   The principle set at the head of the entire theoretical Science of Knowledge: *the self posits itself as determined by the not-self*— is completely exhausted, and all the contradictions it harbored have been overcome. The self cannot posit itself otherwise than as determined by the not-self (no object, no subject). To that extent it posits itself as determined. At the same time it posits itself also as

determinant; for the limiting factor in the not-self is its own product (no subject, no object).   —Not only is the required reciprocity *possible;* what was demanded by the postulate we established is also quite unthinkable without such a reciprocity. What held good before in purely problematic fashion now has an apodictic certainty.   —It is thereby proved, moreover, at the same time, that the theoretical part of the Science of Knowledge is wholly completed; for every science is completed when its basic principle is exhausted; but the principle is exhausted when in the course of inquiry we eventually return to the same.

I, 219

4.   If the theoretical part of the Science of Knowledge is exhausted, then all the elements necessary to explain presentation must have been grounded and established; and from now on we thus have to do no more than apply and connect what has been proved so far.

But before embarking on this course, it is worthwhile, and of much consequence for complete understanding of the entire Science of Knowledge, that we reflect upon the course itself.

5.   Our task was to investigate whether, and under what determinations, it was possible to entertain the problematically established principle: the self posits itself as determined by the not-self. We have attempted this under all possible determinations thereof, as exhaustively enumerated through a systematic deduction; by setting aside the illicit and unthinkable, we have confined the thinkable to an ever more restricted circle, and so step by step have approached ever nearer to the truth, till we finally discovered the only possible way of conceiving what we are obliged to conceive. If now this principle is true in general, that is, without the special determinations it has now acquired—that it is so, is a postulate resting on the supreme principles—if, in virtue of the present deduction, it is true in this *one* way only: then what we have established is at the same time *a primordial fact occurring in our mind.*   —Let me make myself clearer. All the possibilities of thought established in the course of our inquiry, which we thought to ourselves, which we thought to ourselves with consciousness of our thinking thereupon, were also facts of our consciousness, insofar as we were engaged in philosophizing; but they were facts *artificially* brought forth according to the rules of reflection, through the spontaneity of our reflective powers. The present possibility of thought, which alone remains

I, 220

standing after excision of everything proved false, is also, in the first place, a fact of this kind, artificially engendered through the spontaneity of philosophizing; it is so, inasmuch as it has been elevated by reflection into the consciousness (of the philosopher); or, more properly, the *consciousness* of this fact is a fact engendered by artifice. But now the principle set at the head of our inquiry is supposed to be true, that is, there must be something in our mind that corresponds to it; and it must be capable of truth only in the *one* way established, so that there must be something originally present in our mind, independently of our reflection, that corresponds to our thought of this one way; and in this higher sense of the word I call the thought in question a fact, as the other proposed thought-possibilities are not. (For example, the realist hypothesis, that the material of presentation might be given to us somehow from without, admittedly made its appearance in the course of our investigation; we were obliged to think it, and the thought thereof was a fact of the reflective consciousness; but on closer examination we found that such a hypothesis would contradict the principle proposed, since that to which a material was given from without would be no self at all, as it was required to be, but a not-self; so that such a thought could have nothing external corresponding to it, but was completely empty, and, as the thought of a transcendent but not transcendental system, was therefore doomed to rejection).

It should also be noted in passing that, in a Science of Knowledge, facts are admittedly established, whereby the system distinguishes itself from all empty rote philosophy, as the system of a real process of thought; yet that we are not allowed therein simply to postulate something as a fact, but have to offer proof *that* it is a fact, as has been done in the present case. Appeal to facts lying within the scope of ordinary consciousness, unguided by philosophic reflection, produces nothing—if we are only consistent, and do not have the results to be extracted already lying before us—save a deceptive popular philosophy, which is no philosophy at all. But if the facts alleged lie beyond this compass, then we certainly need to know how the conviction was arrived at, that they are indeed present as facts; and we certainly need to be able to impart this conviction, and such imparting of conviction is assuredly proof *that* the facts in question are facts.

I, 221

6. To all expectation, this fact must have consequences within our consciousness. If it is to be a fact within the consciousness of a *self*, then, to start with, the self must posit it *as* present in its consciousness; and since this should have its difficulties, and be possible only in a certain fashion, we shall perhaps be able to indicate the manner in which this positing takes place. —To put the matter more plainly—the self must explain this fact to itself, but can account for it no otherwise than by the laws of its own nature, which are the same laws whereby our reflections hitherto have also been conducted. This manner the self has, of processing this fact within itself, of modifying and determining it, and conducting all its business therewith, is from now on the object of our philosophic reflection. —It will be evident that from this point on our whole reflection stands on a completely different level, and has an entirely new significance.

7. The preceding chain of reflections, and those to come, are to be distinguished, firstly, in terms of their object. So far we have been considering possibilities of thought. It was the spontaneity of the human mind which brought forth, not only the object of reflection—those very possibilities of thought, though according to the rules of an exhaustive, synthetic system—but also the form of reflection, the act of reflecting itself. It turned out that what the mind reflected on, though containing something real in itself, was mixed with empty dross which had gradually to be separated out, till all that remained was the truth adequate to our purposes, which are those of the theoretical Science of Knowledge. —In the future course of our reflection we shall meditate upon facts; the object of this reflection is itself a reflection; namely the reflection of the human mind upon the datum pointed out therein (which admittedly can only be called a datum *qua* object of this mental reflection upon it, for apart from that it is a fact). Hence, in our future meditations, the object of reflection will not first be *brought forth* by that same reflection, but simply elevated *into consciousness*. —It follows at once that from now on we shall no longer be concerned with mere hypotheses, in which the modicum of true content must first be separated from the empty dross; but that everything established henceforward is fully entitled to be credited with reality. —The Science of Knowledge is to be a pragmatic history of the human

I, 222

mind. Till now we have been endeavoring only to gain an entry therein; to succeed in bringing forward a single undoubted fact. We are in possession of this fact; and from now on our perception—not blind, to be sure, but nonetheless given to experiment—can calmly follow the course of events.

8. The two trains of reflection are different also in the direction they take. —Let us first abstract entirely from the artificial reflection of the philosopher, and simply stay with the original necessary reflection which the human mind must engage in about this fact (and which from now on will be the object of a higher philosophic reflection). It will be evident that such a mind can reflect upon the given fact by no other laws than those whereby it was discovered; and thus by the very same laws that have governed our reflections up to this point. The reflection set out from the principle: the self posits itself as determined by the not-self, and pursued its course to the fact; the present reflection, which is natural and to be regarded as a necessary fact, sets out from the fact, and since the application of the proposed principle cannot be decided until that principle has itself been confirmed as a fact (until the self posits itself *as* positing itself to be determined by the not-self), it is obliged to proceed towards the principle. It thereby pursues the entire course described by the former line of reflection, but *in the reverse direction;* and philosophic reflection, which can only follow it, but can give it no law, necessarily takes the same path.

9. If reflection proceeds henceforward in the reverse direction, the fact put forward represents at the same time the point of return for philosophizing reflection; it is the point at which two entirely different trains of thought are united, and at which the end of the first joins on to the beginning of the second. Hence it must contain the ground of difference between the previous line of argument and that which is now to prevail. —Our procedure was synthetic, and remains so throughout: the fact in question is itself a synthesis. This synthesis initially unites two opposites from the first series, which would thus constitute the relationship of the synthesis to that series. —The same synthesis must now also contain two opposites for the second train of reflection, with a view to possible analysis and a synthesis resulting from that. Since there can be no more than two opposites united in this synthesis, the elements united therein

I, 223

as the end of the first series must be the same as those that have again to be separated for purposes of beginning a second. But if that is the whole situation, this second series is no new series at all; it is merely the first in reverse, and our procedure is a merely recapitulatory dissolution, which serves no purpose, furthers our understanding not at all, and fails to advance us a single step. Hence the components of the second series, insofar as they are so, must nonetheless differ in some respect from those of the first, even though they are the same; and this difference they can have acquired in one way alone, namely by means of the synthesis, and as it were in the process of going through it.   —It is worth the trouble, and sets in the clearest light the most important and characteristic point of our system, that we should gain a proper acquaintance with this difference between the opposed elements, insofar as they are members of the first or the second series.

10.   The opposites are in both cases a subjective and an objective; but *before* the synthesis, and *after* it, they figure very differently as such in the human mind. *Before* the synthesis, they are mere opposites and nothing more; the one is what the other is not, and the other is what the one is not; they betoken a mere relationship and that is all. They are something negative and in no sense positive (just as light and darkness were, in our earlier example, at the point Z, if the latter be viewed as a boundary merely *in thought*). They are a mere thought without any reality, and the thought of a mere relation at that.   —As one makes its appearance, the other is destroyed; but since this one can only appear under the predicate of counterpart of the other, so that along with its concept the concept of the other simultaneously enters and destroys it, even the first cannot make its appearance. So nothing at all is present, nor can it be; our consciousness is not occupied, and contains absolutely nothing whatever. (Admittedly, too, we could simply not have undertaken all our previous inquiries without a beneficent deception on the part of the imagination, which interposed a substrate unawares beneath these mere opposites; we ought not to have been able to entertain them, for they were nothing at all, and one cannot reflect about nothing. This deception could not have been obviated, nor should it have been; its product needed merely to be cast out and excluded from the sum of our deliberations, and this has now been

I, 224

I, 225

done.) *After* the synthesis, the opposites are something that can be grasped and retained in consciousness, and as it were occupies the same. (*For reflection,* and by the grace and favor thereof, they are what they also were before, indeed, but unawares and in the face of persistent objection from the same quarter.) Just as the light and darkness in Z above, as the boundary *extended to an instant by imagination,* were admittedly something that did not absolutely destroy itself.

This change occurs in them in the course, as it were, of their progress through the synthesis, and we need to show how and in what manner the synthesis can impart to them something that they did not have before. —It is the office of the synthesizing faculty to unite opposites, to *think* of them as one (for the demand is addressed initially, just as it always has been, to the power of thought). Now this it cannot do; yet the requirement is there; and hence there arises a conflict between the incapacity and the demand. The mind lingers in this conflict and wavers between the two—wavers between the requirement and the impossibility of carrying it out. And in this condition, but only therein, it lays hold on both at once, or, what comes to the same thing, makes them such that they can simultaneously be grasped and held firm; in touching them, and being repulsed, and touching them again, it gives them, in the *relation to itself,* a certain content and a certain extension (which will reveal itself in due course as a manifold in time and space). This condition is called the state of *intuition.* The power active therein has already been denominated earlier the productive imagination.

I, 226

11. We can see here how the very circumstance which threatened to destroy the possibility of a theory of human cognition becomes the sole condition under which such a theory can be established. We saw no prospect of ever being able to unite what was absolutely opposed; we now see that an account of the events in our mind would be simply out of the question without absolute opposites; for the productive imagination, the power on which all these occurrences depend, would be utterly impossible, if absolute opposites, irreconcilables totally unfitted to the self's apprehension, did not enter the scene. And this then also provides illuminating evidence that our system is correct, and exhaustively accounts for what it was called on to explain. The presupposed item can be explained

only by the item discovered, and the discovered item only by what was presupposed. From the very fact af absolute opposition there follows the entire mechanism of the human mind; and this entire mechanism can be explained no otherwise than by the fact of absolute opposition.

12. We also get full light at this point on something already stated, but not yet wholly explained, namely how ideality and reality can be one and the same; how they differ only in the different manner of regarding them, and how the one can be inferred from the other. —Prior to synthesis, the absolute opposites (the finite subjective and the infinite objective) are merely creatures of thought and ideal things, as the term has throughout been employed here. Once they become due for unification through the power of thought, and yet cannot be united, the wavering of the mind, which in this capacity is called imagination, confers reality upon them, since they thereby become intuitable: that is, they acquire reality in general; for there

I, 227   is, and can be, no other reality save that derived through intuition. As soon as we abstract once more from this intuition, which one can certainly do in regard to the mere power of thought, though not for consciousness in general (cf. p. 201), this reality again becomes something merely ideal; it has a merely derived existence, in virtue of the laws of the faculty of presentation.

13. Our doctrine here is therefore that all reality—*for us* being understood, as it cannot be otherwise understood in a system of transcendental philosophy—is brought forth solely by the imagination. One of the greatest thinkers of our age, whose teaching, as I understand it, is the same, calls this a *deception* on the part of the imagination. But to every deception a truth must be opposed, and there must be a means of escaping it. Yet if it is now proved, as the present system claims to prove it, that this act of imagination forms the basis for the possibility of our consciousness, our life, our existence for ourselves, that is, our existence as selves, then it cannot be eliminated, unless we are to abstract from the self; which is a contradiction, since it is impossible that what does the abstracting should abstract from itself. Hence the act is not a deception, but gives us truth, and the only possible truth. To suppose that it deceived us would be to institute a scepticism that told us to doubt our own existence.

Deduction of Presentation

I.   Let us begin by taking a firm stand on the point we have arrived at.

The endlessly outreaching activity of the self, in which nothing can be distinguished, precisely because it reaches into infinity, is subjected to a check; and its activity, though by no means to be extinguished thereby, is reflected, driven inwards; it takes exactly the reverse direction.

Picture the infinitely outreaching activity as a straight line stretching from A through B to C, etc. It might have been checked short of C, or beyond it; but let us suppose it to be checked precisely at C; and, by the foregoing, the ground of this lies, not in the self, but in the not-self.

Under the condition postulated, the direction of the self's activity from A to C is reflected from C to A.

But so long as it is to be only a self, no influence at all can be exerted on it, without reaction on its own part. Nothing in the self can be abolished, so the direction of its activity cannot be either. Hence the activity reflected towards A, *insofar as it is reflected,* must *simultaneously* react towards C.

And thus we obtain between A and C a twofold direction of the self's activity, at variance with itself, wherein the direction from C to A may be regarded as a passivity, and that from A to C as an activity; both being one and the same state of the self.

This state, in which totally opposed directions are united, is simply the activity of imagination: and we now have in perfectly determinate form what we were looking for above, an activity possible only through a passivity, and a passivity possible only through an activity.   —The activity of the self lying between A and C is a *resistant* activity, but such a thing is impossible unless its activity undergoes reflection; for all resistance presupposes something to which resistance is made: it is a passivity, insofar as the original direction of the self's activity is reflected: but no direction can be reflected which is not present as *this* direction, and moreover at every point of the same. Both directions, towards A and towards C, must simultaneously exist, and by the very fact that they do so, our problem above is resolved.

The state of the self, insofar as its activity lies between A and C, is a state of intuition; for intuition is an activity impossible without a passivity, and a passivity impossible without an activity. —Intuition is now determined, though only as such, for philosophic reflection; it remains completely indeterminate in regard to the subject, as an accident of the self; for in that case it would have to be distinguishable from other determinations of the self, which is not possible as yet. It is equally indeterminate in regard to the object, for in that case an intuited something would have to be distinguishable as such from something not intuited, which is likewise impossible so far.

(It is evident that the activity of the self, reexerted in its first original direction, also extends beyond C. But insofar as it goes beyond C, it is not resistant, since the check does not lie beyond C; and hence it is not an intuitive activity either. Thus intuition, and what is intuited, are bounded by C. The activity extending beyond C is not intuition, and its object is not intuited. What they both may be we shall see in due course. Here we are merely concerned to indicate that we are leaving aside something that we shall take up again later on.)

II.   The self is to intuit; now if the intuitant is to be really just a self, this is as much as to say that *the self is to posit itself as intuiting;* for nothing belongs to the self, save insofar as it attributes the same to itself.

That the self posits itself as intuiting, means, in the first place, that in intuition it posits itself as *active.* Whatever else may be meant will emerge of its own accord in the course of inquiry. Now insofar as it posits itself as active in intuition, it posits something opposite to itself which is not active therein, but passive.

I, 230   To guide us in this inquiry, we have only to recall what was said earlier concerning the interplay in the concept of substantiality. The two opposites, the activity and the passivity, are neither to destroy nor to eliminate one another; both are to subsist together, and each is merely to exclude the other.

It is evident that the intuitant, as the active factor, must have something intuited in opposition to it. The question is merely as to how, and in what manner, such an intuited item may be posited.

An intuited item, to be opposed to the self insofar as the latter is intuitive, is necessarily a not-self; and hence it follows in the first place, that an act of the self which posits such an intuited item is *not a reflection,* not an inward-directed but an outward-directed activity, and thus, so far as we can see at present, a production. The intuited, as such, is produced.

It is also apparent that the self cannot be conscious of its activity in thus producing the intuited, as such, since the activity is not reflected or attributed to the self. (It is ascribed to the self only in the philosophic reflection which we are at present engaged in, and which must always be carefully distinguished from reflection of the common and necessary kind.)

The productive faculty is always the imagination; so this positing of the intuited occurs through imagination, and is itself an intuiting (an *ex*tuiting [in the active sense] of an indeterminate something).

Now this intuition is to be opposed to an activity in the intuition, which the self ascribes to itself. There must simultaneously be present in one and the same act an activity of intuiting which the self ascribes to itself by means of reflection, and another which it does not so ascribe. The latter is a mere intuiting; and so, too, should the former be; but it is to be reflected. The question is, how this comes about, and what happens as a result.

Qua activity, the intuiting is directed towards C, but is an intuiting solely insofar as it runs counter to the opposing tendency towards A. If it does not resist, it is no longer an intuiting, but an absolute activity.

Such an activity of intuiting is to be reflected, that is, the activity of the self tending towards C (which is always one and the same activity) is to be directed towards A, and that *as* resisting an opposing tendency (for otherwise it would not be *this* activity, the activity of intuiting).

The difficulty here is as follows: The activity of the self has already been once reflected towards A by the check from outside, and now it again has to be reflected in the same direction, and that by an absolute spontaneity (for the self must posit itself as intuiting, simply because it is a self). Now if these twin tendencies are not distinct, no intuition at all is reflected, there being a mere repetition of the intuiting in exactly the same manner; for the activity is

I, 231

the same: it is one and the same activity of the self; and it has the same direction, from C to A. So if the required reflection is to be possible, they must be distinguishable; and before we can go further, we have to solve the problem of how and whereby to distinguish them.

III. Let us define the problem more closely. Already, prior to investigation, we can see more or less how the first direction of the self's activity towards A can be distinguished from the second. For the first is reflected by a mere check from without, while the second occurs through absolute spontaneity. This we can now survey, indeed, from the level of philosophic reflection at which we have deliberately stationed ourselves from the outset of our inquiry; but our task is just that of presenting this fact (which the possibility of all philosophic reflection presupposes), as a primordial fact of natural consciousness. The question is, how the human mind originally comes to make this distinction between a reflection of activity from without, and another reflection from within. It is this distinction which has to be deduced as a fact, and, by that very deduction, demonstrated.

The self is to be determined by the predicate of being an *intuitant,* and thereby distinguished from what is intuited. This was the requirement we started from, nor could we proceed from any other. The self, as subject of intuition, must be opposed to the object thereof, and so distinguished *ab initio* from the not-self. In this inquiry we clearly have no fixed point, and are revolving endlessly in a circle, unless intuition, in itself and as such, is first stabilized. Only then can we determine how both self and not-self are related to it. The possibility of solving the problem posed above is therefore dependent on the possibility of stabilizing intuition as such.

This latter task is equivalent to the one just proposed, of rendering the first direction towards A distinguishable from the second; and either will provide the solution to the other. Once intuition itself is stabilized, the first reflection towards A is already contained in it; and now, without fear of confusion or mutual elimination, it is not only the first direction that can be reflected towards A, but intuition generally.

Intuition as such is to be stabilized, so that we can conceive it as one and the same. But intuition as such is in no way stable, consisting, rather, in a wavering of the imagination between conflicting directions. That it should be stabilized, is to say that imagination should waver no longer, with the result that intuition would be utterly abolished and destroyed. Yet this must not happen; so that in intuition there must at least remain the product of this state, a trace of the opposed directions, consisting of neither but containing something of both.

Such a stabilizing of intuition, which only becomes an intuition thereby, involves three factors. First, the act of stabilizing or fixating. This whole process occurs, for purposes of reflection, through *spontaneity,* and, as we shall soon see, through the very spontaneity of reflection itself; so the act of stabilizing belongs to the self's capacity for absolute positing, or to reason. —Next, the determinate or thing to be determined; —and this, of course, is the imagination, to whose activity a limit is to be set. —Finally, the outcome of the determination; —the product of imagination in its wavering. Clearly, if the required stabilization is to be possible, there must be a capacity for effecting this; and neither the determinant reason nor the productive imagination are capacities of this sort, so it must be an intermediate faculty between the two. It is the power whereby a transiency is *arrested, settled,* as it were, or brought to a stand, and is thus rightly termed *understanding.* —Understanding is such, simply insofar as something is stabilized therein; and everything stable is stabilized in the understanding. It might be described either as the imagination stabilized by reason, or as reason furnished with objects by the imagination. —Understanding is a dormant, inactive power of the mind, the mere receptacle of what imagination brings forth, and what reason determines or has yet to determine; whatever may have been told of its doings at one time or another.

[In understanding alone (albeit first through the power of imagination) does reality *exist;* it is the faculty of the *actual;* the ideal first becomes real therein: (hence, to *understand* also betokens a relation to something that certainly has to come from outside, without our assistance, but must throughout be merely indicated and intimated.) Imagination produces reality; but there *is* no reality therein; only through apprehension and conception in the understanding does its product become something real. —To that of which we are conscious as a product of imagination, we do not ascribe reality; yet we certainly do this to what we find contained in the understanding, to which we ascribe no power of production at all, but merely that of conservation. —We shall see that in natural reflection, as opposed to the artificial reflection of transcendental philosophy, we are able, in virtue of its laws, to go back only so far as the understanding, and then always encounter in this something *given* to reflection, as the material of presentation; but that we do not become conscious of the manner in which it arrived there. Hence our firm conviction of the reality of things outside us, and this without any contribution on our part, since we are unaware of the power that produces them. If we were conscious in ordinary reflection, as we can indeed become conscious in philosophical reflection, that they first arrive in understanding through the medium of imagination, we should again want to call the whole thing a deception, and would be no less mistaken in this case than we were in the previous one.]

IV.　We resume the thread of our discussion where we dropped it, because it was impossible to carry it further.

The self reflects that activity of its own which proceeds, in intuition, toward C. For reasons given above, this activity cannot be reflected as resisting an opposing tendency from C towards A. Yet nor can it be reflected as an activity extending generally outwards, for then it would be the whole unbounded activity of the self, which

I, 235　cannot be reflected, and not the activity operative in intuition, whose reflection is what we require. It must therefore be reflected as an activity extending to C, but as limited and determined there; which would be the first point.

At C, therefore, the intuitive activity of the self is bounded by the absolute activity operative in reflection. —Yet since this latter activity merely reflects, without being itself reflected (save in our present philosophical reflection), the limitation at C is posited counter to the self and attributed to the not-self. Into the infinite beyond C there is projected a determinate product of the absolutely productive imagination, by means of a dark, unreflected intuition that does not reach determinate consciousness; and this product sets limits to the power of reflected intuition, according to the very rule, and for the very reason, whereby the first indeterminate product was posited at all. This would be our second point. —The product in question is the not-self, by whose counter-positing for present purposes the self in general is first determined *as* a self, —which first makes possible the logical subject of the proposition: the self intuits.

At least in regard to its determination, the activity (thus determined) of the intuiting self is seized and fixated in understanding, with a view to further determination; for without this, contradictory activities of the self would come into collision and mutually destroy one another.

This activity proceeds from A to C, and in this direction is to be apprehended, but by a reflex activity of the self, proceeding, therefore, from C to A. —It will be evident that opposed directions are involved in this apprehension, and hence that it must take place through the power of what is opposed thereto, namely the imagination; and so must itself be an intuition. Which would be our third point. In its present function the imagination is not productive, but merely apprehends (for positing in understanding, not conservation therein) what has already been produced and seized upon in understanding; and is therefore called reproductive.

I, 236   The intuitant must be *determined,* and determined as such, that is, as active; an activity must be *opposed* to it, which is *not the same one,* but another. But activity is always activity, and nothing save its direction can so far be distinguished therein. Such an opposing direction is to be found, however, in the tendency from C to A, occasioned by reflection from without, and conserved in the understanding. Our fourth point.

Insofar as the content of intuition is to be determined thereby, this opposing tendency must itself be intuited; and hence, along with the determination of the intuitant, we also have an intuition, though not reflected, of the *intuited.*

But the intuited itself must be determined *as* an intuited, if it is to be opposed to the intuitant. And this is possible only through reflection. The only question is, which of the outgoing activities is to be reflected; for it must be an outgoing activity that is reflected, and yet the activity proceeding, in intuition, from A to C, yields the intuition of the intuitant.

We observed above, that for purposes of limiting intuition

generally at C, the productive activity of the self must go on beyond C into the indeterminate. This activity is reflected from infinity, through C, back to A. But from C to A there extends the first direction, whose traces are conserved in understanding; which resists the A-to-C activity proper to the self in intuition; and in relation to this must be appropriated to the self's opponent, namely the not-self. This opposed activity is intuited as opposed; which is our fifth point.

This intuited item must be determined as such, and, moreover, as an intuited opposed to the intuitant; by an unintuited, therefore, which is nonetheless a not-self. But a thing of this kind lies out beyond C as an absolute product of the self's activity (the thing in and for itself, as noumenon. Hence the natural distinction between presentation and the thing presented therein). Yet within C and A there lies the intuited, which according to its determination in understanding is apprehended as something real. Our sixth point.

I, 237

They are mutually related as activity and passivity (reality and negation), and hence are united through interdetermination. No intuited, no intuitant, and vice versa. Moreover, if and insofar as an intuited is posited, there is also a positing of an intuitant, and *vice versa.*

Both must be determined, for the self is to posit itself as the intuitant, and to that extent oppose itself to the not-self; but for this purpose it needs a firm ground of distinction between the intuitant and the intuited; yet interdetermination, as our previous discussions have shown, does not provide this.

Inasmuch as *one* of them is further determined, the *other* is likewise, simply because they stand in a relation of interdetermination. But for the same reason, one of the two must be determined *by itself,* and not by the other, since otherwise there is no exit from the circle of interdetermination.

V.   The intuitant as such, that is, as activity, is already determined by the fact that it stands in a relation of interdetermination; it is an activity to which there corresponds a passivity in its opponent, hence an *objective* activity. Any such activity is further determined by a non-objective, and thus *pure* activity, activity absolute and in general.

Both are opposed: both must also be synthetically united, that is, mutually determined by each other: 1)   The objective activity by the absolute activity. Activity in general is the condition of all objective activity; it is the real ground thereof. 2)   Activity in general is utterly indeterminable by objective activity, except by way of its opposite, passivity; hence, by way of an object of activity, and thus by objective activity. Objective activity is the ground of determination, or ideal ground, of activity in general. 3)   Both reciprocally determined by each other, that is, the boundary between them must be posited. This represents the transition from pure to objective activity, and *vice versa*; the *condition* we may reflect on, or from which we can abstract.

I, 238

This condition as such, that is, as boundary between pure and objective activity, is intuited through imagination as fixated in the understanding; both in the manner already described.

Intuition is objective activity under a certain *condition*. If unconditioned, it would not be objective, but pure activity.

In virtue of the determination through reciprocity, the intuited, too, is such only under a certain condition. Failing the condition, it would not be an intuited item, but an absolutely posited one, a thing-in-itself: an absolute passivity, as the counterpart of an absolute activity.

VI.   In relation, then, to the intuitant as to the intuited, intuition is a conditioned act. This feature is thus as yet incapable of distinguishing the intuitant from the intuited, and we now have to determine them further. We are seeking to determine the *condition* for intuition in each case; and whether they may perhaps be distinguished thereby.

That absolute activity becomes, under conditioning, an objective activity, obviously means that the absolute activity, as such, is eliminated and destroyed; and in respect to it there is a passivity present. Hence the condition of all objective activity is a passivity.

I, 239

This passivity must be intuited. But a passivity cannot be intuited save as an impossibility of the opposed activity; a feeling of being compelled to a specific act, of which feeling the imagination is certainly capable. This compulsion is stabilized in understanding as *necessity*.

The counterpart of this activity conditioned by a passivity is a free activity, intuited by imagination as a wavering of imagination itself between performance and nonperformance of one and the same act; between apprehension and nonapprehension of one and the same object in understanding; which is apprehended in the understanding as *possibility*.

Both types of activity, in themselves opposed, are to be synthetically united. 1) The compulsion is determined by freedom; the free activity determines itself to determinate action (self-affection); 2) The freedom is determined by compulsion. Only under the condition of an already present determination by a passivity, does the self-activity, still free in self-determination, determine itself to a determinate action. (Spontaneity can reflect only under the condition of a reflection already brought about by a check from without; but even under this condition it is not *obliged* to reflect). 3) Each determines the other in intuition. Interaction between the self-affection of the intuitant and an affection from without, is the condition for the intuitant to be an intuitant.

By this, then, the intuited is also simultaneously determined. The thing in and for itself is an object of intuition under a condition of reciprocal action. Insofar as the intuitant is active, the intuited is passive; and insofar as the intuited, which to that extent is a thing-in-itself, is active, the intuitant is passive. Moreover, insofar as the intuitant is active, it is not passive, and *vice versa;* and so with the intuited. But this yields no definite determination, and we do not thereby escape from the circle we were in. So we have to determine further. We must attempt, that is, to determine the share of one of the two components in the said interaction on its own account.

I, 240   VII.   The activity of the intuitant, which is paralleled by a passivity in the object, and is thus involved in the interaction, is contrasted to another activity having no corresponding passivity in the object; this latter activity (occurring in self-affection) therefore relates to the intuitant itself; and the first activity must be determined by this.

Such a determining activity must be intuited by imagination and fixated in the understanding, exactly as with the types of activity already referred to.

It is clear that even the objective activity of the intuitant can have no other ground than the activity of self-determination: so if this latter activity can be determined, the former would be also, and with it the intuitant's share in the interaction, and thereby also the share of the intuited.

The two types of activity must mutually determine each other: 1) That which *reverts into itself* must determine the *objective* activity, as has just been shown. 2) The objective must determine the self-reverting activity. However much objective activity there is, to that extent it determines itself to the determination of the object. But the objective activiy admits of being determined by determination of the object, and thence by that which occurs in self-determination. 3) Both are involved, therefore, in an inter-determination, as has now been shown; and again we have no fixed point of determination.

The activity of the intuited in the interplay, so far as it relates to the intuitant, is similarly determined by a self-reverting activity, whereby it determines itself to operate upon the intuitant.

By our earlier argument, the activity proper to self-determination is the determination, by reason, of an imaginative product fixated in the understanding: hence an act of *thought*. The intuitant determines itself to the *thinking* of an object.

I, 241   So far as the object is determined by thinking, it becomes an object of thought.

Now by this it is at once determined as *determining itself;* to an operation upon the intuitant. This determination has only become possible, however, in that a passivity has had to be determined in the intuitant opposed to it. No passivity in the intuitant, no original and self-reverting activity in the object, as thought-of activity. No such activity in the object, no passivity in the intuitant. But, on our previous showing, this type of interdetermination is that of *efficacy*. Hence the object is construed as the *cause* of a passivity in the intuitant, which is its *effect.*   —The inner activity of the object, whereby it determines itself to efficacy, is a mere matter of thought (a *noumenon,* if, through imagination, we provide a substrate for this activity, as we must).

VIII.   This activity of self-determination for purposes of determining a *determinate* object must be subject to further determination; for we still have no fixed point here. It is, however, determined by an activity of the intuitant, of a kind that determines no object as a determinate (= A); an activity directed to no determinate object (and hence, in effect, to an object in general, as mere object).

Such an activity would have to be capable of addressing itself to the object, by determination of itself as A or ∼A. Thus in respect of A or ∼A it would be wholly undetermined, or free; free to *reflect* on A, or to *abstract* therefrom.

Such an activity must first be intuited through imagination; but since it wavers inwardly in the middle between opposites, between the apprehension and non-apprehension of A, it must also be intuited *as* imagination, that is, in its freedom to waver from one to the other (as when one looks upon a *law*—of which here indeed we know nothing as yet—as a deliberation of the mind with itself). —But since, by this activity, one of the two, either A or ∼A, must be apprehended (A posited as something to be reflected on, or to be abstracted from), it must also to that extent be intuited as understanding. —These two, again united in a new intuition and stabilized in understanding, are called *judgment.* Judgment is the capacity, free till now, of reflecting upon objects already posited in understanding, or of abstracting from them, and, on the strength of this reflection or abstraction, of positing these objects more determinately in understanding.

I, 242

Both activities, mere understanding as such, and judgment as such, must again mutually determine one another. 1)   Understanding determines judgment. It already contains the objects that the latter reflects on or abstracts from, and is thus the condition for the possibility of a judgment generally. 2)   Judgment determines understanding. It determines for the latter the object in general as an object. Without it there is no reflecting at all; without it, therefore, there is nothing fixed in understanding, which is first posited through and for purposes of reflection, and so no understanding at all either; and thus judgment in turn is the condition for the possibility of understanding; and consequently 3)   Each *determines* the other. Nothing in understanding, no judgment; no judgment, nothing in understanding *for the understanding;* no thinking of what is thought, *as* such.

In virtue of the interdetermination, the object, too, is now determined thereby. What is thought, as object of thinking, and thus to that extent as passive, is determined by something *not* thought, and thus by a mere thinkable (which must have the ground of its thinkability in itself, and not in what thinks, and is thus to that extent active, while what thinks is passive in relation thereto). Both, the thing thought and the thinkable, are now mutually determined by each other: 1) Everything thought is thinkable; 2) Everything thinkable is thought of as thinkable, and is thinkable only to the extent that it is thought of as such. No thinkable, nothing thought of; nothing thought of, no thinkable. —The thinkable and thinkability as such are mere objects of the faculty of judgment.

Only what is judged to be thinkable can be thought of as a cause of intuition.

What thinks is to determine itself to think of something as thinkable, and to that extent the thinkable will be passive; but then again the thinkable is to determine itself to be a thinkable; and to that extent what thinks will be passive. This again yields an interaction of what thinks and what is thought in thinking; and thus we have no firm point of determination, and must determine what judges to a further extent still.

IX. The activity determinant of an object in general is determined by one which has no object at all, an intrinsically nonobjective activity, opposed to the objective one. The question, however, is how such an activity can be posited, and opposed to the objective activity.

Just as we have already deduced the possibility of abstracting from all *determinate* objects (= A), so here we postulate the possibility of abstracting from *all objects in general*. Such an absolute power of abstraction must exist, if the required determination is to be possible; and the latter must be possible, if self-consciousness and consciousness of presentation are to be possible.

A power of this sort would first have to be capable of being intuited.   —Imagination, by its own nature, wavers in general between object and non-object. That it should be pinned down to having no object would imply a total destruction of the (reflected) imagination, and this destruction or nonexistence of the imagination will itself be intuited by imagination (nonreflected, and thus not attaining to clear consciousness). (The obscure presentation occurring in us, when, for purposes of pure thought, we are bidden to abstract from all admixture of the imagination, is the intuition in question, familiar enough to those who think.)   —The product of such a (nonreflected) intuition has to be fixated in the understanding; but it is supposed to be nothing, no object at all, and so it cannot be fixated. (The obscure presentation of the thought of a mere relationship, without any terms, is something of the kind). So nothing remains beyond the mere rule of reason in general, telling us to abstract; the mere law of an unrealizable determination (through imagination, and for clear consciousness, through understanding); —and hence this absolute power of abstraction is simply *reason* itself. *(Pure* reason, in the theoretical sense, without imagination; the same power that Kant made the object of his investigation in the *Critique of Pure Reason.)*

I, 244

If everything objective is eliminated, we are left at least with what *determines itself,* and is *determined* by *itself,* the self or subject. Subject and object are so far determined by each other, that the one is absolutely excluded by the other. If the self determines itself merely, it determines nothing beyond itself, and if it determines something beyond itself, it does not determine merely itself. But the self is now determined as that which remains over, after all objects have been eliminated by the absolute power of abstraction; and the not-self as that from which abstraction can be made by this same abstractive power: and thus we now have a firm point of distinction between object and subject.

(This then is also, in fact, the manifest source of all self-consciousness, never again to be mistaken, now that it has been pointed out. Everything that I abstract from, everything I can think away (if not all at once, then at least by later abstracting what I now leave over, and then leaving over what I now abstract), is not my self, and I oppose it to my self merely by regarding it as something that I can think away. The more a determinate individual can think away of himself, the closer does his empirical self-consciousness approximate to a pure self-consciousness; —from the child who leaves his cradle for the first time, and thereby learns to distinguish it from himself, to the popular philosopher, who still accepts material idea-pictures, and searches for the seat of the soul, and thence to the transcendental philosopher, who at least entertains and abides by the rule of conceiving a pure self).

I, 245

X.   This activity, determining the self by abstraction of everything that can be abstracted from it, is itself in need of further determination. Since nothing further can be determined, however, in that *from* which nothing can be abstracted, and *in* which there is nothing to abstract from (hence the self is judged *simple)*, the activity will be determinable only by an absolutely nondeterminant activity—and that which it determines, by an absolute indeterminate.

To be sure, such a faculty of absolute indeterminacy, as the condition of everything determinate, has been shown by argument to belong to the imagination; but it cannot possibly be brought to consciousness as such, for then it would have to be reflected, and thus determined by understanding, and hence would be indeterminate and infinite no longer.

In self-determination, the self has been regarded just now as simultaneously determinant and determined. If, by means of the present higher determination, we reflect on the fact that what determines the absolutely determinate must itself be an absolute indeterminate; and moreover, that the self and not-self are absolutely opposed; then, given that the self is regarded as *determinate,* the indeterminate that determines it is the not-self; and given, on the contrary, that the self is regarded as *determinant,* it is itself the indeterminate, and what it determines is the not-self. And hence arises the following conflict:

If the self reflects upon itself, and thereby determines itself, the not-self is infinite and unbounded. If, on the other hand, the self reflects upon the not-self in general (upon the universe), and thereby determines it, it is itself infinite. In presentation, therefore, I, 246 self and not-self are reciprocally related; if the one is finite, the other is infinite, and *vice versa;* but one of the two is always infinite. —(Here lies the ground of the *antinomies* expounded by Kant.)

XI. If, at a still more elevated level of reflection, we reflect that the self is itself the absolute determinant and therefore also that which absolutely determines the foregoing reflection, on which the conflict depends; then the not-self in each case again becomes determined by the self, whether it be expressly determined for purposes of reflection, or whether it be left undetermined in reflection, so that the self may determine itself; and hence the self, insofar as it may be either finite or infinite, is reciprocally related merely to itself: a reciprocity in which it is perfectly united with itself, and beyond which no theoretical philosophy advances any further.

Part III

FOUNDATION OF KNOWLEDGE
OF THE PRACTICAL

§ 5. SECOND DISCOURSE.

In the proposition resulting from the three basic principles of the entire Science of Knowledge, namely, that *self and not-self mutually determine each other,* the following two were contained: first, that *the self posits itself as determined by the not-self;* this we have discussed, and have shown what fact in our mind must correspond thereto; and secondly, that *the self posits itself as determining the not-self.*

I, 247 At the outset of the previous section we could not tell, as yet, whether we should ever be able to endow this latter proposition with meaning, since it presupposed the *determinability,* and thus the *reality,* of the not-self, which we could still give no reason for assuming at that point. Now, however, by this postulated fact, and on the assumption thereof, we have simultaneously postulated the reality of a not-self—*for* the self, of course (seeing that the entire Science of Knowledge, as a transcendental science, neither can nor should go beyond the self)—and the particular difficulty which prevented us from assuming this second proposition is thus removed. If a not-self has reality for the self, and if (what comes to the same thing) the self posits it as real—a thing of which both the possibility and the mode and manner are now demonstrated—then, provided the other determinations of the proposition are thinkable (which admittedly we cannot yet tell at present), the self is also certainly able to posit itself as determining (restricting, limiting) this posited reality.

In discussing the said proposition, that the self posits itself as determining the not-self, it would be possible for us to proceed with it exactly as we did in discoursing upon its predecessor—that the self posits itself as determined by the not-self. The second, like the first, contains a number of opposites; these we could seek out, uniting them synthetically, again synthetically uniting the concepts arising from this synthesis, if they should once more turn out to be opposed, and so on; and we should be certain of completely exhausting our proposition according to a simple and basic method. There is, however, a shorter way of analyzing it, and no less exhaustive for that.

For within this proposition there lies a major antithesis, which spans the entire conflict between the self as intelligence, and to that extent restricted, and the self as an absolutely posited and thus unrestricted entity; and which compels us to adopt as a means of unification a practical capacity of the self. We shall first seek out this antithesis, and unite its opposing constituents. The remaining antitheses will then disclose themselves, and be all the more easily susceptible of unification.

I, 248

I

To discover this antithesis, we take the shortest way, whereupon, from a higher point of view, it will at once appear that we can accept the major principle of the whole practical Science of Knowledge, namely, that *the self posits itself as determining the not-self;* and that this principle acquires from the very outset a more than merely problematic validity.

The self in general is a self; in virtue of its own self-positing (§1), it is absolutely one and the same self.

Now more especially insofar as the self *presents,* or is an *intelligence,* it is, *as such,* certainly also one thing: a capacity for presentation under necessary laws; but to that extent it is by no means one and the same with the absolute, unconditionally self-posited self.

For the self *qua* intelligence, *insofar as it already is this,* is certainly self-determined in regard to its specific determinations within this sphere; to that extent also there is nothing in it save what it posits in itself, and our theory expressly rejects the view that anything occurs in the self to which the latter is related in a merely passive fashion. But *this sphere itself,* regarded in general and as such, is not posited for the self by the self, but by something outside it; the *mode* and *manner* of presentation in general is certainly determined by the self; but *that* the self should engage in presenting at all is determined, as we have seen, not by the self, but by something outside it. For we could in no way think of presentation in general as possible, save on the assumption of a check occurring to the infinitely and indeterminately outreaching activity of the self. Thus, as *intelligence in general,* the self is *dependent* on an undetermined and so far quite indeterminable not-self; and only through and by means of such a not-self does it come to be an intelligence.[1]

I, 249   But the self, in all its determinations, must be absolutely posited by itself, and must therefore be wholly independent of any possible not-self.

Hence the absolute self and the intelligent self (if we may put it as though they consisted of two selves, though they can only constitute one) are not one and the same, but are opposed to each other; which contradicts the absolute identity of the self.

This contradiction must be removed, and can be obviated only as follows: —The intelligence of the self in general, which causes the contradiction, cannot be eliminated without again throwing the self into a new contradiction with itself; for once a self is posited, and a not-self opposed to it, then by all the evidence of the theoretical Science of Knowledge, we have also posited a faculty of presentation, with all the determinations thereof. And insofar as it is already posited as an intelligence, the self, too, is determined solely by itself, as we noted just now, and have proved in the theoretical part. But the *dependence* of the self, *qua* intelligence, requires to be eliminated, and this is con-

---

[1]Should anyone scent a deep meaning and far-reaching consequences in this remark, he is a very welcome reader to me, and may go on peacefully drawing conclusions from it in his own fashion. —A finite being is finite only as an intelligence; the practical legislating, which he is to have in common with the infinite, can depend on nothing outside himself.

Those, too, who, from the scanty outlines of a completely new system, and one that is beyond them to survey, have acquired the facility of detecting —if nothing else, at least the smell of atheism, may halt meanwhile at this explanation, and see perhaps what they can make of it.

ceivable only on the assumption that *this hitherto unknown not-self* that is responsible for the check whereby the self becomes an intelligence, *should be determined on its own account by the self.* In this way the not-self to be presented would be *immediately* determined by the absolute self, while the presenting self would be determined *mediately*, by means of that determination; the self would be dependent solely on itself, that is, it would be self-determined throughout; it would be that as which it posits itself, and nothing more whatever, and the contradiction would be satisfactorily removed. And thereby we should have given a preliminary proof at least of the second half of our proposed major principle, that the self determines the not-self (namely, that the self is the determinant, and the not-self that which gets determined).

I, 250

The self, *qua* intelligence, stood in a causal relation to the not-self, to which the postulated check is to be ascribed; it was an effect of the not-self, as its cause. For the causal relation consists in this, that owing to a restriction of activity in the one (or to a quantity of passivity therein), a quantity of activity equal to that eliminated is posited in its opposite, according to the law of interdetermination. But if the self is to be an intelligence, then a part of its infinitely outreaching activity must be eliminated, and is thereupon posited according to the said law in the not-self. Since, however, the absolute self must be capable of no passivity whatever, and be absolute activity and nothing other than activity, we have had to assume, as just stated, that even this postulated not-self must be determined, and thus passive; and that the activity opposed to this passivity has to be posited in the opposite of the not-self, namely the self; and not indeed in the intelligent self, since this is itself determined by the not-self, but rather in the absolute self. But a relationship of the kind thus assumed is the causal relation. The absolute self must therefore be *cause* of the not-self, insofar as the latter is the ultimate ground of all presentation; and the not-self must to that extent be its *effect*.

1. The self is absolutely active, and merely active—that is our absolute presupposition. From this we have inferred in the first

place a passivity of the not-self, insofar as the latter is to determine the self *qua* intelligence; the activity opposed to this passivity is posited in the absolute self as a *determinate* activity, as the very activity whereby the not-self is determined. And hence, from the *absolute activity of the self,* we have inferred a certain *determinate activity* thereof.

I, 251

2. Everything just alluded to serves at the same time to render the foregoing argument more illuminating still. Presentation in general (if not the specific determinations thereof) is indisputably an effect of the not-self. But there can be absolutely nothing in the self that constitutes an effect; for the self is that which it posits itself to be, and there is nothing in it that it does not posit in itself. Hence the not-self in question must itself be an effect of the self, and of the absolute self at that: —and thus we should then have no operation at all on the self from without, but merely an exertion of the latter upon itself (which admittedly takes a roundabout route, the grounds of which are still unknown to us, though it will perhaps be possible to exhibit them later on).

The absolute self is thus to be cause of the not-self in and for itself, i.e., of that alone in the not-self which remains over when abstraction is made from all demonstrable forms of presentation; of that to which we ascribe the check imposed on the infinitely outreaching activity of the self: for in the theoretical Science of Knowledge it has been shown that, according to the necessary law of presentation, the specific determinations of the presented, *as* presented, are caused by the intelligent self.

The self cannot, however, be cause of the not-self in the same fashion, that is, by an absolute positing.

The self posits itself absolutely, and without any other ground, and *must* posit itself, if it is to posit anything else: for what does not *exist,* cannot posit; but the self exists (for the self) solely and absolutely through its own positing of itself.

The self cannot posit the not-self without restricting itself. For the not-self is completely opposed to the self; what the not-self is, the self is not; and thus insofar as the not-self is

I, 252   posited (or the predicate of 'being posited' is ascribed to it), the self is not posited. If, say, the not-self were posited without quantity, as infinite and unlimited, the self would not be posited at all and its reality would be utterly annihilated, which contradicts what was said above. —Hence it requires to be posited in a determinate quantity, and the reality of the self will be restricted by the amount of reality posited in the not-self. —The expressions *to posit a not-self* and *to restrict the self* are completely equivalent, as was shown in the theoretical Science of Knowledge.

Now according to our assumption, the self was to posit a not-self *absolutely* and without a ground of any kind, that is, it was to restrict itself, in part not posit itself, absolutely, and without any ground. Hence it would have to have the ground for its non-self-positing within itself; it would have to contain the principle of self-positing, and also that of non-self-positing. And thus the self would be essentially opposed to, and in conflict with, itself; it would contain a doubly opposed principle, which is itself a self-contradictory assumption, for then there would be no principle in it at all. The self would be nothing whatever, for it would eliminate itself.

Here we have reached a point from which we can set out more clearly than we ever could before the true meaning of our second basic principle: *a not-self is opposed to the self,* and by means of this the true significance of our whole Science of Knowledge.

In the second principle, only some part is absolute; part, on the contrary, presupposes a fact that cannot in any way be proved a priori, but only from the experience of a given individual.

In addition to the self-positing of the self, there is also to be another positing. A priori, this is a mere hypothesis; *that* such a positing occurs, can be demonstrated by nothing other than a fact of consciousness, and everyone must demonstrate it for himself by this fact; nobody can prove it to another on rational grounds. (He
I, 253 might indeed trace some admitted fact to this highest fact on grounds of reason; but such a proof would do no more than persuade the other that by admission of some such fact he had also conceded this highest fact). It is, however, absolutely and ultimately grounded in the nature of the self, that *if* such a

positing occurs, it must be an *opposition,* and the posited *a
not-self.* —How the self is able to distinguish something from
itself, can be deduced from no higher ground of possibility anywhere, for this distinction itself lies at the base of all derivation
and grounding. It is absolutely certain that every positing that is
not a positing of the self must be a counterpositing; that there is
such a positing, can be demonstrated by anyone only through his
own experience. Hence the argument of the Science of Knowledge
holds absolutely a priori; it establishes only such propositions as
are certain a priori; reality, however, it first obtains only through
experience. For anyone incapable of awareness of the postulated
fact—and we may know for certain that this will not be so for
any finite rational being—the entire Science would have no content—it would be empty to him; yet he would have to concede it
formal correctness.

And thus the Science of Knowledge is possible a priori,
whether or not it is to relate to objects. The object is not a priori,
but is first given to that science in experience; objective validity is
furnished to everyone by his own consciousness of the object,
which consciousness can only be postulated a priori, but not
deduced. —The following must serve merely as an illustration:
—For the deity, that is, for a consciousness in which everything
would be posited by the mere fact of the self having been posited
(though for us the concept of such a consciousness is unthinkable), our Science of Knowledge would have no content, since in
such a consciousness there could be no other positing whatever,
save that of the self; but even for God the science would have
formal correctness, since its form is the form of pure reason itself.

II

We have seen that the required causality of the self upon the
not-self, whereby we were to remove the contradiction disclosed
between the self's independence, as an absolute being, and its
dependence, as an intelligence, itself contains a contradiction. Yet
the first contradiction must be got rid of, and there is no other
way of doing it, save through the causality required; so we must

try to resolve the contradiction embodied in this very requirement, and to this second task we now proceed.

In order to accomplish it, let us first examine more closely
the true meaning of the contradiction in question.

The self *is to exert causality on the not-self,* and first bring
forth the latter for possible presentation by itself, because nothing
is attributable to the self which it does not posit in itself, either
mediately or immediately, and because it has to be absolutely
everything that it is by means of itself. —Hence the demand for
causality is based on the absolute essentiality of the self.

The self *can exert no causality on the not-self,* because the
not-self would then cease to be a not-self (to stand opposed to the
self) and would itself become the self. But it is the self that has
opposed the not-self to itself; and this opposition cannot therefore
be eliminated unless by eliminating something that the self has
posited, and thus by the self's ceasing to be a self, which contradicts the identity of the self. —Hence the contradiction confronting
the required causality is based on the fact that a not-self is, and
must remain, absolutely opposed to the self.

The conflict therefore lies between the self as such in its two
different aspects. It is these that contradict each other, and between them that an intermediary must be found. (In respect of a
self to which nothing was opposed—the unthinkable idea of deity
—a contradiction of this sort would simply not arise). Insofar
as the self is absolute, it is *infinite* and *unbounded.* Everything
that exists it posits; and what it does not posit, does not exist (*for*
it; and *apart from* it there is nothing). But everything it posits is
posited as self; and the self posits it as everything *that* it posits.
From this point of view, therefore, the self includes everything,
that is, an infinite, unbounded reality.

Insofar as the self opposes to itself a not-self, it necessarily
posits limits (§ 3), and itself within these limits. It apportions the
totality of posited being in general to the self and the not-self; and
to that extent thus necessarily posits itself as *finite.*

These two very different acts may be expressed in the following propositions. First: the self posits itself absolutely as *infinite* and unbounded. Second: the self posits itself absolutely as

1, 255

finite and *bounded*. And there would thus be a higher contradiction in the very nature of the self—as evidenced by its first and second acts—from which the present contradiction derives. Once the former is resolved, we also resolve the present contradiction, which depends on it.

All contradictions are reconciled by more accurate determination of the propositions at variance; and so too here. The self must have been posited as *infinite* in one sense, and as *finite* in another. If it were posited in one and the same sense as both infinite and finite, the contradiction would be insoluble; the self would be not one but two; and there would be no way out for us but Spinoza's method, of transposing the infinite outside us. And this would still leave unanswered the question (which Spinoza's dogmatism prevented him even from raising), how at least *the idea* of infinity should ever have been engendered in us.

In what sense, then, is the self posited as infinite, and in what sense as finite?

I, 256   The one attribute, like the other, is ascribed to it absolutely; the mere act of its positing is the ground both of an infinity and a finitude. Merely by positing something, it posits itself—in either case—in this something, and ascribes the latter to itself. Thus we have only to find a difference in the mere act of positing in these two cases, and our problem is solved.

So far as the self posits itself as infinite, its (positing) activity relates to the self as such, and nothing else but that. Its whole activity is directed to the self, and this activity engenders and encompasses all being. Hence the self is *infinite, insofar as its activity returns upon itself,* and thus its activity also is to that extent infinite, since its product, the self, is infinite. (Infinite product, infinite activity; infinite activity, infinite product; this is a circle, but not a vicious one, since it is the one that reason cannot escape from, expressing as it does what is certain absolutely through itself and on its own account. Product and activity and agency are here one and the same (§ 1), and we distinguish them only for purposes of self-expression). The *pure activity* of the self alone, and the *pure self alone,* are infinite. But pure activity is that which has no sort of object, but returns upon itself.

So far as the self posits limits, and itself within these limits, as we said above, its (positing) activity does not relate immediately to itself, but rather to a not-self that is to be opposed thereto (§ 2, 3). Hence it is no longer pure but *objective* activity (which posits an object for itself. The word *ob*ject (*Gegenstand*) admirably designates what it is meant for. Every object of an activity, so far as it is so, is necessarily something opposed to the activity, which *re*jects or *ob*jects to the same. If no rejection or resistance occurs, then there is simply no object of the activity, and no objective activity either; on the contrary, the activity, if it is indeed to be such, is pure, and reverts into itself. It is implicit already in the mere concept of objective activity, that resistance is offered to it, and hence that it is restricted). Thus the self is finite, insofar as its activity is *objective*.

I, 257

Now in both its relations, insofar as it returns upon the agent itself, and insofar as it is directed to an object outside the latter, this activity must be one and the same, the activity of one and the same subject, which in both contexts posits itself to be such. Between the two types of activity there must therefore be a bond of union, whereby consciousness is conducted from one to the other; and precisely such a bond is available in the causal relation that was asked for; namely, that the self-reverting activity of the self should be related to its objective activity as cause to effect, that the self should determine itself to the second activity by means of the first. The first activity would thus relate *immediately* to the self as such, but *mediately* to the not-self, thanks to the resultant determination of the self as a self determinant of the not-self; and the required causality would thereby be realized.

Our first requirement is therefore that the act of the self whereby it posits itself (as outlined in our first principle), should be related to that whereby it posits a not-self (as outlined in our second principle), as cause to effect. Now in general we have not been able to point to such a relation; having found it, rather, to be an altogether contradictory one; for in that case the self, by positing itself, would simultaneously have to posit the not-self, and so not posit itself—which is to abolish itself. —We have expressly maintained that the self opposes some thing to itself ab-

solutely, and without any ground, and only through the uncondi-
tional nature of this act could the proposition asserting this be
called a basic principle. But we noted at the time that at least something in this act was conditioned, namely its product—to wit, that
I, 258   the outcome of the act of opposing must necessarily be a not-self,
and could be nothing else. We now enter more deeply into the
meaning of this observation.

The self posits *absolutely* an object (a contrasted, counterposited not-self). In the *mere positing* of this it is therefore
dependent on itself alone, and on nothing else. So long as a mere
object in general is posited, and by means of this the self, as
merely *limited* in general, the requirements are satisfied; no question here of a *determinate* limit. The self is now absolutely
bounded: but where does its boundary lie? Inside point C, or
outside it? And how, indeed, could such a point be determined? It
depends entirely on the spontaneity of the self, posited by the
word *'absolutely'*. The boundary lies wherever in the infinite the
self posits it to be. The self is finite, because it is to be subjected
to limits; but it is infinite within this finitude because the boundary can be posited ever farther out, to infinity. It is infinite in its
finitude and finite in its infinity. —Thus it is not confined by this
absolute positing of an object, save insofar as it absolutely and
ungroundedly confines itself; and since such an absolute confine-
ment contradicts the absolute infinite nature of the self, it is itself
impossible, and so too is the whole counterpositing of a not-self.

Furthermore, however—it posits an *ob*ject, wherever in infinity it may choose to locate it, and thereby posits an extraneous
activity, independent of its own (positing) activity, and in fact
opposed thereto. In some sense, to be sure (though we do not
ask what), this opposed activity must *lie in the self*, insofar as it is
posited therein; but in another sense also (again we do not ask
what), it must *lie in the object*. So far as it does so, this activity is
to be opposed to some activity ($=X$) of the self; not that whereby
it is posited in the self, for that is the same activity; therefore,
I, 259   *some other one*. Insofar, therefore, as an object is to be posited,
and as a condition *of the possibility of such positing,* there must
be another activity ($=X$) occurring in the self, distinct from that
of positing. What sort of activity is this?

In the first place, an activity that is *not eliminated* by the object; for it has to be opposed to the object's activity; both are therefore to subsist alongside one another, as posited:—an activity, then, whose being is independent of the object, just as the object, in turn, is independent of it. —Such an activity must also be absolutely grounded in the self, since it is independent of the positing of any object, and the latter, conversely, is independent of it; hence it is posited by the absolute act of the self, whereby the latter posits itself. —Finally, by the above, the object is to be capable of being posited out to infinity; this activity of the self that resists it must therefore itself extend into infinity, beyond any possible object, and be itself infinite. —But, as surely as our second principle is valid, an object must be posited. —Hence X is the infinite activity posited by the self in itself; and this is related to the objective activity of the self, as ground of possibility to what is grounded thereby. The object is merely posited, insofar as there is resistance to an activity of the self; no such activity, no object. —It is related as determinant to determinate. Only *insofar* as this activity is resisted, can an object be posited; and so far as it is not resisted, there is no object.

We now examine this activity as regards its relation to that of the object. —Considered in themselves, they are both perfectly independent of each other and utterly opposed; there is no sort of connection between them. But if, as required, an object is to be posited, they must nonetheless be connected through the self that posits it. On this connection, equally, the positing of an object in general depends; so far as an object is posited, the activities are related, and so far as they are not related, no object is posited. —Moreover, since the object is posited absolutely, unconditionally and without any ground (by the act of positing merely as such), the connection also takes place absolutely and without any ground; and only now does it become fully apparent, to what extent the positing of a not-self is absolute: it is absolute, insofar as it is based on this connection that depends entirely on the self. That the activities are absolutely connected, is to say that they are posited as absolutely alike. But since, as surely as an object is to be posited, they are not alike, we can only say that their likeness is absolutely demanded: they *ought* to be absolutely alike. —But

I, 260

since they are not in fact alike, it remains always a question, which of the two is to align itself to the other, and which of them we are to take as the ground of comparison. —It is at once apparent, how we are obliged to answer this question. As the self is posited, so all reality is posited; everything is to be posited in the self; the self is to be absolutely independent, whereas everything is to be dependent upon it. Hence, what is required is the conformity of the object with the self; and it is the absolute self which demands this, precisely in the name of its absolute being.[2]

I, 261   [In what will hereafter be posited as the object, let us grant (we do not ask *how*, or by *what power* of the subject) the activity Y. To it there is *connected* an activity of the self; we thus envisage an activity extraneous to the self ($=\sim$Y), equal and akin to this activity of the self. Where, in this transaction, is the ground of connection? Obviously in the requirement that *all* activity shall be like that of the self, and this demand is grounded in the absolute being of the self. $\sim$Y lies in a *world* in which all activity would *really* be like that of the self, and is an ideal. —Now Y does not conform with $\sim$Y, but is *opposed* thereto. Hence it is attributed to an *object;* and without such connection, and the absolute requirement underlying it, there would be no object for the self, for the latter would be all in all, and for that very reason, as we shall see more fully below, nothing.]

Thus the absolute self is related absolutely to a not-self (our $\sim$Y), which is apparently to be a not-self in form, indeed (so far

---

[2]*Kant's* categorical imperative. If it is clear anywhere that Kant founded his critical enterprise, albeit tacitly, on the very premises that the Science of Knowledge lays down, it is apparent here. How could he ever have arrived at a categorical imperative, as an absolute postulate of conformity with the pure self, unless by presupposing an absolute being of the self, whereby everything is posited, and so far as it *is* not, at least *ought* to be?   —In what they say of the categorical imperative, the majority of Kant's followers seem merely to be echoing the great man, and not yet to have attained clarity as to the ground of the authority of an absolute postulate.   —Only *because* and *insofar as* the self is itself absolute, does it have the right to postulate absolutely; and this right then extends no farther than to a postulate of this its absolute being, from which, indeed, much else may then admit of being *deduced.*   —A philosophy which, at every point where *it* can advance no farther, appeals to a fact of consciousness, is little less shallow than the popular philosophy it derides.

as it is in general something external to the self), but not in content; for it is to be perfectly in conformity with the self. But it cannot conform to the latter, insofar as it is also to be a not-self merely in form; hence this activity of the self related to it is in no way a determination (to real sameness), but merely a *tendency* or *striving* towards determination, which is nonetheless wholly legitimate; for it is posited through the absolute positing of the self.

The result of our inquiry so far is therefore as follows: *in relation to a possible object,* the pure self-reverting activity of the self is a *striving;* and as shown earlier, *an infinite striving* at that. This boundless striving, carried to infinity, is the *condition of the possibility of any object whatsoever:* no striving, no object.

I, 262

We may now see how far this conclusion, drawn from other principles, does justice to the problem we undertook, and how far the contradiction we indicated is resolved thereby. —The self which, regarded in general as an intelligence, is dependent on a not-self, and is an intelligence simply to the extent that a not-self exists, is nonetheless to depend merely on the self; and to find this possible, we again had to assume a causality of the self in determining the not-self, insofar as the latter is to be the object of the intelligent self. At first sight, and taking the word in its full extension, such a causality annulled itself; once it was presupposed, either the self was not posited, or the not-self was not, and hence no causal relationship could occur between them. We attempted to mediate this conflict by distinguishing two opposed activities of the self, the pure and the objective; and by supposing that perhaps the first might be immediately related to the second, as cause to effect; while the second might be immediately related to the object, as cause to effect. And hence we supposed that the pure activity of the self might at least stand *mediately* (through the intermediacy of the objective activity) in a causal relation with the object. Now to what extent has this supposition been confirmed, and to what extent not?

How far, for a start, has the pure activity of the self turned out to be a cause of the objective activity? In the first place, insofar as no object can be posited without an activity of the self, opposed to that of the object, and insofar as this activity must necessarily exist in the subject prior to any object whatsoever, and simply through the subject itself (so that it is the pure activity thereof), the pure activity of the self is, as such, a

I, 263 *condition of any activity that posits an object.* But insofar as this pure activity originally relates to no object at all, and is wholly independent of the object, just as the latter is independent of it, it must be related and compared by an equally absolute act of the self to the activity of the object (which to that extent is not yet posited as an *ob*ject).[3] Now whether, *as* an act, this act is *absolute in form,* i.e., really happens,—(its absolute being is the foundation of the absolute spontaneity of reflection in theory, as of the will in practice, as we shall see in due course)— nevertheless, owing to the absolute positedness of the self, as the essence of all reality, it is again conditioned as to *content* (in that it is a *connecting,* and requires likeness and subordination of that which is subsequently posited as the object): and the pure activity is in this respect a *condition of connecting,* without which no positing of the object is possible. —Insofar as the pure activity is related, through the act just referred to, to a (possible) object, it is, as we said, a striving. That in general the pure activity is posited in relation to an object, is not grounded in the pure activity as such; but that *if* it is so posited, it is posited as a *striving,* does have its ground therein.

(This demand, that everything should conform to the self, that all reality should be posited absolutely through the self, is the

I, 264 demand of what is called—and with justice—practical reason. Such a practical capacity of reason has been postulated hitherto,

---

[3]The claim that, *in itself and as such,* the pure activity relates to an object, and that no special absolute act of connection is needful for this purpose, would be the transcendental principle *of intelligible fatalism;* the most coherent theory of freedom that was possible before the founding of a Science of Knowledge: and this principle would then surely entitle us to the conclusion, with regard to finite being, that no pure activity could be posited, inasmuch as none was manifested, and that finite being was posited as absolutely finite—not through itself, of course, but through something outside it. Were it not that such a concept would be altogether beyond us, the system of intelligible fatalism would hold true of the deity, that is, of a being through whose pure activity its objective activity would also be immediately posited.

but not proved. The injunctions issued now and then to the philosophers, to prove *that* reason was practical, were therefore fully justified. —Now such a proof must be carried out agreeably to theoretical reason itself, and the latter should not be ousted from the case by mere decree. This can be achieved no otherwise than by showing that reason cannot even be theoretical, if it is not practical; that there can be no intelligence in man, if he does not possess a practical capacity; the possibility of all presentation is founded on the latter. And this proof has now just been effected, in showing that, without a striving, no object at all is possible.)

But we still have a difficulty to resolve, which threatens to overturn our whole theory. For the required connection of the tendency of the pure activity to that of the future object—whether it be made immediately, or by means of an ideal projected according to the idea of this pure activity—is impossible, unless already in some fashion the activity of the object should be given to the connecting self. Let it be given in the same fashion, by connecting it to a tendency of the pure activity of the self, and our explanation turns in a circle, and we obtain absolutely no primary ground of connection in general. Such a primary ground must be pointed out—merely in an idea, of course, since it is to be a primary ground.

The absolute self is absolutely identical with itself: everything therein is one and the same self, and belongs (if we may express ourselves thus figuratively) to one and the same self; nothing therein is distinguishable, nothing manifold; the self is everything and nothing, since it is nothing *for itself,* and can distinguish no positing or posited within itself. —In virtue of its nature it *strives* (which again can only be said figuratively in regard to a future connection) to maintain itself in this condition. —There emerges in it a disparity, and hence something alien to itself. (*That* this happens, can in no sense be proved a priori, but everyone can confirm it only in his own experience. Moreover, we are so far unable to say anything further at all of this alien element, save that it is *not* derivable from the inner nature of the self, for in that case it would simply not be anything distinguishable.)

This alien element necessarily stands in conflict with the

I, 265

self's endeavor to be absolutely identical; and if we fancy some intelligent being outside the self, observing the latter in these two different situations, then *for such a being,* the self will appear restricted, its forces rebuffed, as we take to be the case, for example, in the physical world.

But the intelligence positing this restriction is not to be some being outside the self, but the latter itself; and hence we must progress a few steps further, in order to resolve the difficulty we pointed out.   —If the self is the same with itself, and necessarily strives after perfect identity with itself, it must straightway restore this striving, which was *not* interrupted by itself; and thus a comparison would become possible between its states of restriction and restoration of the curbed striving—a mere connection, therefore, of itself to itself, without any assistance from the object— provided a ground of connection between the two states could be pointed out.

Suppose that the self's striving proceeds without check from A to C; then so far as C there is nothing to be distinguished, for there is no distinguishing of self from not-self, and nothing whatever occurs up to that point of which the self could ever become conscious. At C this activity, which contains the primary ground of all consciousness, though never attaining to consciousness itself, is curbed. But it cannot be curbed in virtue of its own inner nature; it therefore goes on beyond C, but as an activity that is curbed from without and sustains itself *only* through its own inner forces; and so on to the point where there is no more resistance, for example, to D. [a)   Beyond D it can no more be an object of consciousness than from A to C, and for the same reason. b)   We are not saying at all here that the self posits its own activity as curbed, and sustained only through itself; but merely that some intelligence outside the self would be able to posit it as such.]

In the interests of clarity, we continue within the limits of the assumption just made. —An intelligence which was to posit, as required, correctly and appropriately—and we, indeed, are ourselves such an intelligence in our present course of scientific reflection—would necessarily have to posit this activity as that of a *self*—a self-positing being, which only has the properties that it

I, 266

posits in itself. Thus the self as such would have to posit in itself both the curbing of its activity and the restoration thereof, as surely as it is to be the activity of a self that is curbed and restored. But *this activity can be posited as restored only insofar as it is posited as curbed; and as curbed, insofar as it is posited as restored;* for both, on the above account, are in inter-determination, Hence, the states to be united are already in and for themselves in a synthetic unity; they cannot be posited at all, except as united. But *that* they are posited at all, is inherent in the mere concept of the self, and is postulated along with the latter. And thus the curbed activity, which has indeed to be posited and thence restored, would simply require positing in and through the self.

All positing of the self would thus proceed from the positing of a merely subjective state; all synthesis, from an inherently necessary synthesis of an opposite in the mere subject. This simply and solely subjective element will reveal itself later on as *feeling.*

I, 267 As condition of the possibility of this feeling, we now go on to posit an activity of the object; hence this activity, at all events, will be given, as above required, to the relating subject by way of feeling, and the needed relation to an activity of the pure self is now possible.

So much by way of solution to the difficulty we proposed. We now return to the point from which we started. No infinite striving of the self, no finite object therein: this was the result of our inquiry, and it appeared to remove the contradiction between the finite, conditioned self, *qua* intelligence, and the infinite and unconditioned self. But if we look at the matter more closely, we find that though the contradiction is indeed removed from the point where we encountered it, between the intelligent and the nonintelligent self, it has in general been merely pushed further out, and now brings higher principles into conflict.

For our task was to resolve the contradiction between an infinite and a finite activity of one and the same self, and this we did by arguing that the *infinite* activity was in no sense objective, but simply self-*reverting,* whereas the *finite* activity was *objective.*

Now, however, the infinite activity itself, as a *striving,* is related to the object, and thus to that extent is itself an objective activity; and since it is nonetheless to remain infinite, while the former finite objective activity is also to subsist beside it, we are left with an infinite and a finite objective activity of one and the same self; but this again is an assumption that contradicts itself. Such a contradiction can be resolved only by demonstrating that the infinite activity of the self is objective in a sense different from that of its finite activity.

The conjecture that will come to anyone's mind at first sight is doubtless this, that the finite objective activity of the self relates to a *real* object, while its infinite striving is directed upon a merely *imaginary* object. And this conjecture will indeed be verified. But since the question thereby receives a circular answer, and a distinction is already presupposed which first becomes possible only by distinguishing these two activities, we must enter rather more deeply into examination of the difficulty in question.

I, 268

As surely as it is to be an object, every object is necessarily determined; for insofar as it is so, it itself determines the self, and its determination thereof is itself determined (has its limits). As surely as it is such, all objective activity is thus determinant, and to that extent also determined, and so finite. Hence, even this infinite striving can itself be infinite only in a certain sense, and in a certain other must be finite.

Now to this striving an objective finite activity is *opposed;* hence the latter must be finite in the very sense that the striving is infinite, and the striving is infinite insofar as this objective activity is finite. To be sure, the striving has an end; but it is not precisely the same end as that of the objective activity. The only question is, what this end may be.

For purposes of its determination, the finite objective activity already posits in advance an activity of the self, opposed to the latter's infinite activity, which will subsequently be determined as the object. Insofar as it operates in general, it is not indeed a dependent, limited and finite activity, for to that extent (by the foregoing) it is absolute; but it is so, to the extent that it posits the *determinate* limits of the object (that it resists the self just so much, and neither more nor less). The ground of its determination, and hence of its determinacy also, lies outside it. —An object determined by an activity so far restricted in this fashion is a *real* object.

In this respect the striving is not finite; it proceeds beyond this boundary determination set out by the object, and by the above reasoning is obliged to do so, if such a boundary determi-

nation is to exist. It determines, not the real world, dependent on an activity of the not-self in reciprocity with the activity of the self, but a world as it would be, if all reality were absolutely posited by the self; hence, an ideal world, posited solely by the self, and not by any not-self whatever.

But how far is the striving nonetheless finite? To the extent that it refers in general to an object, and must posit limits to this object, as surely as the latter is to be such. In the real object, it was not the act of determining in general, but the limits of determination, that depended on the not-self: but in the ideal object, both the act of determining, and the limits, depend solely on the self; the latter is subject to no condition, save that it must posit limits in general, which it can extend out to infinity, because this extension depends solely on itself.

The ideal is an absolute product of the self; it can be elevated out to infinity; but at each determinate moment it has its limits, which at the next determinate moment must be utterly different. The indeterminate striving in general—which to that extent should really not be called striving, for it has no object, though we neither have nor can have a name for it, since it lies beyond all determinability—is infinite; but as such it does not attain to consciousness, nor can it do so, since consciousness is possible only through reflection, and reflection only through determination. But as soon as we reflect upon it, it necessarily becomes finite. The moment we become aware of its finitude, we continue to expand it further; but as soon as we raise the question, is it now infinite? it is reduced by this very question to finitude: and so on *ad infinitum*.

Hence the juxtaposition of *infinite* and *objective* is itself a contradiction. Anything that relates to an object is finite; and anything finite relates to an object. This contradiction would be removable only by a general elimination of the object; but the latter does not disappear, except in a completed infinity. The self can extend the object of its striving to infinity; but if, at a determinate moment, the object was extended to infinity, it would be an object no longer, and the idea of infinity would be realized, which is itself, however, a contradiction.

Nevertheless, the idea of an infinity to be thus completed floats as a vision before us, and is rooted in our innermost nature. We are obliged, as it enjoins us, to resolve the contradiction; though we cannot even think it possible of solution, and foresee that in no moment of an existence prolonged to all eternity will we ever be able to consider it possible. But this is just the mark in us that we are destined for eternity.

And in this way, therefore, the nature of the self is determined, so far as it can be, and the contradictions therein resolved, so far as they are soluble. The self is infinite, but merely in respect to its striving; it strives to be infinite. But the very concept of striving already involves finitude, for that to which there is no *counterstriving* is not a striving at all. If the self did more than strive, if it had an infinite causality, it would not be a self: it would not posit itself, and would therefore be nothing. But if it did not endlessly strive in this fashion, again it could not posit itself, for it could oppose nothing to itself; again it would be no self, and would therefore be nothing.

We shall set forth what has so far been deduced in yet another fashion, in order to give complete clarity to the concept of striving, which is of such great importance for the practical part of the Science of Knowledge.

According to our previous deliberations, there is a striving on the part of the self, which is such only insofar as it encounters resistance, and is itself incapable of causality; a striving, therefore, which so far as it has this character, is simultaneously conditioned by a not-self.

So far as it is incapable of causality, I said: and a causality of this sort is therefore required. That such a demand for absolute

causality must originally be present in the self, has been evidenced by the contradiction between self as intelligence and as absolute being, which cannot be solved without it. And this has furnished an apagogic proof; it has been shown that unless we are prepared to accept the demand for an absolute causality, the identity of the self will have to be given up.

This demand must also be capable of a direct and genetic demonstration; it must not only make itself acceptable by an appeal to higher principles, which would be in contradiction without it, but must actually be susceptible of *deduction* from these higher principles themselves, so that we may perceive *how* such a demand arises in the human mind. —It must be possible to demonstrate, not merely a striving for a causality determined (through a determinate not-self), but a striving for causality in general, which is the ground of the former striving. —An activity extending beyond the object becomes a striving precisely because it proceeds beyond the object, and thus only on condition that an object is already present. It must be possible to provide a ground for this excursion of the self out of itself, whereby an object first becomes possible. This outgoing process, which precedes all resistant activity and is the foundation of its possibility in regard to the self, must be founded simply and solely in the self; and by means of it we first obtain the true point of union between the absolute, the practical and the intelligent self.

Let us set forth an even clearer explanation of the actual point in question: —It is perfectly clear that, insofar as it posits itself absolutely, insofar as it is as it posits itself, and posits itself as it is, the self must be utterly identical with itself, and that to that extent nothing in any way distinct can emerge therein; and from this it certainly follows at once that *if* something distinct is to make its appearance therein, it will have to have been posited by a not-self. But if the not-self is to be able to posit anything at all in the self, *the condition for the possibility of such an alien influence must* be grounded beforehand, prior to any actual effect from without, *in the self as such, in the absolute self;* the self must originally and absolutely posit in itself the possibility of something operating upon it; without detriment to its absolute positing of itself, it must leave itself open, as it were, to some

I, 272

other positing. Hence, if ever a difference was to enter the self, there must already have been a difference originally in the self as such; and this difference, indeed, would have had to be grounded in the absolute self as such. —The apparent contradictoriness of this assumption will resolve itself in due course, and its unthinkability will disappear.

The self is to encounter in itself something heterogeneous, alien, and to be distinguished from itself: our inquiry may proceed most conveniently from this point.

For all that, this alien element is to encountered *in the self*, and can only be encountered therein. If it lay *outside the self*, it would be nothing for the self, and nothing would follow for the self from this. Hence, in a certain respect, it must also be *cognate* to the self; it must be capable of ascription thereto.

The essence of the self consists in its activity; so if this heterogeneous element is also to be capable of ascription to the self, it must in general be an activity of the self, and cannot as such be alien, though its mere *direction* is perhaps alien, having its source not in the self, but outside it. —If, as we have so often supposed, the self's activity extends into the infinite, but is checked at a certain point, though without being abolished thereby, but merely driven back into itself, then this activity, so far as it is such, is and remains always an activity of the self; only the rebuff it undergoes is foreign and contrary to the self. In this connection there remain unanswered only those difficult questions whose solution also enables us, however, to penetrate into the inmost nature of the self: How does the self come by this *outward* direction of its activity into infinity? How can it distinguish an outward direction from an inward one? And why is the recoil inwards regarded as alien and not grounded in the self?

I, 273

The self posits itself absolutely, and to that extent its activity is self-reverting. The direction thereof—if I may be allowed to presuppose something not yet derived, for the sole purpose of greater intelligibility; and if I may also be allowed to borrow from natural philosophy a word that (as will be seen) first enters the latter from our present transcendental viewpoint—the direction, I say, is purely *centripetal*. [One point does not determine a line: the possibility of such determination always requires that two should be given, even if the second lies at infinity, and indicates merely the direction. In the same way, and on the very same grounds, there can be no direction if there are not two such, and two opposite directions at that. The concept of direction is a purely reciprocal concept; *one* direction is none at all, and is absolutely unthinkable. Hence we can ascribe a direction, and a centripetal direction, to the absolute activity of the self, only on the tacit presupposition that we shall also discover a second, centrifugal direction of this activity. On the strictest interpretation, the picture of the self, in our present mode of envisaging it, is that of a self-constituting mathematical point, in which we can distinguish no direction or anything else whatever; which is *altogether where* it is, and whose content and limits (substance and form) are one and the same.] If the nature of the self contains nothing other than this constitutive activity alone, it is what every body is for us. We ascribe to such a body also an *inner* force, posited through its mere existence (by the principle $A = A$); but if we only philosophize transcendentally, and not in some way transcendently, we assume it posited *by us, that* this force is posited by the mere existence of that body (for ourselves); but

I, 274   not that it is posited, *by and for the body itself, that* such a force should be posited, and hence, for us, such a body is without life or soul, and not a self. The self is to posit itself, not merely for some intelligence outside it, but simply *for itself;* it is to posit itself *as* posited by itself. Hence, as surely as it is a self, it must have the principle of life and consciousness solely within itself. And thus, as surely as it is a self, it must contain unconditionally and without any ground the principle of reflecting upon itself; and hence, from the beginning, we have the self in a dual aspect: partly, insofar as it is reflective, and to that extent the direction of its activity is centripetal; partly, insofar as it is that upon which reflection takes place, and to that extent the direction of its activity is centrifugal, and centrifugal out to infinity at that. The self is posited as a reality, and in that there is reflection on whether it has reality, it is necessarily posited as *something,* as a quantum; yet it is posited as all reality, and is thus necessarily posited as an infinite quantum, a quantum exhaustive of infinity.

Thus the centripetal and centrifugal directions of activity are both grounded in like fashion in the nature of the self; both are one and the same, and are distinguished merely inasmuch as there is reflection upon them as distinct. —(All centripetal force in the physical world is a mere product of the self's imaginative power of bringing unity into the manifold according to a law of reason; as will appear in due course.)

But the reflection whereby the two directions could be distinguished is impossible unless a third thing be added, to which they can be connected, or which can be connected to them. —The requirement (we must always presuppose something as yet unproved, if only so that we can express ourselves; for in strictness, no sort of *requirement,* as the opposite of *what actually happens,* is as yet possible)—the requirement, that all reality should be in I, 275   the self, is satisfied upon our presupposition; both directions of the self's activity, the centripetal and the centrifugal, coincide with one another, and are but one and the same direction. (Suppose, by way of elucidation, that we are to explain the self-consciousness of God; this will be possible only on the presupposition that God reflects upon his own being. But since in God *as reflected upon,* everything would be in one and one in everything, and would similarly be so for God *as reflecting,* there would be no distinguishing, in and through God, between the reflecting and the reflected, between consciousness itself and the object thereof; and God's self-consciousness would thus be unexplained, as it would then also remain everlastingly inexplicable and inconceivable to any finite reason, that is, to any reason subject to the law *of determination* of that on which reflection occurs.) Hence no consciousness is derivable from the above presupposition; for the two supposed directions are incapable of distinction.

But now the infinitely outreaching activity of the self is to be checked at some point, and driven back upon itself; and hence the self is not to exhaust the infinite. *That* this occurs, as a fact, is absolutely incapable of derivation from the self, as has frequently been pointed out; but we can show, at all events, that it must occur, if a genuine consciousness is to be possible.

The demand made by the reflecting self in its present capacity, that the self it reflects on should exhaust the infinite, continues to hold and is in no way limited by this check. The question, whether it exhausts the infinite, and the outcome, that it does not really do so, but is bounded at C, are still valid—and only now is it possible to distinguish the two directions as required.

For, by the demand of the absolute self, its (to that extent centrifugal) activity was to extend to infinity; but it is reflected at C, and so becomes centripetal. Any pair of things to be distinguished must be related to a third thing; and now, by relation to this original demand for a centrifugal direction extending to infinity, the distinction becomes possible; for we now encounter in reflection a centrifugal tendency answering to this demand, and a centripetal tendency that resists it (the second tendency, reflected by the check).

At the same time it becomes clear why this second tendency is regarded as something alien, and is derived from a principle opposed to that of the self.

And with this, the problem we set ourselves above is resolved. The original striving after a causality in general within the self is genetically derived from the self's law, that it shall reflect upon itself and shall demand that, in this reflection, it be found to be the whole of reality; both being requisite, as surely as it is to be a self. This necessary reflection of the self upon itself is the basis of all its going forth outside itself, while the demand that it exhaust the infinite is the basis of its striving after causality in general; and both are grounded solely in the absolute being of the self.

As was likewise required, we have thereby discovered in the self as such the ground of possibility for an influence of the not-self upon the self. The self posits itself absolutely, and is thereby complete in itself and closed to any impression from without. But if it is to be a self, it must also posit itself as self-posited; and by this new positing, relative to an original positing, it opens itself, if I may so put it, to external influences; simply by this reiteration of positing, it concedes the possibility that there might also be something within it that is not actually posited by itself. Both types of positing are conditions for an operation of the not-self; without the first, there would be no activity of the self to undergo limitation; without the second, this activity would not be limited for the self, and the latter would be unable to posit itself as limited. Thus the self, as such, is initially in a state of reciprocity with itself, and only so does an external influence upon it become possible.

I, 277   By this, too, we have at last discovered the point of union we were seeking between the absolute, the practical and the intellectual characters of the self. —The self demands that it encompass all reality and exhaust the infinite. This demand of necessity rests on the idea of the absolutely posited, infinite self; and this is the *absolute* self, of which we have been talking. [Here the meaning of the principle, *the self posits itself absolutely,* first becomes wholly clear. There is no reference at all therein to the self given in actual consciousness; for the latter is never absolute, its state being invariably based, either mediately or immediately, upon something outside the self. We are speaking, rather, of an idea of the self which must necessarily underlie its infinite practical demand, though it is inaccessible to our consciousness, and so can never appear immediately therein (though it may, of course, mediately, in philosophical reflection).]

It is equally implicit in the concept of the self, that it must reflect about itself, whether it really includes all reality within itself. It bases this reflection on the foregoing idea, and thus carries the latter out to infinity, and is to that extent *practical:* not absolute, since it actually goes forth from itself, through the tendency to reflection; and yet not theoretical either, since its reflection rests on nothing save this idea deriving from the self as such, and is wholly oblivious of the possibility of a check, so that no real reflection is present. —Hence arises the series of those things that *ought* to be, and are given through the self alone; in short, the series of the *ideal.*

If reflection addresses itself to this check, and the self thus regards its outgoing as restricted, we obtain thereby a quite different series, that of the *real,* which is determined by something other than the mere self. —And to that extent the self is *theoretical,* or an *intelligence.*

Without a practical capacity in the self, an intelligence, too,

I, 278   is impossible; if the self's activity extends only to the checking-point, and not on beyond any possible check, there is nothing that operates as a check in and for the self—no not-self—as we have frequently pointed out already. Conversely, if the self is not an intelligence, it can have no consciousness of its practical capacity, nor any self-consciousness whatever; for, as has just been shown, it is only through the alien direction occasioned by the check that different directions first become distinguishable. (Here, indeed, we are still discounting the fact that, in order to attain to consciousness, the practical capacity must first proceed through the intelligence, must first adopt the form of presentation.)

And thus at last the whole essence of finite rational natures is encompassed and exhausted. The original idea of our absolute being: the endeavor to reflect upon ourselves in accordance with this idea: the restriction, not of this endeavor, but of the *real existence*[1] that this restriction first posits in us, by an opposed principle, the not-self, or by our finitude generally: self-consciousness, and more especially consciousness of our practical striving: determination of our presentations accordingly (with and without freedom); determination thereby of our actions—of the direction of our real sensory capacities: constant enlargement of our limits, to infinity.

And in this connection a further important observation,
I, 279   which alone would be sufficient to set the Science of Knowledge in its true perspective, and to render its characteristic doctrine perfectly clear. According to the account just put forward, the principle of life and consciousness, the ground of its possibility—is admittedly contained in the self; but this gives rise to no genuine life, no empirical existence in time; and any other kind, for us, is

[1]In a consistent stoicism, the infinite idea of the self is taken to be the real self; absolute being and real existence are not distinguished. Hence the stoic sage is all-sufficient and unconfined; he is credited with all the predicates belonging to the pure self, or even to God. According to stoic ethics, we are not to become like God, we actually are God. The Science of Knowledge makes a careful distinction between absolute being and real existence, and employs the former merely as a basis, in order to explain the latter. Stoicism is refuted by showing that it cannot account for the possibility of consciousness. Hence the Science of Knowledge is not atheistic either, as stoicism must necessarily be, if it is thoroughly worked out.

absolutely unthinkable. If such a genuine life is to be possible, we need for the purpose another and special sort of check to the self on the part of a not-self.

According to the Science of Knowledge, then, the ultimate ground of all reality for the self is an original interaction between the self and some other thing outside it, of which nothing more can be said, save that it must be utterly opposed to the self. In the course of this interaction, nothing is brought into the self, nothing alien is imported; everything that develops therein, even out to infinity, develops solely from itself, in accordance with its own laws; the self is merely set in motion by this opponent, in order that it may act; without such an external prime mover it would never have acted, and since its existence consists solely in acting, it would never have existed either. But this mover has no other attribute than that of being a mover, an opposing force, and is in fact only felt to be such.

Thus, in respect of its existence the self is dependent; but in the determinations of this its existence it is absolutely independent. In virtue of its absolute being, it contains a law of these determinations, valid to infinity, and an intermediary power of determining its empirical existence according to this law. The point at which we find ourselves, when we first set this intermediary power of freedom in play, is not dependent on us; considered in its full extension, the series that from this point on we shall traverse to all eternity, is wholly dependent on ourselves.

The Science of Knowledge is therefore *realistic*. It shows that
I, 280   the consciousness of finite creatures is utterly inexplicable, save on the presumption of a force existing independently of them, and wholly opposed to them, on which they are dependent in respect of their empirical existence. Nor does it assert anything beyond this opposing force, which the finite being feels, merely, but does not apprehend. All possible determinations of this force, or not-self, which may emerge to infinity in our consciousness, the Science of Knowledge undertakes to derive from the determinant power of the self, and must indeed really be able to derive them, as surely as it is a Science of Knowledge.

Notwithstanding its realism, however, this science is not transcendent, but remains in its innermost depths *transcendental*. It accounts for all consciousness, indeed, by reference to a thing that is present independently of any consciousness, but it does not forget that, even in the course of this explanation, it governs itself by its own laws, and that, in course of reflecting on this, the independent factor again becomes a product of its own power of thought, and thus something dependent on the self, insofar as it is to exist for the self (in the concept thereof). But in order for this new account of the first explanation to be possible, we again presuppose already a real consciousness, and for this to be possible we again presuppose that something on which the self depends; and if now that very thing, which was initially posited as independent, has become dependent on the thinking of the self, it is not thereby abolished, but merely posited further out, and so we might proceed out indefinitely, without it ever being eliminated. —In respect of their ideality, all things depend upon the self; but in regard to its reality, the self is itself dependent; yet nothing is real for the self, unless it is also ideal; so in it the ideal and the real grounds are one and the same, and this interaction between self and not-self is at the same time an interaction of the self with itself. It is able to posit itself as restricted by the not-self, in that it does not reflect on the fact that it is itself responsible for positing this not-self that restricts it; it can posit itself as itself restricting the not-self, in that it does reflect upon that.

I, 281

This fact, that the finite spirit must necessarily posit something absolute outside itself (a thing-in-itself), and yet must recognize, from the other side, that the latter exists only *for it* (as a necessary noumenon), is that circle which it is able to extend into infinity, but can never escape. A system that pays no attention at all to this circle, is a dogmatic idealism; for it is indeed the aforesaid circle which alone confines us and makes us finite beings; a system which fancies itself to have escaped therefrom, is a transcendent realist dogmatism.

The Science of Knowledge assuredly occupies the mean between the two systems, and is a critical idealism, which might also be described as a real-idealism or an ideal-realism. —We append a few words, to render ourselves, where possible, intelligible to everyone. We said that the consciousness of finite creatures is inexplicable, unless we assume a force present that is independent of them. —To whom is it inexplicable? And for whom is it to become explicable? Who, then, is it that explains this anyway? The finite creatures themselves. In uttering the word *explain* we are already in the realm of finitude; for all *explanation*, that is, not immediate comprehension, but a progression from one thing to the next, is a finite affair, and limitation or determination is simply the bridge we traverse to it, and which the self possesses in itself. —So far as its being and determination are concerned, the opposing force is independent of the self, in that it seeks to modify the practical faculty of the latter, or its drive to reality; but it is still dependent upon the ideal activity, the theoretical faculty, of the self; it exists *for the self* only insofar as it is posited *by the latter,* and otherwise has no existence for the self. Only to the extent that anything is related to the practical faculty of the self, does it have independent reality; so far as it is related to the theoretical faculty, it is incorporated in the self, contained within its sphere, subjected to its laws of presentation. Yet how, furthermore, can it in fact be related to the practical faculty, save by way of the theoretical, and how can it then become an object of the theoretical faculty, unless by means of the practical? Here, then, the principle: no ideality, no reality, and *vice versa,* again receives confirmation, or rather emerges into full clarity. As we can also put it, therefore: the ultimate ground of all consciousness is an interaction of the self with itself, by way of a not-self that has to be regarded from different points of view. This is the circle from which the finite spirit cannot escape, and cannot wish to escape, unless it is to disown reason and demand its own annihilation.

I, 282

The following objection may prove of interest: if, on the foregoing principles, the self posits through its ideal activity a not-self, to account for its own limited nature, and thereby incorporates that not-self into itself, does it not posit the latter as itself limited (in a determinate finite concept)? Posit this object = A. Now the activity of the self in positing this A is necessarily itself limited, since it relates to a limited object. But the self can never limit itself, and therefore cannot do so in the case under review; hence, in limiting A, which it admittedly incorporates, it must itself be limited by a B that is still quite independent of it, and is not incorporated therein. —We acknowledge all this, but point out that even this B can again be incorporated into the self; our opponent concedes this but points out in turn that for this incorporation to be possible, the self must again be limited by an independent C; and so on without end. The outcome of this inquiry would be that to all eternity we could refer our opponent to no single instant at which there was not present outside the self an independent reality for it to strive after; while he, too, could refer us to none at which this independent not-self could not be presented, and thereby made dependent on the self. Now where do we locate our opponent's independent not-self, or thing-in-itself, which the foregoing argument is supposed to have demonstrated? Obviously, nowhere and everywhere at once. It is there only so long as we do not have it, and as soon as we seek to apprehend it, it flies away. The thing-in-itself is something for the self, and consequently in the self, though it ought *not* to be *in the self:* it is thus a contradiction, though as the object of a necessary idea it must be set at the foundation of all our philosophizing, and has always lain at the root of all philosophy and all acts of the finite mind, save only that no one has been clearly aware of it, or of the contradiction contained therein. This relation of the thing-in-itself to the self forms the basis for the entire mechanism of the human and all other finite minds. Any attempt to change this would entail the elimination of all consciousness, and with it of all existence.

I, 283

All apparent objections to the Science of Knowledge, bewildering as they are to any but the acutest reasoners, will have their origin simply in this, that people are unable to master and hold firmly to the idea just put forward. There are two ways in which it can be wrongly apprehended. On the one hand, a person may simply reflect that, since it is an idea, it must surely be located in the self; and then, at least if he is a resolute thinker, he becomes an idealist, and dogmatically denies the existence of all reality outside us; or else, if he clings to his feeling, he may deny what is plainly the case, refuting the arguments of the Science of Knowledge by appeal to the pronouncements of common sense (with which, at heart, it is in agreement, if properly understood) and accusing this Science itself of idealism, because its import has not been grasped. On the other hand, a person may simply reflect that the object of this idea is an independent not-self, and become

I, 284　a transcendent realist; or, supposing him to have got hold of a few of *Kant's* opinions, without having mastered the spirit of this entire philosophy, he will accuse the Science of Knowledge of transcendency, from his own transcendent standpoint, which he has never, in fact, abandoned, and will fail to realize that he is merely turning his own weapons upon himself. —Neither of these courses is the one to follow: we should reflect neither on the one aspect alone, nor the other alone, but on both together, oscillating inwardly between the two opposing determinations of this idea. And this is the business of the *creative imagination,* a faculty that all men are quite certainly endowed with, since without it they would have no presentations at all; though by no means all of them have it at their command, to create therewith in a purposeful manner, or if, in a fortunate hour, the required image should visit their minds like a flash of lightning, to seize it, to examine it, and to register it inerasably for any use they wish. It is this power which determines whether or not we philosophize with insight. The Science of Knowledge is of a kind that cannot be communicated by the letter merely, but only through the spirit; for its basic ideas must be elicited, in anyone who studies it, by the creative imagination itself; as could not, indeed, be otherwise, in a Science that penetrates back to the ultimate grounds of human knowledge, in that the whole enterprise of the human spirit issues from the imagination, and the latter cannot be grasped save through the imagination itself. Anyone, therefore, in whom this whole aptitude is already weakened or deadened beyond hope of recall will admittedly find it forever impossible to make headway in this Science; but the ground of this inability he should look for, not in the Science itself, which is easily grasped, if it is ever grasped at all, but rather in the want of capacity in himself.[5]

I, 285   Just as the aforesaid idea is the foundation-stone of the whole structure from within, so it also guarantees the security of that structure from without. It is impossible to philosophize about any topic whatever without coming upon this idea, and therewith upon the especial territory of the Science of Knowledge. Every antagonist must do battle—blindfold, it may be—upon its terrain and with its weapons, and it will always be easy to strip the bandage from his eyes and let him see the ground on which he stands. The Science is thus perfectly entitled, in the nature of the case, to declare in advance that many will misunderstand it, and more will not understand it at all; that, not only in the present exceedingly defective accounts, but even in the completest that any one man might achieve, it will remain sorely in need of improvement in every part; but that in its main outlines it will not be refuted by any man, or in any age.

§ 6.   THIRD DISCOURSE.

In the striving of the self there is simultaneously posited a counterstriving of the not-self, which holds the former in equilibrium

A few preliminary remarks about method: —In the theoretical part of the Science of Knowledge, we have had to do solely with *knowing;* here we are concerned with the *known.* There, the question was, *how* is a thing posited, intuited, thought, etc; here it is, *what* is posited? Thus if the Science of Knowledge were after

I, 286   all to possess a metaphysic, as a supposed science of things-in-themselves, and such a metaphysic were demanded of it, it would

---

[5]The Science of Knowledge must be exhaustive of the whole of man; it can only be encompassed, therefore, with the totality of all his powers. It cannot become a generally accepted philosophy, so long as education has the effect, in so many men, of killing off one capacity for the sake of another; imagination for the sake of understanding, understanding for the sake of imagination, or both, even, for the sake of memory; while this continues, it must remain confined to a narrow circle—a truth as displeasing to utter as it is to hear, but a truth nonetheless.

have to refer to the practical part of the system. As will become increasingly apparent, it is this alone which treats of an original reality; and if the Science of Knowledge should be asked, how then, indeed, are things-in-themselves constituted, it could offer no answer, save, as we are to make them. Now this in no way renders our science transcendent; for everything that we shall also point out in this connection we find in ourselves, and bring forth from ourselves, because there is something *in us* that can be fully accounted for only by something *outside us*. We know that we think it, and think it according to the laws of our mind; and hence that we can never escape from ourselves, never speak of the existence of an object without a subject.

The striving of the self must be infinite, and can never have causality. This can be conceived of only on the supposition of a counterstriving, holding the former in balance, that is, having the same quantity of internal force. The concept of such a counterstriving, and of the equilibrium in question, is already implicit in the notion of striving, and can be evolved therefrom by analysis. Without these two conceptions, it is in contradiction with itself.

1.   The concept of striving is the notion of a cause that is not a cause. But every cause presupposes *activity*. Everything that strives has force; if it did not, it would not be a cause, which contradicts the foregoing.

2.   The striving, insofar as it is such, necessarily possesses its determinate quantity as an activity. It aspires to be a cause. If it does not become one, it fails in consequence to attain its goal, and becomes *limited*. If it were not limited, it would become a cause and would not be a striving, which contradicts the foregoing.

3.   The striving is not limited *by itself*, for it is implied in the concept of striving that it aspires to causality. If it limited itself, it would not be a striving. Every striving must therefore be limited by a force opposed to that of the striving itself.

I, 287

4.   This opposing force must equally have the character of a striving, that is, in the first place, it must aspire to causality. Unless it did so, it would have no point of contact with its opponent. And yet again, it must not possess causality; if it did, it would utterly

abolish the striving of its opponent by annihilating the force of the latter.

5. Neither of these two contrary strivings can possess causality. If one of them did so, it would annihilate the force of its opponent, and they would cease to contend with each other. Hence the forces of both must maintain an equilibrium.

§ 7. FOURTH DISCOURSE.

The self's striving, the not-self's counterstriving, and the equilibrium between them, must be posited

A) The self's striving is posited as such.

1. It is posited in general, as *something,* by the general law of reflection; not, therefore, as *activity,* as a thing moving or darting about, but as something fixed and stable.

2. It is posited as a *striving.* Striving aspires to causality; it must be posited, therefore, as essentially causal in character. But this causality cannot be posited as extending to the not-self; for in that case a real efficacious activity would be posited, and not a striving. It would thus be capable only of reverting upon itself, of producing only itself. But a self-productive striving that is fixed, determinate and definite in character is known as *a drive.* (The concept of a drive implies 1.) that it is founded in the internal nature of that to which it is ascribed; hence, that it is brought forth by the causality of the latter upon itself, i.e. through the fact of its own self-positing. 2.) that, precisely for this reason, it is something fixed and enduring. 3.) that it aspires to causality outside itself, but that, insofar as it is to be merely a drive, it has no causality solely through itself. —Hence the drive is merely in the subject, and by nature does not issue beyond the latter's sphere.)

That is how the striving must be posited, *if* it is to be posited; and— whether this happens immediately with or without consciousness— it must *be* posited, if it is to reside in the self, and if a consciousness (based, by the foregoing, on a manifestation of the striving) is to be possible.

B) The self's striving cannot be posited unless a counterstriving of the not-self is posited; for the former striving aspires to causality, yet has none; and the ground of this deficiency does not lie in itself, for otherwise its striving would be no striving at all, but rather nothing. Hence, if posited, this ground must be posited outside the self, and again merely as a striving; for otherwise the striving—or drive, as we now know it—of the self would be suppressed, and could not be posited.

C) The equilibrium between the two must be posited.

We are not saying here that there has to be a balance between them; that has already been shown in the preceding paragraphs. All we are asking is: *What* is posited, in and through the self, when we posit this balance?

The self strives to fill out the infinite; at the same time, its law and tendency is to reflect upon itself. It cannot do this without being limited, and limited, in regard to the *drive,* by a *relation thereto.* Suppose the drive to be limited at point C; then at C the *tendency to reflection is satisfied,* but *the drive towards real activity is restricted.* The self then limits itself, and is thrown into interaction with itself: the drive urges it onward, while it is arrested by the reflection, and reins itself in.

I, 289

The two together yield the manifestation of a *compulsion,* or *inability.* An inability entails a) a continuance of striving; for otherwise the thing I cannot do would have no existence *for myself;* it would be altogether out of my sphere. b) limitation of real activity; hence, real activity itself, for what does not exist cannot be limited. c) that the limiting factor should lie (or be posited), not *in me,* but *outside me;* for otherwise there would be no striving. We should then have, not an inability, but an *unwillingness.* —So this manifestation of inability is a manifestation of equilibrium.

The inability, as manifested in the self, is called *a feeling.* Combined within it we have, first of all, *activity*—I feel, and am that which feels, and this activity is one of reflection. —Secondly, restriction—I feel, am passive and not active; there is a compulsion present. Now this restriction necessarily presupposes a drive to push on further. What wills nothing further, requires nothing further, reaches no further, is—*for itself* of course—not restricted.

Feeling is entirely *subjective*. To *explain* it, indeed—though this is an act of theorizing—we require a *limiting factor;* but not to deduce it as it is to appear in the self—not to account for the *presentation* or *positing* thereof in the self.

[Here we encounter in broad daylight what is beyond the grasp of so many philosophers, who despite their supposedly critical outlook have not yet freed themselves from transcendent dogmatism; *that* and *how* the self can evolve, entirely from itself, whatever is to occur therein, without ever emerging from itself or breaking out of its own circle; as must necessarily be the case, if the self is to be a self. —There is a feeling in the self; this represents a restriction of the drive; and if it is to be positable as a determinate feeling, distinct from other feelings (which at this point, admittedly, we do not yet see to be possible), it must be the restriction of a determinate drive, distinct from other drives. The self must posit a ground for this restriction, and posit it outside itself. It can posit the drive as restricted only by something utterly opposed to it; and hence it is evidently the drive which determines *what* is to be posited as object. If the drive is determined as Y, for example, not-Y must necessarily be posited as object. —But since all these functions of the soul take place according to necessary laws, we do not become aware of our own action, and are necessarily bound to assume that we have received from without what we have in fact ourselves produced by our own forces, and according to our own laws. —This process has objective validity nonetheless, for it is a procedure that all finite reason has in common, and there is and can be no other objective validity than that. The pretension to any other rests upon a crude and manifestly demonstrable deception.

In the course of our inquiry we do indeed appear to have broken out of this circle; for in explanation of striving in general we have postulated a not-self wholly independent of the self and striving against it. The ground for the possibility and legitimacy of this procedure is as follows: Everyone who has joined us in undertaking the present inquiry is himself a self, and one that has long since engaged in the acts here deduced, and thus has already long ago posited a not-self (of which he is now to be persuaded, by the very inquiries we are prosecuting, that it is his own product). Of necessity, he has already concluded the whole enterprise of reason, and now freely engages himself, as it were, to go through the calculation again; to scrutinize the path, that he once took himself, in the person of another self, whom he arbitrarily posits, stations at his own original starting-point, and makes the subject of his experiment. The self under investigation will itself arrive eventually at the point where the observer now stands; there they will both unite, and by this union the circuit in question will be closed.]

§ 8. FIFTH DISCOURSE.

Feeling itself must be posited and determined.

A few general remarks to begin with, in preparation for the highly important inquiry now to be set on foot.

1. The self initially contains a striving to fill out the infinite. This striving resists termination in the *individual* object.

2. The self has an inherent law that it should reflect upon itself as filling out the ·infinite. But it cannot, in fact, reflect upon itself, or on anything else whatever, if the thing in question is not limited. The fulfilment of this law, or—what comes to the same thing—the satisfaction of the drive to reflection, is therefore *conditioned*, and depends upon the object. It cannot be satisfied without an object— and may thus be also described as a drive *towards the object*.

3. Through limitation by means of a feeling, this drive is at once satisfied and not satisfied.

    a) *Satisfied;* the self was absolutely bound to reflect upon itself; it reflects with absolute spontaneity, and is therefore satisfied, as regards the *form* of the action. There is something in the feeling, therefore, that can be related or ascribed to the self.

    b) *Not satisfied,* in regard to the *content* of the action. The self was to be posited as filling out the infinite, but it is posited as limited. This now emerges with equal necessity in the feeling.

    c) The positing of this lack of satisfaction is, however, *conditioned* by an excursion of the self beyond the boundary set for it by

I, 292 the feeling. Something must be posited outside the sphere posited by the self, which also pertains to the infinite, and to which, therefore, the drive of the self is also addressed. This must be posited as not determined by the self.

We are to ask how this excursion, the positing, therefore, of this nonsatisfaction, or—what amounts to the same—the feeling, is possible.

I.   As surely as the self reflects upon itself, it is in fact limited, that is, it fails to occupy the infinity which it nonetheless strives to fill. It *is* limited, we said—for a possible observer, that is, though not yet for itself. Let us act ourselves as these observers, or—what comes to the same—let us posit in place of the self a thing that is merely observed, an inanimate thing; though otherwise it is to have the properties we presuppose as attaching to the self. Posit, therefore, an elastic sphere = A, and assume that it is compressed by another body. In that case
   a)   You posit in the sphere a force which, so soon as the opposing pressure is withdrawn, will assert itself, and that without any external aid; which therefore has the ground of its efficacy entirely in itself.   —The force is there; it struggles, in and upon itself, for expression; it is a force directed in and upon itself, and is thus an inner force, for that is the name we give to such a thing. It is an immediate striving for causality upon itself, though because of the external resistance it has no causality. It is an equilibrium of the striving and the mediate counterpressure in the body itself, and thus what we earlier called a *drive*. In the supposed elastic body we have therefore posited a drive.
I, 293   b)   We posit the same in the resistant body B—an inner force that stands up to the counterexertion and resistance of A, and is thus itself restricted by this resistance, though it has its ground entirely in itself.   —We posit a force and drive in B, exactly as in A.
   c)   If one of the two forces were increased, the opposing force would be weakened; if one were weakened, the other would be increased; the stronger would express itself completely, and the weaker would be utterly driven out of the former's field of action.

Now, however, they preserve a perfect equilibrium, and their point of contact is the point of balance in question. Were it to be shifted in the slightest degree, the whole relationship would be destroyed. II. That is the position with an object (we call it *elastic*) that strives without reflecting. The topic of our present inquiry is a *self*, and we shall see what the consequences of that may be.

The drive is an inner force, determining itself to causality. The inanimate body has no causality whatever, save *outside* itself. This is to be held in check by the resistance, and under this condition the outcome of its self-determination is therefore nil. This is precisely the case with the self, insofar as it aspires to a causality outside itself; and its case would not differ in any respect, if it *merely* demanded an external causality.

But the self, precisely because it is such, also has a causality upon itself, namely that of positing itself, or the capacity for reflection. The drive is itself to determine *the force of that which strives;* now insofar as this force is to manifest itself *in the striving thing itself*, as reflection must do, the determination by the drive must *necessarily give rise to a manifestation;* otherwise, no drive would be present, which contradicts our assumption. Hence, the drive necessarily leads to the act of the self's reflection upon itself.

I, 294

[An important conclusion, which sheds the clearest light upon our inquiry. 1.)   The above-mentioned original *duality* in the self —of striving and reflection—is thereby intimately unified. All reflection is based on the striving, and in the absence of striving there can be no reflection.   —Conversely, in the absence of reflection, there is no striving *for the self,* and so no striving *of the self,* and no self whatever. The one is a necessary consequence of the other, and the relation of both is a reciprocal one. 2.)   We see more definitely here that the self must be finite and limited. No restriction, no drive (in the transcendent sense): no drive, no reflection, (transition to the transcendental): no reflection, no drive, and no limitation and nothing that limits, etc., (in the transcendental sense): so runs the circuit of the self's functions, and the inwardly linked reciprocity of the latter with itself. 3.)   Here, too, it becomes truly evident, what *ideal* and *real* activity are, how they differ and where their boundary lies. Viewed as a drive, and a drive founded solely in the self as such, the original striving of the self is both *ideal* and *real* at once. It is directed to the self as such, for the striving occurs through its own force; and to something outside the self: but in this there lies nothing to distinguish. Through limitation, whereby only the *external* direction is eliminated, but not the *internal,* this original force is as it were divided: and the remainder which reverts back into the self is the *ideal* force. The *real* will likewise be posited in due course. —And so here then there appears once more in its fullest light the principle: no ideality, no reality, and *vice versa.* 4.) The *ideal* activity will shortly prove to be the *presenting* activity. The relation of the drive to this activity is therefore to be designated the *presentational drive.* This latter is thus the first and highest manifestation of the drive, and through it the self first becomes an intelligence. And so indeed it would also necessarily have to conduct itself, if ever any other drive were to come to *consciousness,* and occur in the self *as a self.* 5.)   From this, then, we may further derive in a most enlightening manner the subordination of theory to the practical; for it follows that all *theoretical* laws are based on *practical* laws, or rather, since there can be only one of the latter, on one and the same law; whence we obtain the completest system of the whole of man's nature; it follows that if the drive itself should be susceptible of enhancement, insight is also enhanced, and *vice versa;* it follows that, even in the context of theory, there is an absolute freedom of reflection and abstraction, and the possibility of directing one's attention to something and withdrawing it from something else *as a matter of duty,* without which there can be no morality whatever. There is a radical extirpation of that fatalism which rests on the assumption that our acting and willing are dependent on the system of our presentations, in that it is here shown, on the contrary, that our system of presentations depends on our drive and our will: and this, indeed, is also the only way of thoroughly refuting that view. —In short, this system introduces throughout the whole man that *unity* and *connection* which so many systems fail to provide.]

III.   Now in course of this reflection on itself, the self as such cannot come to consciousness, since it is never immediately conscious of its own action. Yet it is henceforth present, as a self; for some possible observer, of course; and here then lies the boundary whereby the self, as living, is distinguished from inanimate bodies,

though these, too, can also have a drive in them.   —There is something present, *for which* a thing might be, though it is not as yet
present *for itself*. But there is necessarily present for it an inner
driving force, though since there can be no consciousness of the self,
or of any relation thereto, this force is merely *felt*. A situation that
cannot, indeed, be described, but can certainly be felt, and in regard to which everyone must be referred to his own inner feeling.
[The philosopher may refer men to their private feelings, not in
I, 296   respect of the *that* (for once a self is granted, this must be rigorously demonstrated), but merely in regard to the *what*. To postulate
the occurrence of a specific feeling is a shallow way of proceeding.
Later on, this feeling will admittedly reveal itself, albeit not
through itself, but through its consequences.]

Here, we were saying, the living is divided from the dead. The
feeling of force is the principle of all life; the transition from death
to life. To be sure, in existing merely, life is still very far from complete; but for all that, it is already distinct from inanimate matter.
IV.

a)   This force is felt as an *impelling drive:* the self, as we
said, feels itself driven, and driven *out abroad from itself.* (Where
this *out* and *abroad* come from, we cannot yet discern here, though
it will soon become evident.)

b)   Just as before, this drive must *effect what it can. Real*
activity it does not determine, that is, it produces no causality upon
the not-self. But *ideal* activity, depending solely on the self, is
something it *can* determine, and *must,* as surely as it is a drive.
—Hence the ideal activity goes outward, and posits something as
object of the drive; as that which the drive would bring about, if it
possessed causality.   —(*That* this production must occur through
ideal activity, is demonstrated; *how* it will be possible, is still quite
beyond our discernment at present; and presupposes a multitude of
other inquiries.)

c)   This production, and the agent therein, still makes no
appearance at all here in consciousness; so nothing whatever results
from it as yet; neither a *feeling* of the drive's object—a thing entirely impossible—nor yet an *intuition* thereof. No result of any
I, 297   kind occurs; all that we obtain here is an explanation of how the

self is able to feel itself *driven towards something unknown;* and the way is opened to what follows.

V.   The drive was to be *felt* as a drive, that is, as something that lacks causality. But insofar as it impels at least to a production of its object through ideal activity, it possesses causality after all, and is to that extent not felt as a *drive.*

Insofar as the drive aspires to real activity, it is nothing that can be noticed or felt; for it has no causality. To that extent, also, it is therefore not felt as a drive.

Let us combine these two: —no drive can be felt, unless ideal activity is directed to the object thereof; and such activity cannot be so directed, unless the real activity is limited.

Both principles together yield the self's reflection on itself as a *limited* thing. But since in this reflection the self is not conscious of itself, the reflection in question is a mere *feeling.*

We thus have a complete deduction of feeling. It is characterized by a feeling of force which does not yet make itself manifest; by an object thereof, which equally fails to manifest itself; and by a sense of compulsion or incapacity; and this is the manifestation of feeling that we were required to deduce.

§ 9.   SIXTH DISCOURSE.

Feeling must be further determined and limited.

I.

1.   The self now feels itself limited, that is, it is limited *for itself,* and not merely, as hitherto, or as in the case of the inanimate elastic body, limited merely for an observer outside itself. Its activity is eliminated *for itself*—we repeat, *for itself;* for though we, from our higher standpoint, can indeed see that by absolute activity it has produced a drive-object outside itself, the self we are investigating is not aware of this.

I, 298

This total annihilation of activity is foreign to the character of the self. As surely as it is a self, therefore, it must restore this activity, and restore it *for itself,* that is, it must at least put itself in the position of being able, if only in some future course of reflection, to posit itself as free and unlimited.

In accordance with our deduction thereof, this restoration of its activity occurs through absolute spontaneity, solely as a result of the self's nature, without any special inducement. With absolute spontaneity a reflection ensues upon the reflective act, which the present act will soon prove to be; the one act is broken off, so that another may take its place—when it feels, in the manner just described, the self also acts, but does so without consciousness; in place of this act another is to be substituted which at least makes consciousness possible. The self acts therein absolutely because it acts.

(Here lies the boundary between mere life and intelligence, as earlier between death and life. From this absolute spontaneity alone there arises the consciousness of the self.   —Not by any law of nature, nor by any consequence of such laws, do we attain to reason; we achieve it by absolute freedom, not through a *transition,* but by means of a *leap.*   —In philosophy, therefore, we must necessarily start from the self, since this we cannot deduce; and hence the materialists' project, of deriving the appearance of reason from natural laws, remains forever incapable of achievement.)

2.   It will at once be evident that the required act, occurring simply and solely through absolute spontaneity, can be nothing but an act occurring through ideal activity. But every act has an object,

I, 299   as surely as it is an act. The present act, to be founded simply and solely on the self, and to depend on the self alone in all that conditions it, can have for its object only some factor present in the self. But nothing is present therein save feeling. Hence it necessarily refers to feeling.

The act occurs with absolute spontaneity, and is to that extent, for a possible observer, an act of the self. It is directed to *feeling,* that is, in the first place, to *that which reflects* in the foregoing reflection which constituted feeling.   —Activity is directed to activity; what reflects in this reflection, or *what feels,* is therefore posited *as the self;* the selfhood of what reflects in the present function, which as such makes no appearance in consciousness, is transferred thereto.

The self, by our previous argument, is that which determines itself. Hence, what feels can be posited as a self only insofar as it is determined to feel by the *drive* merely, and thus by the self, and is thus self-determined; that is, solely insofar as it feels *itself,* and *its own power within itself.* —Only what feels is the self, and only the drive, insofar as it gives rise to feeling or reflection, belongs to the self. Whatever lies beyond this boundary—if anything does lie beyond, and we know at all events that something does, namely the *outward* drive—is excluded; and this must certainly be noted, since the excluded element will require further consideration in due course.

What is *felt,* therefore, in and for the present reflection, will likewise be the self, since what *feels* is self only to the extent that it is self-determined, that is, feels itself.

II. In our present course of reflection, the self is posited as self solely insofar as it is at once what *feels* and what is *felt,* and therefore stands in reciprocity with itself. It has to be posited as self, and must therefore be posited in the manner described.

1. What *feels* is posited as *active* in the feeling, insofar as it is the reflecting element, and to that extent what is felt in this feeling is *passive;* it is the object of reflection. —At the same time, what *feels* is posited *as passive* in the feeling, insofar as it feels itself *driven;* and to that extent the felt, or the drive, is *active;* it is the *driving* factor.

2. This is a contradiction that requires to be reconciled, and is capable of reconciliation only in the following manner. —What feels is *active* in relation to *what is felt;* and in this respect it is *solely* active. (That it is driven to reflection, does not come to consciousness therein; though it finds a place in our philosophic inquiry, the drive to reflection receives no attention at all in the original consciousness. It is incorporated into the object of that which feels, and in reflection on the feeling it is not distinguished.) But now it also has to be *passive,* in relation to a drive. This is the outward drive, by which it is really impelled, to produce a not-self through ideal activity. (Now in this function it is in fact active, but just as before with its passivity, so now this activity it engages in is not reflected on. For *itself,* in reflection on itself, it acts under compulsion, notwithstanding that this appears to be a contradiction, though one that will dissolve in due course. Hence the felt compulsion to posit something as really present.)

3. What is *felt* is *active,* by way of the drive impelling the reflective factor to reflection. In the same relation to this factor it is also *passive;* for it is the object of reflection. But there is no reflection on the latter, since the self is posited as one and the same, as *feeling itself,* and no further reflection takes place on the reflection itself. Hence the self is posited as passive in another relation: namely insofar as it is *limited,* and to that extent the limiting factor is a not-self. (Every object of reflection is necessarily limited; it has a determinate quantity. But in and in course of reflection, this limitation is never derived from the reflection itself, because to that extent there is no reflection upon the latter.)

I, 301

4. Both must be one and the same self, and be posited as such. Yet the one is regarded as active in relation to the not-self, while the other, in the same relation, is regarded as passive. In the one case, the self produces a not-self through ideal activity; in the other, it is limited thereby.

5. The contradiction is easily reconciled. The productive self was itself posited as *passive,* and thus as what is felt in reflection. *For itself,* therefore, the self is always *passive* in relation to the not-self, is quite unaware of its own activity, and does not reflect thereon. —Hence the reality of the thing appears to be felt, whereas it is only the self that is so.

(Here lies the ground of all reality. Only through that relation of feeling to the self, which has now been demonstrated, is the reality either of the self, or the not-self, possible for the self. Anything which is possible solely through *the relation of a feeling,* without the self being conscious, or able to be conscious, *of its intuition thereof,* and *which therefore appears to be felt,* is *believed.*

As to reality in general, whether that of the self or the not-self, there is only *a belief.)*

§ 10. SEVENTH DISCOURSE.

The drive itself must be posited and determined.

Just as we have now explained and determined feeling, so the drive also must be determined, since it is linked with feeling.

By means of this explanation we shall make progress, and gain a footing within the domain of the practical.

1. That the drive is posited means, as we know, that the self reflects upon it. Now the self can reflect only upon itself and on that which is in it and for it—which is, as it were, accessible thereto. Hence the drive must already have established something in the self, and contrived, indeed, to install itself therein, *insofar as the reflection just outlined has already posited it as the self.*

2. What feels is posited as the self. The latter was determined by the felt original drive to issue forth from itself and produce something, at least by ideal activity. Now, however, the original drive is by no means bent upon mere ideal activity, but upon *reality;* and the self is therefore determined by it to the production *of a reality outside itself.* —Now this determination it cannot fulfil, since the striving is never to have causal efficacy, but is to be kept in balance by the counterstriving of the not-self. Hence, insofar as it is determined by the drive, it is *restricted* by the not-self.

3. The self has a persistent tendency within it to reflect upon itself, as soon as the condition of all reflection—a limitation—makes its appearance. The condition enters at this point; thus the self must necessarily reflect upon its own current state. —Now in this reflection the reflective element forgets itself, as usual, and hence it does not attain to consciousness. Moreover, this reflection occurs upon a mere impulse; hence it contains not the least manifestation of freedom, and becomes, as before, a mere feeling. The only question is, what sort of feeling?

4. The object of this reflection is the self, the self as driven, and hence, *idealiter,* as internally active; driven by an impulse lying within itself, and thus altogether lacking in choice and spontaneity. —But this activity of the self is directed to an object, which it cannot *realize,* as a thing, nor even *represent* through ideal activity. Hence it is an activity *that has no object whatever,* but is nonetheless *irresistibly driven out towards one,* and is merely *felt.* But such a determination in the self is called a *longing;* a drive towards something totally unknown, which reveals itself only through a *need,* a *discomfort,* a *void,* which seeks satisfaction, but does not say from whence. —The self feels a longing in itself; it feels itself in want.

I, 302

I, 303

5. Both feelings, the feeling of *longing* now derived, and the previously exhibited feeling of *limitation and compulsion,* must be differentiated and related one to another.   —For the drive is to be determined; now the drive reveals itself through a specific *feeling,* and so this feeling has to be determined; but it can only be determined through a feeling of some other kind.

6.   If the self were not restricted in the first feeling, the second would evince no *mere longing,* but *causality;* for the self would then be able to bring forth something outside itself, and its drive would not be confined to a mere self-determination of the self from within. Conversely, if the self did not feel itself as *longing,* it could not feel itself to be *restricted,* for it is only through the feeling of longing that the self issues forth from itself—only through this feeling is something first posited, in and for the self, which is to exist outside it.

(This longing is of importance, not only for the practical, but for the entire Science of Knowledge. Only thereby is the self *in itself*—driven *out of itself;* only thereby is an *external world* revealed *within it.)*

7.   Both are therefore synthetically united; the one is impossible without the other. No limitation, no longing; no longing, no limitation.   —Both are also totally opposed to each other. In the feeling of limitation the self is felt only as *passive,* while in that of longing it is also felt as *active.*

8.   Both are based on the drive, and on *one and the same* drive in the self. The drive of the self, as limited by the not-self, and only on that account capable of a drive, determines the power of reflection, and hence arises the feeling of a compulsion. The same drive determines the self to issue out of itself by ideal activity, and to bring forth something external to itself; and since the self is restricted in this respect, the result is a *longing,* and, owing to the power of reflection that is thereby put to the necessity of reflecting, *a feeling of longing.*   —The question is, how one and the same drive could engender such an opposite. Only through the difference of the forces to which it addresses itself. In its first function it is directed solely to the mere power of reflection, which only comprehends what is given to it; in its second, to the absolute, free striving founded in the self as such, which sets out to create, and through

I, 304

ideal activity actually does so; only that so far we are not yet acquainted with its—product, nor are capable of knowing the same.
9. The longing is thus the *original, wholly independent manifestation* of the striving that lies in the self. *Independent,* because it has no regard to any restriction, and is not held up thereby. (An important observation; for it will later become apparent that this longing is the vehicle of all practical laws; and that they are to be identified only by whether or not they can be derived therefrom.)
10. In longing, the limitation at once gives rise to a feeling of compulsion, which must have its ground in a not-self. The object of longing (that which the drive-determined self would really bring about, if it had causality, and which we may provisionally call the *ideal)* is in complete conformity and congruence with the striving of the self; that which could be posited, however (and doubtless is posited), through a relating of the feeling of limitation to the self, is at loggerheads with it. So the two objects are themselves opposed to one another.
11. Since there can be no longing in the self without a feeling of compulsion, and *vice versa* the self in both is synthetically united, is one and the same self. Yet under the two determinations it is manifestly thrown into conflict with itself; is both *limited* and *unlimited, finite,* and *infinite* at the same time. This contradiction must be eliminated, and we now proceed to state the issue more clearly, and to resolve it in a satisfactory manner.
12. The longing aspires, as we said, to realize something outside the self. This it cannot do; nor, so far as we can see, is the self able to do such a thing, under any of its determinations. —Yet this outgoing drive must effect what it can. And it is able to operate on the ideal activity of the self, determining it to issue forth from itself and produce something. —As to this power of production, it is not in question here; it will shortly receive a genetic deduction; but we do need an answer to the following question, which is bound to strike everyone who is pursuing the inquiry along with us. Why, quite apart from the fact that we originally set out from an outgoing drive, did we not make this inference sooner? The answer to this is as follows: *In a manner valid for itself* (and this is all we are talking of here, having already made this inference above, in regard to a possible observer), the self cannot direct itself *outwards*

I, 305

without first having limited itself; for till then there is, for it, neither inside nor outside. This self-limitation took place through the *self-feeling* that we have deduced. Thereafter it is equally incapable of directing itself outwards unless the external world reveals itself somehow to the self *within that self*. This, however, first occurs through longing.

13. The question arises, *how* the self's ideal activity, determined by longing, will produce, and *what* it will produce. —The self contains a determinate feeling of limitation $= X$. —It also contains a longing directed out upon reality. But reality is manifested for the self only by way of feeling: hence the longing is directed towards a feeling. Now the feeling X is not the feeling longed for; if it were, the self would not feel itself as *limited* or as *longing;* and would not feel itself at all; —but rather would have the opposite

I, 306   feeling, $\sim X$. The object that would have to be present, if the feeling $\sim X$ were to occur in the self (and which we shall itself entitle $\sim X$), would have to be produced. This would be the ideal. —Now if, on the one hand, the object X (the ground of the feeling of restriction X) could itself be felt, it would be easy to posit the object $\sim X$ by a mere act of counterpositing. But this is impossible, since the self never feels an object, but merely feels itself; yet can only produce the object through ideal activity. —If, on the other hand, the self could somehow conjure up in itself the feeling $\sim X$, as such, it would be in a position itself to make immediate comparison of the two feelings, to note their difference, and to refer them to objects, as the ground thereof. But the self cannot conjure up feelings in itself; for if so, it would have causality, which it is not supposed to possess. (This fits in with the principle of the theoretical Science of Knowledge, that the self cannot limit itself.) —The problem, then, is nothing less than this, that from the feeling of limitation, which cannot in any way be further determined, we should conclude immediately to the object of the longing totally opposed to it: that, solely under the guidance of the first feeling, the self should bring forth this object through ideal activity.

14. The object of the feeling of limitation is something real: the object of the longing has no reality, but is required to have it in consequence of the longing, since the latter aspires to reality. Both are opposed to each other, since the self feels limited by the one,

whereas in accordance with the other it strives to escape from limitation. What the one is, the other is not. So much, and no more, can be said for the moment of both.

15. Let us pursue the inquiry more deeply. —According to the above, the self, by free reflection on the feeling, has posited itself as a self, on the principle that whatever posits itself, whatever is both determinant and determinate at once, is the self. —In the course of this reflection, therefore (which was manifested as self-feeling), the self has *determined,* has utterly circumscribed and limited, itself. In so doing, it is *absolutely determinant.*

16. The outgoing drive accommodates itself to this activity, and becomes therefore in this respect a drive to the *determination* or *modification* of something external to the self, namely the reality already given by feeling in general. —The self was at once the determinate and the determinant. That it is impelled outwards by the drive, is to say that it must be the *determinant.* But all determination presupposes a determinable matter. —The equilibrium must be preserved; so the reality continues to remain what it was, *reality,* something that can be related to feeling; and for reality as such, as mere *matter,* there can be no conceivable modification, save destruction and total elimination. But its existence is the condition of life; the lifeless can contain no drive, and from the living there can proceed no drive to the destruction of life. Hence the drive that manifests itself in the self is directed, not to *matter* in general, but to a certain *determination thereof.* (We cannot say, a *different matter,* for materiality is absolutely simple, but must speak, rather, of *matter with different determinations.*)

17. It is *this* determination by the drive which is felt as a *longing.* Hence the longing aspires not at all to the production of matter as such, but to its modification.

18. Obviously enough, the *feeling* of longing was impossible without reflection upon the determination of the self by the drive aforementioned. This reflection was impossible without limitation of the drive, and of the very drive to determination which alone finds expression in longing. But all limitation of the self is merely felt. The question is, what kind of feeling it can be, whereby the *drive to determine* is felt as limited.

19. All determination occurs through ideal activity. Hence, if the

I, 308   required feeling is to be possible, an object will already have had to be determined through this ideal activity, and this act of determining will have had to be related to feeling. —At this point the following questions arise: 1.) How is the ideal activity to arrive at the possibility and actuality of this determining? 2.) How is this determining to be able to relate itself to feeling?

To the first we answer: We have already pointed above to a determination of the self's ideal activity by means of the drive, which must constantly effect as much as it can. In consequence of this determination, the activity must serve to *posit*, in the first place, *the ground of limitation*, as an object determined, moreover, entirely by itself; for which very reason, such an object neither comes, nor can come, to consciousness. And besides, a drive to mere determination has just come to light in the self; and in virtue thereof the ideal activity must at least begin by striving to set about *determining* the object posited. —We cannot say *how* the self is to determine the object, in consequence of the drive; but this much at least we know, that in virtue of this drive stemming from its inmost nature, it is to be the *determinant*, the *one and only absolutely active factor* in the determining-process. Now, even apart from the already-known feeling of *longing*, whose presence alone is enough to settle the question, is it possible, on purely a priori grounds, for this drive to determination to have causality, to attain fulfilment, or not? Upon its limitation there depends the possibility of a longing; upon the possibility of that, the possibility of a feeling; and on that —life, consciousness and mental existence in general. Hence, as surely as the self is a self, the drive to determination has no causality. Yet, no more than in the previous case of striving in general, can the ground of this lie in itself, for if so, it would not be a drive; so

I, 309   it must lie in a counterdrive of the not-self *to determine itself*, in an efficacy of the latter, which is wholly independent of the self and its drive, which goes *its own* way, and conforms to *its own* laws, as does the drive of the self.

If, therefore, there is an object, and if its determinations are brought forth in themselves, that is, through the intrinsic inner efficacy of nature (as we meanwhile assume hypothetically, but will shortly show to be true *for the self*); and if, moreover, the ideal (intuitant) activity of the self is impelled outward by the drive, as we have demonstrated, then the self will and must determine the object. In this determination it is guided by the drive, and sets about to determine the object in accordance with the latter; but it is subject at the same time to the operation of the not-self, and by this, by the actual constitution of the thing, it is limited to being more or less *un*able to determine this thing in accordance with the drive.

By this restriction of the drive, the self is limited; as in every limitation of striving, and in the same manner, there arises a feeling —in this case a feeling that the self is limited, not by *matter,* but *by the constitution of matter.* And with that we have an answer to the second question, how the restriction of determination might be related to feeling.

20.   Let us elaborate and give sharper definition to what has just been said.

a)   As was shown earlier, the self determined itself through absolute spontaneity. It is this determining activity that the drive now in question turns to and drives abroad. If we are to gain a thorough acquaintance with the way the drive determines the activity, we need above all to be thoroughly familiar with the *activity itself.*

b)   In action it was simply and solely *reflective.* It determined the self as it found it, without changing anything therein; it was, as we might say, merely *depictive.* The drive neither can nor should interpolate anything that is not present therein; hence it simply impels the activity to copy what is there, as it stands; to intuit the thing merely, but in no way to modify it by real efficacy. The requirement is merely to bring forth in the self a determination, as it exists in the not-self.

I, 310

c)   Yet for all that, the self reflecting on itself was bound in *one* respect to contain its own yardstick of reflection. For it addressed itself to that which *(realiter)* was *at once determinate* and *determinant,* and posited this as a self. That anything of the kind was present, did not depend on it, so far as it was considered merely in its reflective capacity. But why, then, did it not reflect on less, on the determinate alone, or the determinant alone? And why not on more? Why did it not extend the scope of its object? The reason for this could not have lain outside it, if only because the reflection took place with absolute spontaneity. Hence it must have had what every reflection possesses—the limitation thereof—solely in itself. —That this was the case, emerges also from another consideration. The self was to be posited. The 'simultaneously determinate and determinant' was posited as the self. The reflecting agency had this yardstick within it, and brought it along to the task of reflection; for, *in that it reflects by absolute spontaneity*, it is itself at once the determinant and the determinate.

Now does the reflecting agency also have the same sort of inner law for determining the not-self? And what law is this?

This question is easily answered by reference to the grounds already put forward. The drive is addressed to the reflecting self, just as it is. It can add or subtract nothing, and its inner law of determination remains the same. Everything that is to be object of its reflection and *(ideal)* determination must *(realiter)* be 'determinate and determinant at once'; and so too with the not-self that is to be determined. The subjective law of determination is therefore this; *that something should be at once determinate and determinant, or determined by itself:* and the drive to determination is addressed to finding this to be so, and can be satisfied only on this condition.   —It demands *determinacy*, complete *totality* and *wholeness*, which consists simply in this property. That which, *insofar as* it is *determinate*, is not also simultaneously the determinant, is to that extent an effect; and this effect is excluded from the thing as something *alien*, cut off by the boundaries that reflection draws, and explained by *something else*. That which insofar as it is *determinant*, and is not at the same time *the determinate*, is to that extent a *cause*, and the determining relates to *something else*, and is thereby excluded from the sphere that reflection ascribes to the thing. Only insofar as the thing stands in reciprocity with itself, is it a thing, and the same thing. This property is carried out of the self and over to the thing by the drive to determination; and this is an important observation.

(The most commonplace examples serve to illustrate the point. Why are sweet or bitter, red or yellow, etc., *simple* sensations, which cannot be resolved into others—or why, in general, are they self-subsistent sensations, and not mere constituents of some other one? The reason for this must obviously lie in the self *for which* they are simple sensations; the self must therefore contain a priori a law of *limitation* in general).

d) Despite this similarity in the law of determination, the difference between self and not-self remains. If we reflect on the self, that which reflects and that which is reflected on are identical, one and the same, determined and determinant; if we reflect on the not-self, the two are opposed; for that which reflects is self-evidently always the self.

e) Here, too, we obtain strict proof that the drive to determination aims, not at real modification, but simply at ideal determination, determination for the self, or copying. Whatever can be the object of this drive must, *realiter,* be completely determined by itself, and there is nothing left for a real activity of the self to do; on the contrary, such an activity would be in open contradiction with the determination of the drive. If the self modifies *realiter,* we are not given what ought to be given.

21. The only question is, how and in what manner is the determinable to be given to the self; and in answering this question we again enter more deeply into the synthetic connection of the acts to be set forth here.

The self reflects upon itself, as both determinate and determinant, and to that extent limits itself (the limitation extends precisely so far as do the determinate and the determinant): but there can be no *limitation* without a *limitant.* This limitant, to be opposed to the self, cannot be produced—as was postulated in our theoretical inquiry—by any ideal activity, but must be given to the self and lie therein. But now something of the kind is present in the self, namely that which was excluded in this reflection, as we showed above. —The self posits itself as self, only insofar as it is the *determinate and the determinant:* but it is such only in an ideal respect. Its striving toward real activity is limited, however, and is to that extent posited as an internal, confined, self-determining force (*i.e.,* as simultaneously determinate and determinant), or, since it is without manifestation, as intensive matter. We reflect upon it, as such; it is thereupon carried outside by an act of counterpositing, and the intrinsically and originally *subjective* is transformed into something *objective.*

a) We obtain full understanding at this point of the origin

of the law, that the self cannot posit itself as determined without opposing to itself a not-self.   —We could, indeed, have argued from the very beginning in accordance with this now abundantly familiar law: if the self is to determine itself, it must necessarily oppose something to itself; but since we are here in the practical part of the Science of Knowledge, and so must be mindful everywhere of drives and feelings, we were obliged to derive this law itself from a drive.   —The drive that originally proceeds outward effects what it can, and since it cannot exert itself upon real activity, it operates at least upon ideal activity, which by nature cannot be in any way restricted, and drives it outwards. Hence arises the counterpositing; and in this way, in and through the drive, all the determinations of consciousness hang together, and in particular also the consciousness of the self and not-self.

b)   The subjective is transformed into something objective; and conversely, everything objective is originally something subjective.   —A perfectly apt example cannot be furnished; for we are talking here of a *determinate* in general, which is also nothing whatever but a determinate; and such a thing is quite unable to appear in consciousness, the reason for which we shall shortly discover. Every determinate, as surely as it is to appear in consciousness, is necessarily a *particular*. But the foregoing claim can be demonstrated quite clearly in consciousness by means of examples of the latter sort.

Let a thing, for example, be *sweet, sour, red, yellow,* or the like. Such a determination is manifestly something purely *subjective;* and we hope that no one who so much as understands those terms will dispute it. Anything sweet or sour, or red or yellow, is absolutely incapable of being described, and can only be felt, nor can it be communicated by any description to someone else, for everyone must relate the object to his own feelings, if ever a knowledge of my sensation is to arise in him. All that can be said is that *the sensation of bitter, sweet, etc., is in me,* and nothing more. —But then suppose further that the other person relates the object to his own feeling; how then do you know that the knowledge of *your* sensation thereby arises in him, that he senses in the same way as yourself? How do you know that sugar, for example, produces exactly the same impression on his taste that it does on yours?

To be sure, you give the name *sweet* to what occurs in you when you eat sugar, and he and all your fellows also call it sweet as you do; but this is a merely verbal agreement. For how do you know that what you both call sweet is exactly the same for him as it is for you? There is no settling such a question this side of eternity; the issue lies in the realm of pure subjectivity, and is not objective at all. Only when the sugar is synthesized with a determinate taste, *in itself subjective, but* objective solely *in virtue of its determinacy in general,* is the matter transferred to the sphere of objectivity.   —Such purely subjective relationships to feeling are the source of all our knowledge; without feeling, there can be no presentation at all of an external thing.

This determination *of yourself* you now carry over at once to something *outside you;* what is actually an accident of your self, you transform into the accident of a thing required to be external to you (necessitated by laws that the Science of Knowledge has sufficiently set forth), *a matter that must be extended in space, and occupy the latter.*   —That this matter itself may indeed be only something entirely subjective that occurs in you, is a thing you should long ago have come at least to suspect; if only because, without any new feeling being added from such matter, you can straightway carry over to it something that by your own admission is entirely subjective (such as sweet, red, etc.); and further because, without a subjective property to be transferred to it, such a matter simply does not exist for you, and is thus nothing more for you than the bearer you need for the subjective property that is to be carried over from yourself.   —In that you transfer the subjective thereto, it is doubtless present in and for yourself. But now if it was originally there outside you, and had entered into you from without, so as to make possible the synthesis that you have to undertake, it must

I, 315 somehow have entered you by way of *the senses.* But the senses furnish us merely a subjective datum of the kind described above; matter, as such, in no way belongs to the senses, but can only be framed or thought through productive imagination. To be sure, a tyro in abstraction may possibly object, it is neither seen, nor heard, nor tasted, nor smelt; but it falls under the sense of touch *(tactus).* But this sense evinces itself only through the sensation of a resistance, an inability, which is subjective; *that which resists,* one would hope, is not *felt,* but merely *inferred.* Touch extends only to the surface, which reveals itself always through some subjective factor, for example, that it is rough or delicate, cold or hot, hard or soft, and the like; it does not penetrate to the interior of the body. Why then, in the first place, do you spread this heat or cold that you feel (together with the hand you feel it by) over a whole broad area, and do not locate it at your single point of contact? And how, again, do you contrive to assume an interior to the body, within the surfaces, though you do not feel it? This obviously comes about through the productive imagination.   —Yet you take this matter to be something objective, and rightly so, since you all agree as to its presence, and are bound to do so, seeing that the production thereof is based on a universal law of all reason.

22.   The drive was directed to the self-reflected activity, *as such,* whereby the self determines itself *as a self.* It is therefore expressly implied in determination by the drive, that it should be the *self* that determines the thing—hence, that the self should reflect upon itself in the course of this determination. It must reflect, that is, posit itself as the determinant.   —(We shall return to this reflection. Here we regard it merely as an aid to further advance in our inquiry.)

I, 316   23.   The activity of the self is one, and cannot be directed to several objects at once. It was to determine the not-self, which we shall refer to as X. Now *in course of this determining,* the self, through the same activity, of course, is to reflect upon itself. This is impossible, unless the act *of determination* (of X) be interrupted. The self's reflection on itself occurs with absolute spontaneity, and so, therefore, does the interruption. The self, through absolute spontaneity, breaks off the act of determination.

24.   The self is thus restricted in the determining, and there arises from thence *a feeling.* It is *restricted,* for the drive to *determination* extended outward without any determination, that is, into the infinite.   —It contained in general the rule of reflecting on what was *realiter* determined by itself, as one and the same; but no law that the latter—in the present case X—should extend to B or C and so on. This determination is now interrupted at a specific point, which we shall designate as C. (What sort of limitation this may be, can be decided in due course; but beware of conceiving it as a

spatial limitation. We are speaking of an intensive limitation, i.e. of that which distinguishes the sweet from the bitter, and so forth). There occurs, therefore, a *restriction* of the drive to determination, as the condition of a feeling. There is also *a reflection* thereupon, as the second condition thereof. For insofar as the free activity of the self breaks off the determining of the object, it addresses itself to the determining and the limitation, the whole extent thereof, which only becomes an extent in this way. But the self is unaware of this freedom of its act, so that the limitation is therefore ascribed to the thing.   —It is a feeling of limitation of the self through the *determinacy* of the thing, or the feeling of a *determinate,* or *simple.*

I, 317

25.   We now describe the reflection which replaces the determination that has been interrupted, and is betrayed as interrupted by the occurrence of a feeling.   —In it, the self is to posit itself as a self, that is, as that which determines itself in course of the act. It will be apparent that what is posited as product of the self can be nothing other than an intuition of X, an image thereof, but in no sense X itself, as is evident on theoretical grounds, and even from what has just been said. That it is posited as product of the self in its freedom, means that it is posited as *contingent,* as something that did not necessarily have to be as it is, but might also have been otherwise.   —If the self were conscious of its freedom in imaging (by itself reflecting in turn upon the present reflection), the image would be posited as contingent *in relation to the self.* Such a reflection does not occur; it must therefore be posited as contingent *in relation to another not-self,* which till now has remained wholly unknown to us. We proceed to a fuller account of what is here stated in general terms.

In order to conform to the law of determination, X would have to be self-determined (determined and determinant at once). Now this is in accordance with our postulate. Furthermore, in virtue of the feeling that obtains, X must extend to C and no further; but it also determines up to that point. (The import of this will soon be apparent.) This determination has no basis at all in the *idealiter* determinant or intuitant self. It has no law for this. (Does the self-determinant actually extend only this far? It will appear in part that, regarded simply in itself, it goes further, that is, out to infinity; yet even if there were to be a distinction there, in the thing, how does it enter into the sphere of influence of the ideal self? How does it become accessible thereto, since the latter has no point of contact at all with the not-self, indeed is only active *idealiter* insofar as it lacks such a point of contact, and is not delimited by the not-self? —In popular terms: Why is *sweet* something *other* than *bitter*, and opposed thereto? Both, in general, are *determinates*. But apart from this common characteristic, what is their ground of distinction? It cannot lie solely in the ideal activity; for no concept is possible of both. Yet in part at least it must lie in the self; since it is a distinction *for the self*.)

I, 318

Hence the ideal self oscillates with absolute freedom over and within the boundary. Its bounds are wholly indeterminate. Can it remain in this state? By no means; for now, according to the postulate, it is to reflect upon itself in this intuition, and thus posit itself as *determined* therein; for all reflection presupposes determination.

The rule of determination in general is assuredly familiar to us; a thing is determined only insofar as it is determined by itself. Hence, in this intuition of the X, the self would have to set its own limits to the intuition. It would have to determine itself, to posit the point C, indeed, as the boundary-point, and X would thus be determined by the absolute spontaneity of the self.

26. Nevertheless—and this is an important argument—X is something that by the law of determination in general is self-determined, and only so far as it is so is it actually an object of the postulated intuition.   —To be sure, we have so far spoken only of the internal determination of the entity in question; but the *external* determination of the limit follows immediately from this. X = X, insofar as it is at once determinate and determinant, *and goes so far, to the extent that it is such,* e.g., to C. If the self is to limit X correctly and appropriately to the matter in hand, it *must* limit it at C, and hence it could not be said that the limitation comes about through absolute spontaneity. Both principles are self-contradictory, and might oblige us to draw a distinction.

27.   Nevertheless—the limitation of X at C is merely *felt* and not *intuited*. The freely posited must be *intuited* merely, and not *felt*. Yet the two, intuition and feeling, have no connection. Intuition *sees,* but is *empty;* feeling *relates to reality,* but is *blind.*   —Yet X must be limited both as it is limited and in accordance with the

I, 319

truth. What is called for, therefore, is a unification, a synthetic connection, between feeling and intuition. We shall pursue this latter inquiry still further, and will thereby arrive unawares at the point we are in search of.

28. The requirement was, that the intuitant should limit X by absolute spontaneity, and yet in such a fashion that X should appear as limited entirely by itself. This requirement will be satisfied if the ideal activity, by its absolute power of production, should posit a Y out beyond X (at point B, C, D, etc., for the determinate boundary-point can neither be posited by the ideal activity itself, nor be immediately given to it). —This Y, as posited counter to an internally determinate item, a something, must 1.) itself be something, that is, at once determined and determinant, according to the laws of determinacy in general; 2.) be opposed to, a limitant of, X, that is, so far as X is determinant, Y is not related thereto as the determinate, and so far as it is determined, Y does not relate thereto as the determinant, and *vice versa*. It is not to be possible to conjoin them, to reflect upon both as on one. (It should be noted, indeed, that we are not referring here to relative determination or limitation, in which relation they admittedly stand; but to inner determination, in which they do not. Every possible point of X stands in reciprocity with every other point thereof; and so too with Y. It is not the case, however, that every point of Y stands in reciprocity with every point of X, or *vice versa*. They are both something, but each is something different; and only thereby do we first arrive at posing and answering the question, *what* are they? Without counterposition, the entire not-self is something, but not a determinate or particular something, and the question, *what* is this or that? has in such a case no meaning whatever; for only through counterposition does it obtain an answer.)

It is this to which the drive determines the ideal activity; the law of the required act is easily deducible according to the rule given above, namely, that X and Y should mutually exclude one another. So far as this drive is merely directed, as here, to the ideal activity, we may name it *the drive to interdetermination*.

29. The boundary-point C is posited solely through feeling; hence the Y lying beyond C, insofar as it is to start precisely at C, can also be given only through relation to feeling. It is feeling alone

that unites the two at the boundary.   —The drive to interdetermination is therefore simultaneously directed to a feeling. In it, *ideal activity and feeling* are thus internally united; in it, the whole self is one.   —We can to that extent entitle it *the drive towards change in general.*   —It is this which finds expression in *longing;* the object of longing is *some other thing, opposed* to what is present.

In longing, ideality and the drive to reality are inwardly united. Longing is directed *to something else;* this is possible only on the presumption of a previous determination through ideal activity. It also evinces the drive to reality (as restricted), since it is *felt,* and not thought or represented. Here we see how in a feeling a drive *outwards,* and thus the intimation of an external world, may come about; because in fact it is modified through ideal activity, which is free from any limitation. We also see here how a theoretical function of the mind may be traced back to the practical capacity; which would have to be possible, if the rational being is ever to become a complete whole.

30.   The feeling does not depend on us, since it derives from a limitation, and the self cannot limit itself. Now, an opposed feeling is due to enter. The question is, will the external condition enter, under which alone such a feeling is possible? It must do so. For if it does not, the self feels nothing *determinate,* and hence feels *nothing at all;* it is not alive, therefore, and is no self, which contradicts the presupposition of the Science of Knowledge.

31.   The feeling of an *opposite* is the condition for satisfying the drive, since *the drive towards change of feelings* in general is *longing.* What is longed for is now determined, though only by the predicate that it is to constitute *something else,* a change, for feeling.

32.   Now the self cannot feel in two ways at once; for it cannot be *limited at C* and at the same time *unlimited at C.* Hence the altered state cannot be *felt as* an altered state. The other would thus have to be intuited solely by ideal activity, as something different and opposed to the current feeling.   —Intuition and feeling would therefore be always necessarily present simultaneously in the self, and both would be synthetically united at one and the same point.

Moreover, the ideal activity cannot take the place of a feeling, or engender one; so it could only determine its object as *not* being what was felt, as susceptible of all possible determinations other than that present in the feeling. Hence, for ideal activity, the thing remains always determined in a merely negative fashion; and what is felt remains equally undetermined thereby. No means of determination is conceivable in this context, save a negative determination extended to infinity.

I, 322

[That is in fact the situation. What, for example, does *sweet* mean? In the first place, something connected, not with vision, hearing and so on, but with *taste*. What taste is, you have to know already through sensation, and can realize it through imagination only in a dim and negative fashion (in a synthesis of *everything that is not taste*). Moreover, under what does relate to taste, it is not *sour, bitter*, etc., or however many specific determinations of taste you may be able to enumerate. But even were you to have enumerated all the taste-sensations known to you, you could still always be given new ones, hitherto unfamiliar, of which you will then judge: they are not *sweet*. Hence the boundary between sweet and all the taste-sensations known to you still remains always an infinite one.]

The one question still to be answered would be this: How is it brought home to the ideal activity that the state of the feeling subject has altered?   —To anticipate, this is evinced through the satisfaction of longing, through a feeling;   —from which circumstance, many important consequences will ensue.

§ 11.   EIGHTH DISCOURSE.
The feelings themselves must be capable of being opposed.

1.   By ideal activity, the self is to oppose an object Y to the object X; it is to posit itself as altered. But it posits Y only at the instigation of a feeling, and *another* feeling at that.   —The ideal activity is dependent solely on itself, and not on the feeling. A feeling, X, is present in the self, and in this case, as shown, the ideal activity is unable to limit the object X, or specify *what* it is. Now, by our postulate, a new feeling = Y is to arise in the self; and hereupon

I, 323   the ideal activity is to determine the object X, that is, be able to oppose to it a determinate Y. The change and alteration in feeling is thus to be capable of exerting influence on the ideal activity. The question is, how this can come about.

2.   The feelings themselves are *different,* for any observer outside the self; but they are to be different for the self as such, that is, they are to be posited as opposed. This is solely the affair of the ideal activity. Both feelings would thus have to be posited, so that they can be posited as a *pair,* synthetically united, yet also opposed. We therefore have to answer the following three questions: a) How is a feeling posited? b)   How are feelings synthetically united by positing? c)   How are they opposed?

3.   A feeling is posited through ideal activity: this can be conceived of only as follows: The self, without any self-consciousness, reflects upon a restriction of its drive. Hence arises, in the first place, a feeling of self. It reflects further upon this reflection, or posits itself therein, as the determined and determinant at once. By this the feeling itself now becomes an ideal act, in that the ideal activity is transferred thereto. The self feels, or more properly *senses something,* namely matter.   —A reflection already alluded to above, whereby X first becomes an object. Through reflection on *feeling,* the latter becomes *sensation.*

4.   *Through ideal positing,* feelings are synthetically united. Their ground of relation can be none other than the ground of the reflection upon both feelings. The said ground of reflection was this: because otherwise the drive to interdetermination would not be satisfied, could not be posited as satisfied, and because, if this does not occur, there is no feeling, and then no self whatever.   —Thus the synthetic ground of union of the reflection on both is this, that without reflection on *both,* there could be reflection on *neither of them,* as feelings.

The condition under which reflection on the individual feeling will not take place, is at once apparent.   —Every feeling is necessarily a limitation of the self; so if the self is not limited, it does not feel, and if it cannot be *posited* as limited, it cannot be posited as feeling. Thus, if the relationship between *two feelings* were to be that *the one* was limited and determined solely *by the other,* then— since nothing can be reflected on without reflecting on its limits, while in this case each feeling is the limit of the other—it would be impossible to reflect on either without reflecting on both.

5.   If feelings are to stand in this relationship, there must be something in each of them that points to the other.   —And in fact we have actually found such a relation. We have pointed out a feeling that was conjoined with a longing; hence, with a drive to *alteration*. If this longing is to be completely determined, then the *other*, that is *longed for*, must be exhibited. Now another such feeling has also, in fact, been postulated. In itself, the latter may determine the self as it pleases: insofar as it is an object, and the *determinate* object, of longing, it must relate to the first feeling, and in respect of the latter be accompanied by a feeling of *satisfaction*. The feeling of longing cannot be posited without a satisfaction, to which it is directed; or the satisfaction, without presupposing a longing that is satisfied. At the point where longing ceases, and satisfaction begins, the boundary lies.

6.   It remains only to ask, how the satisfaction reveals itself in the feeling.   —The longing arose out of an impossibility of determination, since there was a want of limitation; in it, therefore, ideal activity and the drive to reality were combined. As soon as another feeling arises, then 1.)   The required determination, the complete limitation of X, becomes possible, and actually occurs, since the drive and the power for it are present; 2.)   From the very fact of its occurrence, it follows that another feeling is present. In the feeling as such, *qua* limitation, there is no difference at all, nor can there be. But from the fact that something becomes possible, that was not possible without a change of feeling, it follows that the state of the feeling subject has been altered. 3.)   *Drive* and *action* are now one and the same; the determination demanded by the former is possible, and occurs. The self reflects *upon this feeling*, and *on itself* therein, as at once the determinant and the determinate, as wholly at one with itself; and such a determination of feeling we may speak of as *inclination*. The feeling is accompanied by inclination.

7.   The self cannot posit this concurrence of drive and action without distinguishing the two; yet it cannot distinguish them without positing something in which they are opposed. But now there is an instance of this in the preceding feeling, which is therefore necessarily accompanied by a *disinclination* (the opposite of inclination, the expression of a disharmony between drive and action).   —Not

every longing is necessarily accompanied by disinclination, but if it is satisfied, there is disinclination for what preceded; it becomes stale and insipid.

8. The objects X and Y, that were posited by ideal activity, are now no longer characterized merely by opposition, but also by the predicates of evoking *disinclination* or *inclination*. And so we go on determining *ad infinitum*, and the inner determinations of things (which relate to feeling) are nothing more than degrees of the disinclining or inclining.

9. So far, this harmony or disharmony, inclination or the reverse (as a concord or discord of two differing items, though not as a feeling), is present merely for a possible observer, and not for the self as such. Yet both must also be present for the latter, and posited by it—whether ideally merely, through intuition, or through a relation to feeling, we do not yet know at this point.

·10. If anything is to be either posited ideally, or felt, we must be able to exhibit a drive for it. Nothing that is in the self is there without a drive. So there will have to be evidence of a drive towards the harmony in question.

11. Harmony is provided by anything that can be reciprocally viewed as determinate and determinant. —But the harmonizing factor must be, not one, but a duality making for harmony; so the relationship will be as follows: In itself and in general, A must be simultaneously determinate and determinant, and so must B. But both must contain yet another specific determination (of how far), in respect of which A is the determinant if B is posited as the determinate, and *vice versa*.

12. A drive of this sort is to be found in the drive to *interdetermination*. —The self determines X by means of Y, and *vice versa*. Examine your action in the two determinations. Each of them is evidently determined by the other, since the object of each is determined by the object of the other. —This drive may be described as the self's *drive to interdetermination* through itself, or the drive to absolute *unity* and completeness of the self within itself. —(The circuit is now completed: drive to determination, initially of the self; then, by means of this, of the not-self;—since the not-self is a manifold, so that nothing specific can be fully determined in and through it as such—drive to determination thereof by interchange;

I, 326

drive to interdetermination of the self through itself, by way of this interchange. There is thus an interdetermination of the self and the not-self, which, in virtue of the unity of the subject, must become an interdetermination of the self by itself. Hence, in accordance with the schema already established earlier, the self's modes of action have been enumerated and exhausted, and this guarantees the completeness of our deduction of the main drives of the self, since by it the system of drives is rounded off and concluded.)

I, 327

13. The harmonizing, reciprocally self-determined factor is to be both drive and action. a) Both are to be capable of consideration as in themselves at once determinate and determinant. A drive of this sort would be one which absolutely gave birth to itself, an absolute drive, a drive for drive's sake. (If expressed as a law, as for purposes of this very determination it must, at a certain point of reflection, be expressed, it is a law for law's sake, an absolute law, or the categorical imperative. —*Thou shalt absolutely.*) The *indeterminacy* in such a drive is easily located; for it drives us out into the indeterminate, without an aim (the categorical imperative is merely formal, and has no object whatever). b) That an *action* is at once determinate and determinant, signifies that it is performed because it is performed and in order that it shall be, that is, with absolute self-determination and freedom. The entire grounds of the action, and all its conditions, lie in the action itself. —The indeterminacy herein is likewise at once apparent: there is no action without an object; hence the action would have simultaneously to furnish its own object, which is impossible.

14. Now the relation between the two, the *drive* and the *action*, is to be that of reciprocal determination. Such a relationship requires, in the first place, that the action should *admit of being regarded as an outcome* of the drive. —The action is to be absolutely free, and hence irresistibly determined by nothing whatever, and so not by the drive either. Yet it may be so constituted that it can be viewed as determined thereby, or not. Now *how* this harmony or disharmony finds expression is the very question we have to answer, and whose answer will present itself forthwith.

Again, the relationship requires that the *drive* should admit of I, 328 being posited as determined by the action. —In the self, nothing can be simultaneously present in opposition. But drive and action are here in opposition. As surely, therefore, as an action occurs, the drive is broken off or delimited. Hence arises a *feeling*. The action addresses itself to the possible ground of this feeling, positing and realizing the same.

Now if, as above required, *the drive* determines *the action,* it also determines the *object;* the latter is adapted to the drive, and is what it required. The drive is now *(idealiter)* determinable through the action; it admits the predicate of having been such that it addressed itself to this action.

The harmony exists, and a feeling of *inclination* ensues, which in this case is a feeling of *contentment,* of repletion, of utter completeness (which lasts only a moment, however, since the longing necessarily recurs). —If the action is not determined by the drive, the object is *contrary* thereto, and there results a feeling of *disinclination,* of discontent, of the subject divided against itself. —Even now, the drive can be determined through the action; but only negatively; it was not a drive addressed to this action.

15.   The action here referred to is, as always, a merely ideal act, through presentation. Even our sensory efficacy in the world of sense, which we *believe in,* comes to us mediately only, by way of presentation.

Index

Absolute. *See* Act; Activity; Positing; Self

Abstraction, 9, 27–28, 32–33, 72, 98–99, 105, 108, 111, 147, 151, 156–157, 165, 168, 187, 202, 214–216, 259

Accident, 23, 117, 136, 146–148, 154–155, 176, 180, 184–185, 204, 275

Act, absolute, 14, 37, 103, 125, 150, 156, 164, 171, 188, 205, 211, 221–222, 241, 261–262
see also Activity; Positing
primordial, 40, 42, 93–94, 97, 99, 129–130
of the self, 21–22, 33–34, 36–37, 63, 69, 97, 103, 107, 120–121, 149–150, 154, 177, 186, 249, 255, 262, 273, 277, 284
two series of, 17, 30, 33–36, 40, 62–63, 199–200, 256

Action, 63, 162, 245, 259, 283–286
objective, 164

Activity, xv–xvii, 21, 41, 66, 129–136, 139, 152–153, 170, 188–191, 252–254, 276
absolute, 124, 150, 164, 205, 208, 211, 221–222, 261
determinate, 164, 222
diminished, 140, 145–146, 149, 154, 164
finite, 235–237
ideal, 63, 65, 248, 258–270, 273–274, 278–284
independent, 141–144, 148, 150–152, 155, 157, 165, 173, 229
infinite, xvii, 192–194, 203, 205, 208–209, 220–222, 226, 235–237, 240, 243
mediate, 169
nondetermining, 215
of the not-self, 139–141, 145, 148–149, 152, 159–160, 163–164, 237

of the object, 228–229, 232–233, 235
objective, 164, 175, 210–213, 215, 227, 231, 235–237
objectless, 63, 130, 215, 226, 232, 265
opposed, 210–211, 230
pure, 97, 129, 210–211, 226–227, 231–233
real, 65, 254, 258, 260–261, 265, 273–274
resistant, 203–205, 210, 240
self-reverting, xvii, 33–34, 36–37, 63, 130, 158, 203, 213, 226–227, 231, 235, 240, 253

Actuality, 207

Aenesidemus, 54, 118

Affection, 59–60, 62, 130, 147, 150, 173–174, 212

Affirmation, 112, 174

Alienation, 154, 233

Allgemeine Literatur Zeitung, 41, 43, 84

Amazement, 194

Analogy, 127

Analysis, xiii, 28, 57, 111–112, 120–121, 124, 185, 199, 219, 252

Animal, 114

Annulment, 13, 15, 106–107, 110, 122, 124, 128, 131, 161, 163, 165–168, 174, 186, 231, 238, 248, 253, 261

Antinomies, 217

Antithesis, 111–113, 116, 120–121, 186, 193, 219

Apodictic, 196

Apperception, 46–49, 73

Apprehension, 193, 201, 207, 209, 212, 214

A priori, xi, 26, 28, 112, 223–224, 233, 270, 273

Aristotle, xiv–xv, 65, 70

Atheism, 220, 245

Attention, 259

Bacon, Francis, 3
Beauty, 115
Beck, Jakob Sigismund, 24, 53, 60 –61, 91.
Becoming, 165
Being, 21, 36, 95, 98–99, 108, 134, 163, 172, 230, 232, 243, 245
see also Existence
Belief, 15, 40, 81, 264, 286
Berkeley, George, 19
Body, 66, 116, 166, 241, 257, 259, 276
Boundary, 187–188, 191–194, 201, 211, 225–226, 228, 237, 256, 259, 263, 278–279, 283
see also Limitation

Canon, 148
Categorical imperative, 46, 230, 285
Categories, xvi, 22, 51, 54, 62, 100, 105
Causality, 17–19, 22, 54, 66, 78, 131, 136, 221, 224–225, 227, 231, 238–239, 243, 252–254, 257–258, 260–261, 265–268, 270
see also Efficacy
Cause, 17–18, 131, 140, 146, 213, 215, 221–222, 227, 252, 272
Centrifugal, and centripetal, 240– 243
Certainty, 77, 94–96, 99, 110, 226
Check, 189–192, 195, 203–206, 212, 220–222, 234, 240, 242–246
Child, 216
Circle (in thinking), 93–94, 139, 147, 206, 212, 226, 233, 236, 247–248, 255
Clash (of opposites), 187–189, 191, 193
Cogito, 100
Combination, 111, 113–114, 283
see also Conjoining; Unity
Commonsense, 82, 119, 161, 250

Comparison, 116, 119, 133, 185, 234, 268
Completion, 286
Compulsion. *See* Feeling of compulsion
Concept, 34, 36, 38, 47, 67–68, 71–72, 74–75, 104–105, 108, 114, 120–121, 127, 178, 192, 200, 207, 248
generic, 116, 126
Conflict, 124, 147, 160, 193–194, 201, 204, 219, 223, 225, 233, 235, 267
Conjoining (of opposites), 111–113, 185, 189, 191–193
see also Unity
Conjunction, 110–111, 114–115, 119, 133, 144–145, 149, 162, 166, 230, 232–234, 242, 273
see also Relation
Consciousness, vii–viii, x, xv, 6–7, 9, 11, 21, 33, 35–40, 47–50, 62, 93, 98, 101–103, 106–107, 109, 117, 119, 121, 123–124, 156, 161, 168, 185, 188, 193, 196–198, 200–202, 205, 215– 216, 224, 234, 237, 241–242, 244–248, 253, 259–260, 262– 265, 270, 274
see also Self-consciousness
Contentment, 286
Contingency, 7, 61, 166, 179–180, 183, 185, 277
Contradiction, xiii, 67, 111, 123– 124, 129, 137, 140–141, 148, 169, 195, 220, 224–226, 231, 235–238, 249, 252, 263, 267
Conviction, 5, 78, 81–83, 197
Copula, 94
Copying, 271, 273
Counterpositing, 103–106, 108, 110, 125, 149, 188, 193, 209, 268, 273–274, 279

Counterstriving, 238, 251–253, 265
  see also Resistance
Critical philosophy, viii, xvi, 3, 22–
  24, 92, 102, 115, 117–119,
  171, 230, 255
Critique of Pure Reason, 45–46,
  48–49, 51–52, 56, 58, 60, 82,
  112, 171, 216
Critique of Practical Reason, 46

Death, 38, 260, 262
Deception, 82, 130, 170, 200, 202,
  208, 255
Decree (of reason), 106, 137, 233
Deduction, xi, 25–26, 106, 121, 196,
  206, 224, 230, 239, 261–262,
  267
Definition, 116
Degree, 126, 130, 138
Demand, 27, 32, 108, 201, 225, 229–
  230, 232, 238–239, 242–244
Dependence, 118, 220, 224, 246–247
Derivation, 50, 103, 116
Descartes, René, 100–101
Destruction, 187, 269
  see also Annulment
Determinability, 179–187, 190, 192–
  194, 217
Determinacy, 50, 61, 115, 123, 132,
  134–135, 138, 140, 164, 173,
  175, 181, 184, 190, 236–237,
  272, 274–275, 277–278, 282–
  285
Determination, 50, 68, 94, 99–100,
  110, 115, 117, 119, 123–127,
  132, 135, 138, 140, 142–144,
  155, 157, 159, 170–171, 173,
  179–183, 188–190, 193–196,
  204, 208–209, 212–213, 216–
  217, 220–221, 227, 231, 236–
  237, 242 ,245, 248, 269–278,
  280–284
Direction, 203–204, 206, 209, 240–
  241, 245, 259

Disappearance, 165
Disharmony, 283–285
Disinclination, 283–284, 286
Dissatisfaction, 256–257, 265, 286
Distinction (ground of), 110–111,
  114, 116, 119, 149, 234,
  277–278
Divisibility, xiii, 108–110, 112, 116–
  117, 119, 128, 133
Dogmatism, ix–x, xiv, 9–20, 23–24,
  27, 40, 53, 56, 58–59, 61, 69,
  78, 117–119, 146–147, 156,
  161–162, 226, 247, 250, 255
  see also Realism
Doubt, 32, 117,202
Drive, xvii–xviii, 253–261, 263–267,
  270–271, 274, 285–286
  absolute, 285
  to change, 280, 283
  to completion, 284
  to determination, 269–270, 272,
    276–277, 284
  enhancement of, 259
  to harmony, 284
  to interdetermination, 279–280,
    282, 284–285
  to interplay, 284
  to object, 256
  to presentation, 259
  to reality, 248, 280, 283
Duty, xviii, 259

Eberhard, Johann August, 53
Education, 76–77, 251
Effect, 131, 146, 163, 213, 221–222,
  227, 231, 239, 272
Efficacy, 41, 55, 135, 138–139, 145–
  146, 148, 152, 159–160, 162,
  164, 167, 174–175, 213, 253,
  257, 265, 270–271, 286
  see also Causality
Egoism, xv, 84
Elasticity, 257–258, 261
Empiricism, 12

Endurance, 177, 185, 253
Equilibrium, 251–254, 257–258, 269
Eternity, 238, 246
Exclusion, 154, 175–180, 182–184, 187, 189, 200, 204, 263, 272, 279
Excursion, (of self), 239, 243–244, 254, 256–257, 260, 265–267
Existence, 15, 31–34, 45, 65–70, 78, 94–95, 97–98, 100–101, 129, 146–147, 165, 167, 202, 207, 222, 238, 241, 245–246, 249, 252, 270
see also Being
Existence (validity for), 17–18, 31–33, 70, 98–99, 101, 171, 190, 202, 214, 218, 222, 225, 233–234, 241, 247–248, 254, 257, 259–261, 266–267, 271, 278
Experience, ix–xi, xviii, 6, 8, 10–11, 26–27, 34, 53, 223–224, 233
Experiment, 30, 108, 188, 199, 256
Explanation, 21, 27, 61–62, 148, 188, 198, 201, 248, 255
Extension, 189, 201, 275
External world. *See* World

Fact (of consciousness), 96, 100, 102–103, 140, 151, 170, 196–199, 206, 218, 223, 230, 242
Fatalism, 13, 146, 232, 259
Feeling, xviii, 61, 130, 190, 235, 246, 250, 254–257, 260–265, 268–271, 274–281, 286
of compulsion, 211–212, 254, 261, 263, 266–267
of force, 260–261
moral, 118
Fichte, Immanuel Hermann, xx
Fichte, Johann Gottlieb, vii–xx
Filling, xvii, 175, 244, 254, 256–257
Finite, xvi, 60, 192–194, 202, 217, 220, 225–226, 228, 232, 235–238, 247–248, 258

Finitude, 42, 137, 169, 171, 245–246
Fixation, 186, 194, 206–207, 209, 211–212, 216, 253
Fixity, 179–180, 182–185
see also Rest
Forberg, F. K., 43
Force, 234, 241–242, 246, 252–253, 257–259, 273
feeling of (*see* Feeling)
Freedom, x, 6, 11–15, 21–22, 25, 27–28, 32, 35, 41–42, 69, 76, 78–79, 114–115, 173, 211–212, 214, 232, 245–246, 259, 262, 265, 277–278, 285

Given, 190, 208
God, 19, 45, 101, 224–225, 232, 242, 245
Grimblot, F., xix
Ground, 7–8, 27, 110–111, 114–115, 117–118, 144, 151, 164, 169–170, 180, 183, 223, 229–230, 239, 246, 248, 254–255, 268, 270, 282
ideal, 145–147, 161–163, 177, 211, 247
primary, 233–234
real, 40, 62, 146–147, 161–163, 170, 173, 177, 211, 247
Grounding principle. *See* Principle

Harmony, 18, 284–286
preestablished, 140, 169
Heuristic, 152
Hiatus (in consciousness), 13, 19–20, 144, 156, 158
Hume, David, 118
Hypothesis, 25, 27, 197–198, 223

'I am,' xv, 96–97, 99, 102, 105, 114, 129–130
Idea, 173, 194–195, 233, 238, 249–250

of God, 225
self as (*see* Self)
Ideal, 101, 115, 233, 237, 244, 267–268
  ground, (*see* Ground)
  and real, (*see* Real)
Idealism, viii–x, 9–16, 19, 21–24, 56, 78, 156, 169, 188–189, 250
  critical, x–xi, 21–22, 64, 147, 162, 164, 171, 177, 247
    quantitative, 172, 174
  dogmatic, 140, 147–148, 160, 164, 247, 250
  practical, 147
  qualitative, 169–170
  quantitative, 169–171, 174, 176
  transcendent, 140–141
  transcendental, 21, 24–28, 31, 37–38, 40–41, 48, 53–55, 58–59, 61–62, 69, 80, 105
Ideality, 202, 247, 258–259
Identity of consciousness, 49, 99, 106–107, 220, 225, 234, 239
  principle of, (*see* Principle)
Image, 15, 277
Imagination, xviii, 6, 20, 23, 130, 150, 165, 168, 186–188, 193–194, 200–203, 205, 207–208, 211–217, 242, 250–251, 281
  productive, 188, 193, 201, 207–208, 275–267
  reproductive, 193, 209
Impression, 21, 58, 170, 243
Inability, 254, 261, 271
Inclination, 15, 283–284, 286
Incompatibility, 165
Increase (and decrease), 128, 140, 145–146
Incursion, intrusion (of opposites), 157–158, 162, 165–166, 187, 189
Independence, 13–15, 162, 230, 247, 267

Indeterminability, 192
Individuality, xv, 49, 71–75, 84, 101
Infinite, xvi, 42, 137–138, 148, 192–194, 202, 208, 217, 220, 223, 225–226, 228–230, 235–238, 241–244, 252, 256–257, 267, 277, 281
  approach to, 113, 115
  completed, 195, 238
  finite, 228, 236
  judgment, 115
Influence, 166, 239
  on the self, 173, 239, 243–244
Insight, 250, 259
Instant, 165, 187–188, 194, 201, 237, 286
Intelligence, self as. *See* Self
Interaction, and passion, 142–144, 150, 246
Interdetermination, 127–131, 135, 138–139, 141–145, 148–149, 155, 175, 210, 212, 214, 235, 279–280, 282, 284–285
Interest, 15
Interplay, 148, 150–159, 164–166, 173–175, 177–180, 187–188, 190–191, 193–194, 213
  see also Reciprocity
Intuitant, 204, 206, 209–212, 214, 270, 277, 279
Intuition, 35–36, 46–48, 61, 63, 68, 201–202, 204–213, 251, 260, 264, 271, 277–280, 284
  intellectual, xi, 38–42, 44–47, 83
Iron, 151, 162, 175–176, 178–180, 182–184

Jacobi, Friedrich Heinrich, 54, 56–57, 77
Judgment, 24, 97, 103, 111–112, 114, 214–215

Kant, Immanuel, viii–ix, xii, xvi, 3–5, 12, 24, 43–62, 71–73, 82,

Kant, Immanuel (cont'd)
100, 112, 115, 119, 127, 147,
171, 216–217, 230, 250
Knowledge, 118, 250–251, 275
Kroeger, A. E., xix

Law, 21–23, 25, 83, 95, 169, 199,
214, 216, 246, 252, 255–256,
262, 270, 272–273, 276, 285
of positing, 172–174, 274
practical, 32, 118, 220, 259, 267
theoretical, 259
Leap, 18, 262
Leibniz, Gottfried Wilhelm, ix,
52, 82–83, 102, 140
Life, 38, 40–41, 185, 202, 241, 245–
246, 262, 269–270, 280
living, 259–260, 262
Light, 138, 187, 200–201
Likeness, 110, 136, 229–230, 232,
240
Limitation, xii, xvi, 60–61, 66, 108,
117, 119, 143, 153, 164, 169,
186, 189, 208–209, 236–237,
244, 248, 252, 254–259, 265–
267, 273, 278–280, 282–283
of not-self, 122, 225, 248–249,
277
of self, 122, 125, 140, 225, 249,
258, 261, 264, 268, 270–271,
see also Restriction
Line, 203, 240–241
Logic, 20, 23, 66–68, 93–94, 99–100,
118
Longing, 265–270, 280, 283, 286

Magnet, 151, 162, 178–179, 183
Maimon, Solomon, 100, 102, 118
Man, viii, 15, 61, 114–115, 250, 259
Manifold, 18, 22, 39, 48–49, 201,
233, 284
Materialism, 13, 18–19, 262
Materiality, 269
Mathematics, 20, 128–129

Matter, 13, 61, 69, 161, 197, 260,
269, 271, 273, 275, 282
Measure, 132–133
Mediation, 137, 231
Medicus, F., xx
Memory, 251
Metaphysics, 32, 65, 67, 251
Method, x–xiii, 29, 127, 196, 251
Mind, 110, 117, 188, 196, 198–199,
202, 206, 239, 249–250, 252,
280
Modification, 269, 271, 273
Moore, George Edward, xix
Moral law, 40–42
Morality, 259
Motion, 18, 175–176, 178–179, 184

Nature, 162, 233, 270
law of, 262
Necessity, xvii–xviii, 6, 20–21, 25,
31, 41, 78, 95, 118, 211
Need, 101, 265
Negation, 105, 108, 115, 119, 125–
126, 130–131, 133, 135, 138,
141, 148, 156, 161, 163, 169,
174, 200, 210, 281
positive, 130
real, 128
relative, 129
negative judgment, 112
Nonbeing, 108, 163, 165
Nonpositing. *See* Positing
through positing, 152–153, 160,
174
Nonsatisfaction, 256–257
Nothing, 109, 122, 132, 187, 200,
216, 225, 230, 233, 238, 254,
280
Not-self, x, xvi, xviii, 34–35, 60,
104, 106–109, 116–118, 122–
128, 130, 134, 137–140, 146–
147, 149, 152–153, 160–162,
170, 172–173, 176–177, 182,
185, 189–190, 195, 203, 205–

206, 208–210, 216–222, 224–
225, 230, 237, 245–246, 248–
249, 252–253, 255, 263–264,
266, 270–271, 273–274, 276–
279, 284
Noumenon, 55, 210, 213, 247

Object, 4, 9–10, 15, 22–23, 39, 47,
58–60, 72, 98, 105, 130, 150,
154, 164, 168–169, 182, 184,
195–196, 202, 211–214, 216,
224, 227–239, 248, 252, 255–
256, 260–261, 264, 267–268,
270–271, 274, 281, 284–285
Objectivity, 31, 35–36, 63, 65–66,
186, 188–189, 224, 237, 255,
273–276
see also Activity, objective
Opposition, 103–105, 108–114, 116,
120, 131; 133, 141, 167, 187–
188, 199–201, 204, 209, 223–
225, 230, 236, 280–282, 284
essential 165–168, 170, 172, 192,
201–202
Ought, 41, 102, 119, 147, 229–230,
244, 285
Organization, 114

Paradox, 166
Particular, 274
Passivity, 21, 124, 130, 132–135,
138–139, 141–142, 144, 148,
152–154, 157, 160–161, 163–
164, 173, 203–204, 210–212,
215, 221, 254, 263–264, 266
Perception, 199
Philosophy, ix, 6–9, 11, 16, 19, 26–
28, 35, 37, 39, 61, 66–67, 80,
89, 110, 146, 162, 217, 230,
249–250, 262
philosophizing, 35, 65, 162, 196–
197, 199, 249–251
popular, 197, 216, 230

Point, 240–241
Positing. *See also* Self-positing,
xiii–xiv, 160–165, 172, 225
and passim
absolute 72, 94–97, 103, 113, 125–
126, 129–130, 149, 153–154,
164, 207, 211, 222, 228, 231–
232, 237, 239, 243–244
of feeling, 282
ideal, 282
infinite, 226, 228
mediate, 167–168, 170–173, 188
by nonpositing, 109, 152–153,
159–161, 163, 167–168, 172
of object, 176, 182, 184, 223, 228–
229, 248, 270
as positing, 158, 171, 195, 199,
243, 253, 277
Possibility, 196, 198, 212
Postulate, 196, 224, 230, 232, 260
Predicate, 67, 95–97, 114, 135, 173
Presentation, xviii, 6–7, 14, 16–22,
25, 31, 35, 39–41, 46–47, 70,
73, 98, 101, 105, 118, 146–
147, 161–162, 164, 169, 173,
177, 183, 188–189, 195–197,
202, 208, 210, 215, 219–220,
222, 225, 233, 245, 248, 255,
259, 275, 286
Principle, basic, 12, 25, 93–94, 109–
110, 114, 119–120, 123, 140,
153, 164, 218, 227–228, 232,
235, 239
of contradiction, 66–67, (*see also*
Contradiction)
grounding, 21–22, 110–112, 120,
145, 169–170
of identity, 93–94, 107, 120, 154,
219
of opposition, 105–107, 120, 141,
143–144, 160, 223, 228
Producing, 204, 208, 210, 260–261,
263, 268–269

Producing (cont'd)
  power of, 195, 207, 267, 276, 279
  product, 113, 131, 226, 237, 256,
    266, 277
Proof, 20, 77–78, 93–94, 99, 102,
    106, 110, 113, 197, 223, 233,
    239
  apagogic, 239
Propaedeutic, 101, 171

Quality, 129, 146, 148, 161, 165,
    185–186
Quantity, 108, 119, 126, 128–130,
    133, 145–146, 148, 161, 185–
    186, 223, 252, 264
  negative, 109, 128, 130
Quantum, 128, 132–134, 138, 144–
    145, 148, 154, 182, 241

Rational being, 8, 14, 73, 83, 224,
    245, 280
Real, and ideal, 17, 65, 202, 207,
    236–237, 244, 247–248, 258–
    259
  ground (*see* Ground)
  -idealism, 247
  realization, 265
Realism, ix, 31, 55, 62, 146–147,
    162, 189, 197, 246–247, 250
  dogmatic, 146, 160, 164
  qualitative, 170, 173, 177
  quantitative, 170–171, 173–174,
    190
Reality, viii, 11, 28, 53, 100, 108–
    109, 116, 119, 122, 124–125,
    128, 130–133, 136, 138–139,
    141, 148, 154, 156, 160, 164,
    167–170, 184–185, 198, 202,
    207–208, 210, 218, 223–225,
    230, 232, 237, 241–242, 244,
    248, 252, 264–256, 268–269
Reason, xiv, 24, 27, 40, 48, 74–75,
    83, 147, 224, 226, 242, 248,
    255–256, 262, 276
  practical, xiii, 24, 32, 123, 232–
    233, 248, 259

  theoretical, xiii, 14, 101, 123, 194–
    195, 207, 213, 216, 233, 248,
    259
Reciprocity, 142, 144, 146, 148,
    150–153, 155–157, 165, 167,
    174, 178, 196, 211, 217, 237,
    244, 258, 263, 272, 279
  see also Interplay
Reflection, xvii–xviii, 60–61, 93–94,
    112, 144, 150–151, 187, 193–
    194, 198–199, 201, 203, 208,
    212, 214, 232, 237, 241–244,
    253–254, 256–259, 261–266,
    269, 271–273, 276–278, 282–
    283
  drive to, xvii, 254, 256, 263, 265
  philosophic, 120–121, 123–124,
    152, 196–199, 204–206, 208,
    244, 255–256, 263
Regulative validity, 119
Reinhold, Karl Leonhard, 51–53,
    55–56, 60–61, 101
Relation, 23, 127, 129, 140, 157,
    172, 181, 184, 187, 200, 216,
    277
  see also Conjunction
Reproduction, 193
Resistance, 192, 227, 234, 236,
    238–239, 257–258, 275
  see also Counterstriving
Rest, 130, 176
Restoration (of activity), 234–235,
    261–262
Restriction, xvii–xviii, 119, 122,
    222–223, 234, 237, 245, 254–
    255, 257, 265–266, 268, 271,
    276–277
  see also Limitation

Satisfaction, 254, 256, 282–283
Schelling, Friedrich Wilhelm
    Joseph, 41, 53, 83–84
Schlegel, Friedrich, 43
Schulz, F., 46–47, 53, 55–56
Science, 89, 171
Science of Knowledge, vii, xi, xiii,

xvi, 7, 12, 17, 20, 24, 28–31, 34, 38–39, 42–46, 48, 50, 52, 61–62, 64–65, 69, 71–73, 75–76, 80, 85, 91, 97, 99, 109–110, 112–113, 116–117, 119–120, 122–123, 129, 137, 173, 197, 218, 222–224, 230, 245–247, 249–252, 266, 268, 275, 280
  practical, xvi, 113, 119, 123, 148, 164, 190, 195, 219, 238, 274
  theoretical, 113, 119, 123, 147, 164, 186–187, 195–196, 198, 220, 222, 251
Self, viii–xviii, 10, 13–15, 33–37, 50, 52–53, 65–66, 71–75, 83–84, 95–101, 103, 106–119, 122–143, 145–150, 152–154, 159–164, 167–174, 176–177, 182–186, 188–196, 198–199, 202–210, 216–249, 252–278, 280–285
  absolute, x–xiii, xv–xvii, 98, 109, 111, 116–117, 119, 169, 219–221, 224–225, 230, 233, 239–240, 243–245
  finite, xii, 171, 192, 226, 234–235
  as Idea, 83–84, 115, 119, 148, 244–245
  ideal, 278
  infinite, xi, 192–193, 195, 225–226, 238, 245
  as intelligence, 8–10, 17–18, 20–23, 25, 33, 70, 188, 190, 219–222, 224, 231, 233–235, 239, 244–245, 259, 262
  practical, 147, 219, 239, 244–245, 248, 280
  pure, 46, 50, 73–76, 119, 216, 226, 230, 245
  real, 162, 245
  state of, 203–204, 207, 235, 265, 278
  theoretical, 148, 244, 248, 280
Self-affection, 212

Self-consciousness, vii, ix, xv, 10–11, 15, 35, 37–38, 41, 46–47, 49–51, 216, 244–245
  see also Consciousness
Self-determination, xii, xvi, 10, 124–125, 132, 190–191, 195, 212–213, 216, 258, 263, 266, 269–274, 276–277, 285
Self-feeling, 260, 264, 268–269, 282
Self-limiting, xii, 190–191, 193, 222–223, 254, 268–269
Self-positing, xiv, xvii, 37–38, 60, 97–98, 115, 124–125, 129, 163, 176–177, 182, 188, 193, 195, 222–224, 227, 234–235, 238–239, 241, 243–244, 253, 258, 269, 272
Sensation, 18, 38–39, 45, 47, 49, 55, 58, 60–61, 130, 162, 245, 272–278, 281–282, 286
Simultaneity, 203
Skepticism, 14, 54, 100, 117–118, 202
Something, 47, 61, 98, 109, 128, 185–186, 205, 241, 253, 269, 279–280
Soul, 18–19, 66, 216, 241, 255
Space, 23, 42, 51, 66, 166, 171, 201, 275, 277
Spinoza, Baruch, ix, xi, xiv, 81, 83, 101–102, 117–119, 146, 226
Spontaneity, 49, 135, 150, 188, 190, 196, 198, 205–207, 212, 228, 232, 256, 262, 265, 271–272, 276, 278–279
Stoicism, 245
Striving, xvii, 135, 191, 231–234, 236–239, 243, 245, 249, 251–257, 266–267, 273
Subject, x, xv, 9, 33, 47, 73, 108–109, 173, 182, 188–189, 194–196, 202, 216, 232, 235, 252–253, 285
  absolute, 98–99
  logical, 95–97

Subjectivity, 273–276
Sublime, 40, 194
Substance (substantiality), 22–23,
    117–119, 131, 136, 139–140,
    146–148, 153, 165, 174–177
    182, 184–185, 194, 204
Substrate, 83, 98, 119, 154, 165,
    185, 193, 200, 213
Synthesis, xiii, 23, 28, 48, 57, 72–
    73, 111–113, 116, 120–121,
    124, 132, 135, 137, 155, 157,
    159–160, 162, 166–167, 172–
    174, 185–186, 190–191, 193–
    194, 199–201, 219, 235, 266–
    267, 275, 279–282
  synthetic a priori judgment,
    112
System, 4–5, 11, 15–16, 29, 45,
    50–51, 55–57, 62, 81, 90–92,
    101, 113–114, 117–119, 146,
    197–198, 200–202, 259

Task, 106–107, 115, 189–190
Taste, 116, 274–275, 281
  judgment of, 115
Temporality, xiii, 129–131, 165
Tendency, 209, 231, 233, 244, 254,
    265
Terminology, 90
Theory, 201, 259
Thesis, 73, 111, 115, 186, 193
  thetic judgment, xv–xvi, 72, 114–
    116, 164
Thing, 15, 17–19, 23, 100, 117, 119,
    154–155, 162, 168, 247, 272,
    275, 277
Thing-in-itself, x, xvi, 9–11, 13, 16,
    45, 53–56, 58–59, 61–62, 70–
    71, 75, 82, 117, 140, 148,
    160, 162, 164, 176–177, 210–
    212, 247, 249, 251–252
Think, 10, 17, 37, 48–49, 63–65, 68,
    73, 78–79, 100, 134–135,
    196–197, 200–201, 213–215,
    252
  thinkable, 123, 196, 215, 219

Thou, 49, 72, 172–173
Thought, laws of, 22–23, 25–26, 55,
    93–95, 107–108, 118, 198
Time, 23, 42, 51, 66, 131, 139, 165,
    171, 185, 194, 201, 245
Totality, 27, 125, 130, 132, 144,
    148–149, 153–154, 175–181,
    183–184, 194, 225, 272
Touch, 275–276
Transcendency, 21, 117, 197, 241,
    246–247, 250, 252, 258
Transcendental, 258
  philosophy, xi–xii, 21, 202, 208,
    216, 218, 240–241, 247
  see also Idealism
Transference, 152, 154, 159–160,
    168, 273, 275
Transition, 151, 155–158, 160, 211,
    262
Truth, 81, 196–198, 202

Understanding, 59, 207–212, 214,
    216–217, 251
Unity, 59, 101–102, 118–119, 125,
    195, 235, 242, 259, 280, 284
  of opposites, 107, 110, 120, 185,
    195, 199, 201
  see also Combination; Con-
    joining
Universe, 217
  see also World
Unlikeness, 229–230
Unthinkability, 215, 225, 242
Unwillingness, 254

Want, 265
  of reality, 132
Wavering, of the imagination, xviii,
    185, 194, 201–203, 207, 211,
    214–215, 250
  of the self, 278
Will, xiii–xiv, 6, 20, 25, 232, 259
World, xvi–xvii, 83, 230, 237
  external, ix, xviii, 15, 21, 82, 266,
    268, 280
  physical, 234, 242